THE GREAT COWBOY STRIKE

THE GREAT COWBOY STRIKE

Bullets, Ballots & Class Conflicts in the American West

Mark Lause

VERSO

First published by Verso 2017
© Mark Lause 2017

1 3 5 7 9 10 8 6 4 2

Verso
UK: 6 Meard Street, London W1F 0EG
US: 20 Jay Street, Suite 1010, Brooklyn, NY 11201
versobooks.com

Verso is the imprint of New Left Books

ISBN-13: 978-1-78663-196-1
ISBN-13: 978-1-78663-198-5 (UK EBK)
ISBN-13: 978-1-78663-197-8 (US EBK)

British Library Cataloguing in Publication Data
A catalogue record for this book is available from the British Library

Library of Congress Cataloging-in-Publication Data
A catalog record for this book is available from the Library of Congress

Typeset in Adobe Garamond by Hewer Text UK Ltd, Edinburgh
Printed in the US by Maple Press

Contents

Preface

Strikes by the iconic American cowboy confront us with the inescapable realities of class, politics, and violence in the West. Exploring these events and their impact provides an opportunity to examine how these issues converge. And this process poses key questions about how we remember the past.

That memory made the cowboy into a well-cultivated symbol of a rugged American past. That image entered into a symbiotic relationship with the culturally smudged self-image of the United States itself as the well-armed enforcer of virtue, justice, and fair play. In fact, the cowboys were grossly underpaid and overworked seasonal agricultural laborers.

Beyond a remarkably small circle of specialists, class—much less class conflict—touches the least explored of these large questions we hope to address, barely acknowledged in the West. More conservative scholars generally associate the appearance of social class as a concept with the migration of radical exiles and their "foreign" ideas from Europe. More liberal ones identify it with the great cities of the Eastern Seaboard, rather than with regions generally seen as more industrially backward and less settled.

Yet these newcomers to the West carried with them the old social order, its assumptions and its practices. The very first of them brought hired and bound labor with them. In the aftermath of the Civil War companies of unprecedented capital and power brought vast numbers of railroad workers to labor across great expanses of the transportation system, with particularly significant clusters at moving construction sites. Mining communities drew large numbers of hired workers in pursuit of the region's mineral riches. During this period, cowboys assumed a vastly more visible and regionally distinctive importance that belied their smaller numbers and greater isolation than other communities of laborers. This alone makes them an almost irresistible subject.

A touchstone of the increased visibility of genuine cowboys was their strike of 1883. Contemporary newspapers, chroniclers of Western lore, and serious scholars alike have found the event worthy of attention. Several have described it—erroneously—as "the only cowboy strike in history." Others—equally erroneously—have described it as the "first organized protest against big business on the Great Plains."[1]

The 1883 strike in the Texas Panhandle certainly had greater claim to this honor than the rodeo performers' strike in Boston. This latter event in 1936 took place during a period rife with what were then called "labor-management disagreements," and represented a rare intrusion into an eastern metropolis by a trade usually associated with the rural heartland of the nation.[2] The Texas strike took place over half a century earlier.

More importantly, the early work stoppage represented part of a strike wave that swept across much of the American West from 1883

1   Quoted in John Lawton McCarty, *Maverick Town: The Story of Old Tascosa* (Norman: University of Oklahoma Press, 1968), 109. See McCarty, *Maverick Town*, 107–14; Robert K. DeArment, *Deadly Dozen: Twelve Forgotten Gunfighters of the Old West* (Norman: University of Oklahoma Press, 2003), 157; and Jack Weston, *The Real American Cowboy* (New York: Schocken, 1985), 103, part of a good account that runs from 99 to 104. See also Ruth Alice Allen, *Chapters in the History of Organized Labor in Texas* (Austin: University of Texas Press, 1941); B. Byron Price, "Community of Individualists: The Panhandle Stock Association, 1881–1891," in *At Home on the Range*, ed. John R. Wunder (Westport, CT: Greenwood, 1985); Donald F. Schofield, *Indians, Cattle, Ships, and Oil: The Story of W. M. D. Lee* (Austin: University of Texas Press, 1985).

2   For an account of the organization of rodeo performers, see Gail Hughbanks Woerner, *The Cowboys' Turtle Association: The Birth of Professional Rodeo* (Walnut Springs, TX: Wild Horse Press, 2011).

to 1886. One contemporary observer flatly acknowledged "many labor strikes on the range." Literary scholar Jack Weston described "slowdowns, threats, intimidating behavior, and collective defiance" as part and parcel of life among the cowboys.[3] *The Great Cowboy Strike* supports these assessments of an endemic labor discontent where the very existence of social classes seems to be understated, if not ignored by most writers on the region.

Understanding these struggles—and how they came to be so obscured—requires seeing their context: in the broader insurgencies that politically challenged the unquestioned power of the large ranchers, the railroad owners, and the mine bosses. The Patrons of Husbandry (also called the Grange) began in Minnesota. The more political Industrial Brotherhood—which eventually became the Knights of Labor—and the Farmers' Alliance emerged from immediate postwar conditions in Missouri, Kansas, and Texas.

These groups based in the West generated the largest political insurgencies of the period. Greenbackism in the Midwest and Populism in the western heartland aimed at displacing one of the major political parties with one that would place people before profits. Each attained some real successes but faced obstacles that thwarted their efforts (and later permitted often grotesque misrepresentations of their goals).

There existed a working-class component of these insurgencies, particularly associated with what labor historians have called "the Great Upheaval." The Knights of Labor attained unprecedented numbers, reaching nearly 800,000 members. The group not only produced the modern American Federation of Labor but also sparked a dynamic wave of labor parties in 1886, including Henry George's campaign for mayor of New York and numerous local efforts that showed remarkable potential as a national third party. To a great extent, the presidential election of 1888 was a test as to whether these efforts could come to fruition.

The full meaning of the cowboy strikes escapes us without facing this political insurgency. As we shall see, the Greenback movement in Texas, broadly associated with the Farmers' Alliance, sheltered and

---

3 Quoted in Weston, *The Real American Cowboy*, 124; see also 91, 88, and 96.

defended the cowboy militants. The strike movements in Wyoming also directly influenced the rise and course of Populism there.

Scholars regularly downplay the importance of these insurgencies. These third parties disappeared, we are told, because the adoption of their concerns by one or the other of the major parties made them irrelevant. That the major parties frequently adopted and co-opted the rhetoric of insurgents is obvious; a reference to some of the most modest proposals of the Greenbackers or Populists, however, could still end the career of any major party politicians today.

The often ignored institutionalization of political violence in the nineteenth-century United States provides a much better explanation for the demise of opposition of all sorts. Starting with the ethnic cleansing essential to settlement, an ideology centered around civilizing nature and its savagery sanctioned the use of unrestricted violence against any persons and practices that got in the way of the imperatives of the marketplace.

This observation is hardly novel. In addition to Patricia Limerick's *Legacy of Conquest*, Richard Slotkin's trilogy—*Regeneration Through Violence, The Fatal Environment*, and *Gunfighter Nation*—reveals the importance of the West on eastern thinkers.[4] Using Custer's Last Stand as a metaphor for non-Native Americans' fear of "savagery" prevailing on the frontier, Slotkin points to the roots of a mythology that sanctioned efforts to neutralize conflicts arising from industrialization and imperial expansion.

Recognition of coercive violence as an innate, systemic feature of social control over the population provides the missing link between the racial violence aimed at indigenous peoples (and African Americans) and that employed on foreigners. Seeing lynchings in the postwar South as simply a large number of confused responses to accusations of rape, for example, misses the social and political intent of the unrestrained brutality visited on lynching victims. Tolerating such

---

4   Richard Slotkin, *Regeneration Through Violence: The Mythology of the American Frontier, 1600–1860* (Middletown, CT: Wesleyan University Press, 1973); *The Fatal Environment: The Myth of the Frontier in the Age of Industrialization, 1800–1890* (New York: Atheneum, 1985); and *Gunfighter Nation: The Myth of the Frontier in Twentieth-Century America* (New York: Atheneum, 1992).

activities—rendering them legally unaccountable—suited the needs of the ruling elite to intimidate sections of the population that could cause them considerable difficulties if they became unmanageable.

So, too, numerous "feuds" across the West actually represented political conflicts carried beyond the ballot by bullets. This was blatantly true for most of the so-called "Range Wars."[5] Particularly in Texas, these touched the lives and experiences of many cowboys, including the strikers.

One can barely discuss labor struggles—or political insurgencies— in the West during these years without encountering coercive violence. The powers-that-be proved to be far more likely to respond to a serious threat to their power by arranging for someone to shoot it down, rather than by compromising their own hold on power and wealth— and on the future of the country.

History—well, popular memory and the commercialized marketing of the past described as "heritage" in the United States—remembers all this very differently, of course. The reasons for this are quite straightforward. The ongoing security of legitimacy required the projection of violent intentions onto the designated targets of institutionalized violence. Southern Democratic leaders, for example, discussed a War of Northern Aggression. The Civil War did not result from their seceding from the Union and firing on U.S. troops, both nothing more than prudent self-defense against violent seizure of the government in Washington by antislavery voters. Later, these Southern Democrats donned their sheets and asserted their defense of law and order against the alleged brutal savagery of the former slaves and their well-wishers.

No less so, postwar elites generally represented themselves as struggling against the implicitly violent imposition of unjust restrictions on them and their property, profits, and prerogatives. After blazing a trail of corpses, shattered lives, dashed hopes, and broken promises, they described celebrating U.S. history as a grand highway to progress. No book-length study can provide such an explanation, but we hope that this book underscores the need to do so.

5 Harry Sinclair Drago, *The Great Range Wars: Violence on the Grasslands* (New York: Dodd, Mead & Co., 1970).

Introduction

How the West Was Made

In 1869, the Ingalls family moved out into the empty expanses once known as the "Great American Desert." They settled on the Kansas prairie, some thirteen miles southwest of what would later become Independence. The modern tourist can still sigh wistfully in a period schoolhouse recalling how the Ingalls children poured over their McGuffey readers there. One of them, Laura, became a schoolteacher herself and wrote their *Little House on the Prairie* into the fictional landscape of a series of very popular children's books.

The American West was not won but made. Residents of the United States did not simply push a line of settlement westward across a geographic area. Rather, they radically reshaped the environment of that area and, even more radically, conjured a way of thinking about the region that ascribed mystical transformative powers to it. They cleared troublesome occupants—buffalo, wolves, and Indians—to build their towns, railroads, and booming cattle trade, which introduced the kind of savagery they told themselves they wanted to civilize. The railroads that cut through their cow towns physically demarcated the respectable aspirants to middle-class civilization from those parts of town to which they hoped to confine the seasonal tide of savagery that drove the longhorns from the range to the rails.

Remarking the West: Eco-Cleansing

The first wave of permanent small farmers and ranchers faced severe crises. In 1862, the Homestead Act permitted landless persons to occupy parts of unclaimed public lands and gain ownership if they developed them. Vast numbers began turning up after the Civil War.

The Ingalls and their contemporaries had arrived at what would become the geographic heart of the United States. Indeed, only a few years after the family settled there, others established the town of Lebanon, later recognized as the geographic center of the contiguous forty-eight states. Long deemed unsuitable for farming, an earlier government survey had designated it a "desert." Though it was not actually a desert in the modern sense, it inspired a succession of mirages.

At the time the Ingalls moved to Kansas, the line of white settlement seemed to be moving inexorably and irreversibly westward. The movers and shakers had largely completed the "civilization" of Missouri, Arkansas, and much of Texas. The tide seemed to be moving rather predictably and relentlessly across western Kansas, along the northern end of the cattle trails from western and northern Texas at their southern starting point, with the Indian Territory between them. The spread of settlement from the scattered towns and mining communities of the Mountain West lagged a bit and migration to the upper reaches of the West—Wyoming and its neighbors—came even later.

To the Ingalls and their neighbors, it seemed as though ownership of the very land beneath their feet quaked continually. The Ingalls' farm sat on land recently taken from the Osage Indians. The authorities rationalized this by casting the native peoples there as merely nomadic savages who had no use for the land themselves. However, that description fit neither the Osage nor the Cherokee, who had been given the land by the U.S. government. In fact, they shrewdly held on to the land in the most "civilized" fashion in response to the increase in market values as the whites encroached. Of course, violence or the threat of violence underscored everything about such transactions.

In a larger sense, the entirety of Euro-American history came apart when the line of its settlement reached the area. The white masters of the continent had few concerns about slavery until the prospect of Kansas statehood thrust the question to the fore and the balance of sectional power toppled into civil war. The winners oversimplified that conflict into a struggle for freedom and equality before resuming their onslaught on the native peoples of the West.

The recent experience of civil war had not only stalled westward settlement but actually reversed it over much of the heartland. It depleted the populations of what had been settled districts in the eastern Indian Territory, southwest Missouri, and much of Arkansas, all of which were resettled and repopulated in the aftermath of the conflict.

Six years before and thirteen miles away from the Ingalls farm, one of the more grisly scenes of civil war had transpired. Although the Osage people remained overwhelmingly loyal to the Union during the Civil War, Confederate emissaries made overtures to and secured a treaty with one faction, threatening their already tenuous relationship with the U.S. authorities. On May 22, 1863, Charley Harrison, a thug who had run Denver's Criterion Saloon, tried to lead a handful of other guerrillas from Captain William C. Quantrill's band back toward Colorado, claiming commissions from the Confederate Army to recruit there. As the guerrillas passed through Osage lands, they took a few potshots at the Indians to discourage their pursuit. Unimpressed, the Osage followed in a two-mile running fight that ended with the massacre of the guerrillas.[1] The victors decapitated the white corpses and presented them to the local U.S. Army, ostensibly as a sign of loyalty but also, no doubt, as an expression of the tough negotiating stance they intended to take on the future of the land.

Nevertheless, the American heartland actually drew from this self-inflicted disaster a triumphalist faith in progress. A few years before

---

1 "Massacre of Confederate Officers," *Osage Magazine* 2 (February 1910) and "Massacre of Confederate Officers: The Sequel," *Osage Magazine* 2 (May 1910). These guerrillas were self-appointed "colonels" and the myth persists, reflected in Kansas Historical Markers. Donald S. Frazier, *Blood and Treasure: Confederate Empire in the Southwest* (College Station: Texas A&M University Press, 1995), 15.

the Ingalls children attended their little one-room schoolhouse in Kansas, in Wisconsin the young Frederick Jackson Turner came to share his father's interest in local history and settlement.

God's will, Manifest Destiny, and Social Darwinism are distinct concepts, but all generated a faith in progress that rationalized the U.S. holy war of the market economy on the natural world. Expanding American civilization both destroyed the existing world and built a new one, as determined by the God-given laws of supply and demand.

Insofar as settlers drew less comfort from simplistic religious or nationalist principles, they were bolstered by the discovery of a well of knowledge in the natural world. Tapping into underground reserves of water provided the basis for illusions of "scientific agriculture" based on irrigation. At the close of the decade that brought the Ingalls to the region, the government issued official tracts reinforcing the claims of developers that "rain follows the plow." In reality, farming came to be dependent on draining the massive but finite Ogallala Aquifer, underground waters gathered through an unimaginably long prehistory.[2] Science provided mirages for the Great American Desert that were no more substantive than those of faith.

Over time, those illusions became even less substantial. Over a century after Laura Ingalls Wilder wrote her children's books, television transformed them into a kind of therapeutic comfort for the millions of adult Americans shocked by several decades of confrontation with an unrelentingly changing world. Well known as a real-life proponent of what the media touted as "traditional family values," Michael Landon portrayed the Ingalls paterfamilias, combining the patrician values and vision of the Cartwrights in *Bonanza* with the troubled experience of an often desperately poor brood of sodbusters. One wonders what Wilder and her contemporaries might have made of it.

By the time the Ingalls showed up, the Osage Indians, their agents, or people pretending to be their agents had begun to sell "claims" to land-hungry white settlers like them. In many cases, the settlers discovered that they had been misled only after they had begun

2 Henry F. Mason, "County Seat Controversies in Southwestern Kansas," *Kansas Historical Quarterly* 2 (February 1933), 45–6.

working the land. The fate of such families turned on the pace at which the railroad companies pursued new projects. These gigantic corporations, confident in their legal might and weaponry, understood full well that white settlers would seem much more picturesque than the railroads and encouraged families such as the Ingalls to settle on Indian lands. Both the practical engine and symbol for progress, the railroads had also become the touchstone of popular discontent.

The ideological roots of settler resistance grew from the antebellum struggle to secure the admission of Kansas as a non-slave state, which drew disproportionately from the reform-minded across the North who maintained these political impulses after the war. Figures such as Samuel Newitt Wood emerged from the war as prominent political leaders in Kansas. Wood came from a family of Ohio Quakers associated with the Underground Railroad, and was drawn to the West by the antebellum conflict over slavery in the Kansas Territory. A proponent of armed resistance by the Free Staters, he became a prominent Republican leader and was appointed to a customs job in New Mexico by newly elected president Abraham Lincoln. He established an excellent military record during the war and held office in state government during and after it. From this position, he espoused woman suffrage, justice for farmers, and other reforms.[3]

In the aftermath of the war, some of these veteran radicals sought to revive the fighting spirit of the old Republican Party. In July 1870, figures such as the old land reformer William V. Barr and wartime radical Hugh Cameron helped to launch the Kansas Labor Union, a state affiliate of the National Labor Union. By September, the Democrats were courting these dissenters by passing resolutions around the issue.[4] However, the ballot would not resolve such questions.

More deeply, perhaps, the discontent of the West shared a critique rooted in the Founders' concerns about centralized government, executive authority, and the polarization of wealth and power. This created

3   Wood established the first newspapers in Cottonwood Falls (the *Kansas Press*) and Council Grove (the *Council Grove Press*).

4   On the Kansas Labor Union Convention at Leavenworth, see Daniel W. Wilder, *Annals of Kansas*, 2nd ed. (Topeka, KS: T.D. Thacher, 1886), 522. For the Democratic resolution, see p. 527.

serious friction over the land that the Ingalls family had bought, occupied, and worked "in good faith." An account by a transplant from
New York identified as "G. Campbell"—likely Greenback leader D.
G. Campbell, according to a census records at the time—recalled a
secret Settlers' Protective Association in 1872. Outsiders knew of it
simply as "the Settlers' League" or "the Settlers' Alliance."[5] From the
beginning, it struggled to navigate intergroup dynamics that recalled
those of the Civil War.

Early in 1874, the government appointed the lawyer George R.
Peck, who had formerly worked for the railroad corporations, as the
U.S. District Attorney for the area. Per Campbell's account, the Grand
Council of the Settlers' League got Peck to Parsons, where they
"pledged him" to a fair resolution. Campbell's account pointedly
avoids describing how this pledging was carried out, implying that
some intimidation may have been involved.[6] In the end, the government ruled against the claims of the railroad, but this did not prevent
the removal of those who had settled with the Osage before the
agreement.

Great changes were afoot. Though all acknowledged that the
people—white men with property, at any rate—had every right to
protest, the rich and the powerful exercised their own rights to dispose
of all complaints as they saw fit.

Iron Horses and Cow Towns

Railroads brought unprecedented capital to bear in shaping a largely
impoverished West. Faced with these powerful forces, both the Ingalls
and the Osage moved on. In the wake of the Drum Creek Treaty of
1870, the whites who remained began building towns among the
farms. Developers from Oswego ostensibly purchased the townsite
for a county seat from the Osage for only $50 in September 1869.

---

5 See Wilder, *Annals of Kansas*, 359, 366, 402, 481, 581; N. A. Dunning, *The
Farmers' Alliance History* (Washington, DC: Alliance Publishing Co., 1891), 10–11.
6 Dunning, *The Farmers' Alliance History*, 11, 12.

They originally called the town "Colfax" after the vice president, but eventually chose "Independence" for the seat of the new Montgomery County.

Speculation, economic and political, inspired the chartering of other towns, some of which remained paper communities for some time. To the south of Independence, James A. Coffey had a trading post at the nearby Osage camp of Talley Springs, and the nearby projected railroad terminal took the name Coffeyville. Northbound blacks—the "Exodusters"—escaping the collapse of Reconstruction in the South began to settle a few miles north of Coffeyville in 1881. Their Daniel Votaw community, named for a Quaker philanthropist, granted each family eight acres. After a hard first winter, the town began to function well. By the fall of 1883, black and white children attended the same school, and their "Jubilee Singers" led local celebrations of freedom.[7] A small private museum in Coffeyville preserves what remains of that early exuberance.

Other communities came to dominate the state's development. Near Votaw, the railroad established Cherryville, which became Cherry Vale and then Cherryvale, which was named the county seat of Montgomery County in 1871. A developing Cowley County included the newly founded Winfield on land leased from Chief Chetopah. Railroad towns absorbed the nascent settler economy and assumed control over the surrounding farmlands.

In July 1866, Congress voted to subsidize western railroads with massive land grants. This allowed for extensive branches from the Pacific railroad south into Kansas and a second line along the southern route from Springfield, Missouri, through the Indian Territory.

Across the West, whites waged a more general war of extermination against much of the native flora and fauna. Buffalo hunters advanced to finish the extermination of the gigantic herds of bison that had been a predominant species on the plains only a quarter century before. Despite the demand for meat, buffalo beyond the line of the railroad lost their lives mostly for their hides. Of course, removing

7 Daniel C. Fitzgerald, *Faded Dreams: More Ghost Towns of Kansas* (Lawrence: University Press of Kansas, 1994), 107.

and preparing what could be a hundred-pound hide from a massive animal proved very complicated. One estimate suggested that, depending on the location, three to ten beasts died for every complete, salable buffalo hide that got to market.

Meanwhile, in one of those bloody paradoxes that the market creates, the booming population of the country created a great demand for beef, particularly in the West. Whites and those Indians confined to their nations had introduced vast numbers of domestic cattle before the Civil War, which had deflated the available manpower. This left large numbers of cattle roaming untended across the margins of the frontier, where civilians and soldiers on both sides began developing the means to manage and process them.

In 1866, cattle in Texas sold at around four dollars a head, while the price in the North and East ran about ten times that. Soon, Joseph G. McCoy of Illinois, a former student at Knox College, began connecting the dots. In the following year, Abilene entrepreneurs added stockyards, and large cattle drives north to the Kansas railheads became an annual odyssey.[8] Such were the Homeric roots of the Great American Horse Opera. As is always the case, though, the larger operations with more resources fared better and had every interest in extending that advantage.

Certainly, the boom in cattle prices offered some hope to the defeated large landholders of Texas, who found themselves living in conditions that fell more than a bit shy of paradise. The start of the beef bonanza came only thirty years after the Texas War for Independence that severed the state from Mexico, and only twenty years after the U.S. war with Mexico to secure Texas. Later, Texas had attempted to secede from the Union after losing the national election and found itself subjugated, if not economically devastated, and experiencing a federally managed Reconstruction that had yet to turn in its favor.

By the later 1860s, though, those with heavy investments in cattle began gathering and driving their herds to where demand would fetch

---

8 Harry S. Drago, *Wild, Woolly & Wicked: The History of the Kansas Cow Towns and the Texas Cattle Trade* (New York: Bramhall House, 1960), 10–11.

a bigger and better price. This required rapidly rebuilding the region's supply of horseflesh, which had been thoroughly depleted by the war. It also placed cattle owners into direct business with the entrepreneurs of a state particularly associated with John Brown and radical abolitionism.

The pressures exacerbated tensions with the remaining native peoples, particularly the Comanche, who established a massive trade reselling U.S. horses in Mexico. What the whites called Indian "wars" had never actually been conflicts on that scale. Rather, very small raiding parties of Indians periodically slipped through areas that the whites had already come to regard as "settled" in terms of their own hegemony and standards of real estate.

In the summer of 1868, the Southern Cheyenne and allied Arapaho, Kiowa, Comanche, Northern Cheyenne, Brulé and Oglala Lakota, and Pawnee attacked white settlements in western Kansas. The army and the state authorities responded vigorously. This muzzled the conflict and prompted the Indians to move south beyond their reach.

The first cattle drive from Texas took the old Shawnee trail through the Indian Territory, ending at Baxter Springs. These southern cow towns nestled in well-watered and wooded hills, more reminiscent of the Ozarks than the open plains.[9] Even more dramatically than in the East, rapid economic development, industrialized commerce, and good eats pushed American history forward.

In short order, Kansas established a quarantine on the longhorns, whose ticks brought "Texas fever" to domestic herds in the state. For this reason, the cattle drives began entering Kansas farther west, with spurs of the railroad chasing after them. This created a succession of "cow towns." The older Chisholm Trail had to run as far north as Abilene, where the train tracks separated a "Kansas Abilene" from a "Texas Abilene." In the latter, on October 5, 1871, James Butler "Wild Bill" Hickok got into a gunfight at night with a number of hooligans, during which he mortally wounded Phil Coe

9 David Dary, *Cowboy Culture: A Saga of Five Centuries* (New York: Knopf, 1981), 198, 204.

and inadvertently killed his own deputy coming up behind him in support.[10]

Soon, however, southbound extensions of the railroads created new railheads at Newton and Wichita. The line pushed on to Chetopa and Coffeyville before reaching Caldwell, founded in 1871 and briefly marking the end of the trail. However, cattle drives also brought meat on the hoof to Waterville, Junction City, Solomon, Salina, and Brookville farther west.[11]

Two major considerations inspired the drives to use a new Western Trail by the mid-1870s. The state of Kansas once more extended the quarantine line still further west, essentially creating the most famous of the cow towns, Dodge City. Like its predecessors, Dodge grew from encampments of buffalo skinners and a related army post. Fort Dodge on the north bank of the Arkansas River, however, sat at a vital crossroads because it also straddled the Santa Fe Trail, which ran from Independence, Missouri, into New Mexico. West of Dodge, one could take several fords across the Arkansas River to the south, joining up with the Cimarron Cutoff, or Desert Route, which was the shortest way to Santa Fe—the alternative being the Mountain Route through Colorado. Five miles west of the fort, "Buffalo City" provided a temporary camp to those engaged in that slaughter. Dodge City began in 1871 and in September 1872, the Atchison, Topeka, and Santa Fe railroad brought the tracks through the city. For the next fifteen years, Dodge City occupied a unique place in the American West.[12]

The Red River War of 1874 provided the second great reason for the cattle trail to shift west. Renewed violence on the frontier took the authorities by surprise. Proponents of extermination declared the "peace policy" of the Grant administration a failure. In response, the U.S. Army moved against roughly 1,800 Cheyennes, 2,000

10 David Dary, *More True Tales of Old-Time Kansas* (Lawrence: University Press of Kansas, 1987), 104–7.

11 John L. McCarty, *Maverick Town: The Story of Old Tascosa*, 2nd ed. (Norman: University of Oklahoma Press, 1968), 40–1.

12 Stanley Vestal, *Dodge City: Queen of Cowtowns* (Lincoln: University of Nebraska Press, 1952).

Comanches, and 1,000 Kiowas roaming the plains and capable of fielding about 1,200 warriors.

The "war" consisted of military columns scanning the area with the express purpose of locating and removing the highly mobile bands of largely noncombatant Indians. On June 27, Comanche chiefs led a few hundred warriors against a small outpost of buffalo hunters. Some twenty-eight men and one woman sheltered in a few buildings known as Adobe Walls. A much larger conflict had taken place there a decade earlier, but the small number of whites in the Second Battle of Adobe Walls used their buffalo guns to bring down the Indians before they came close enough to use their own weapons, and the attack failed.[13]

Other fights took the conflict consistently in the same direction. When warriors under Lone Wolf attacked a patrol of Texas Rangers in July, their fight in the Lost Valley produced light casualties but brought a crushing federal response. On September 28, the army located a large group of Indians, overwhelmingly civilians, in the Palo Duro canyon and launched a ruthless attack on them, breaking their war-making power. With peace, even the Palo Duro itself became a natural corral for the longhorns.

By 1875, then, Dodge processed half a million heads of cattle passing through on a clear trail coming north from Texas. A year later, the town only had 1,200 people, but had licensed nineteen establishments for selling liquor and strove to emphasize the clearly visible class structure. The town drew the ambitious nineteen-year-old William Barclay "Bat" Masterson, who came to town as a teamster before working as a bartender and occasional gambler, though he also served as a scout for Nelson Miles. Masterson arrived early enough to win the contract to grade the Santa Fe Trail as it passed over Front Street.

Like Abilene and other cow towns, Dodge City actually had two main streets and two downtowns, as the railroad cut through the middle of town over Front Street. The north side held the main commercial street, one appropriate for a proper, civilized small town

13   T. Lindsay Baker and Billy R. Harrison, *Adobe Walls: The History and Archaeology of the 1874 Trading Post* (College Station: Texas A&M University Press, 1986).

with a respectable, churchgoing population. Everything to the south (or on the Texas side) was "wide open." Here roared the saloons, casinos, dance halls and brothels that established the town's reputation as "the wickedest little city in America."

Armed violence was central to this reputation, even before Dodge became a town. On April 6, 1870, Levi Richardson and "Cockeyed Frank" Loving staged the town's first shoot-out. Masterson, Wyatt Earp, Hickok, and others built their reputations in Dodge. By 1875, they began filling the little cemetery on "boot hill" on a slight rise south of town and overlooking the Arkansas river.[14]

Yet, locals always generally associated the violence in town with the untamed wilderness where several wars had been waged to the south. Some years before, in 1868, the U.S. Army had established Camp Supply about a hundred miles south of Fort Dodge for its operations against the Southern Plains Indians. From there, George Armstrong Custer launched his campaign against Black Kettle's camp of Cheyenne and Arapaho on the Washita River.[15] Fort Supply remained a vital outpost in the Indian Territory.

Another 120 miles beyond Fort Supply, the Fort Casement outpost offered some crude protection to Charles Rath, Bob Wright, and Lee Reynolds, who brought more buffalo hunters down from Dodge. They camped and worked in "Hidetown," establishing the origins of Mobeetie, Texas, near the state line. Though Mobeetie never had more than a few hundred residents, it had the first courthouse in the Panhandle, with Temple Houston as local prosecutor, by 1880. Local Indians ostensibly told the whites that Mobeetie meant "sweet water," though a Comanche later claimed that the word meant "buffalo dung."

Buffalo chips or no, the printer-turned-gunman Bill Thompson, brother of Ben Thompson, ran the main dance hall by the mid-1870s. Masterson came south to launch his career as a faro dealer. An army sergeant shot at him over a woman, who threw herself in front of the bullet; it killed her and hit Masterson, giving him a lifelong limp.

---

14 Dary, *More True Tales*, 107–8.

15 Robert C. Carriker, *Fort Supply, Indian Territory: Frontier Outpost on the Plains* (Norman and London: University of Oklahoma Press, 1970), 161.

Masterson's returning shot, however, took the life of his assailant.[16] Having killed his rival, Masterson returned to Dodge and a career as a lawman.

Two other settlements merit notice. One part of the cattle trail crossed the Canadian River about 120 miles west of Mobeetie, where the movement of the large herds fertilized the new town of Tascosa. Another 200 miles west sat Las Vegas, New Mexico, the last big town on that leg of the Santa Fe Trail and only about seventy miles shy of the end of it. Although Las Vegas was nearly 400 miles west by southwest from Dodge, a "Dodge City gang" came to power there.[17]

Tascosa grew on lands that only a few years earlier had been untouched by white settlement. Charles Goodnight quickly occupied Palo Duro Canyon as a natural enclosure for large herds on their way north. From the moment of their arrival in the region, the big ranchers functioned as law unto themselves. Goodnight hired Nicolás Martínez—called Colas, a former Comanchero—as a reliable henchman. One of the first of the legendary bad men of the Panhandle, Sostenes l'Archevêque was said to be a mixed-race man who despised the Anglo-Americans who had killed his father. Martínez settled this problem for his employer by burying it in the fall of 1876.[18]

Jesús María Trujillo established a homestead on what became Trujillo Creek, about eight miles from its confluence with the Canadian River. That November, Casimero Romero had moved a large sheep-raising operation further east, bringing retainers and support personnel along with him. His kind of stock-raising, though, did not require the large-scale privatization of land ownership. However, as the route of the cattle drives shifted westward, they found the ford over the Canadian River about forty miles northwest of Amarillo a natural spot for a permanent outpost.[19]

16 Dary, *More True Tales*, 111.
17 On Las Vegas, see Howard Bryan, *Wildest of the Wild West: True Tales of a Frontier Town on the Santa Fe Trail* (Santa Fe: Clear Light Publishers, 1988).
18 McCarty, *Maverick Town*, 19–21, 26–7.
19 Ibid., 40.

It was but a matter of time until the big Anglo operations spread north. During the cattle drive of 1877—only a few years after Indian removal—a rancher named George W. Littlefield reached that point when he found that the size of the herds that had already reached Kansas had pulled down his selling price. Littlefield decided to winter his cattle in the grasslands of the Panhandle and bring them even closer to Dodge City the following spring. So his new LIT ranch took form and began sprawling across the open range that ran for twenty-five miles along the river, with a complex on Pescado Creek a few miles west of the ford. This complex soon included a few buildings and formed the real beginnings of Tascosa. In a matter of months, they began forming the Panhandle Stockholders' Association.

Not only did new rail links lure larger herds north but overgrazing in the south pushed them in that direction. Soon, herds of considerable size began functioning around Fort Supply. In Kansas, the Comanche Pool represented another attempt still further north, near Medicine Lodge. The Goodnight-Loving Trail veered west through New Mexico up through Colorado to Cheyenne, and large herds emerged where the army had been clearing other Indian populations from the upper Plains in territories such as Wyoming, Montana, and the Dakotas.

This process transformed the West in these years. Initially, all of this activity represented the "open range," where cattle continued to roam freely as they had throughout the war years in the Indian Territory. As had been the custom, cattlemen came to treat this free-range beef as if it were as unowned as wild animals. Anyone with a branding iron and a place to put these mavericks could capture, brand, and domesticate them. Almost nobody regarded this as theft or rustling, and almost everybody on the open range engaged in the practice, from the big rancher down to the lowliest young cowboy aspiring to build his own herd.

This practice, however, was as doomed as the buffalo or the Indian . . . and destroyed almost as quickly.

Law and Disorder

Kansas authorities zoned their cow towns to reflect their perception of violence as containable. In reality, however, civic regulations could not separate the civilization they strove to root in the West from violence visited upon the original inhabitants. The almost instantaneous nature of these American developments also left little time to establish a hierarchy over Mexicans and African Americans different from that which had worked so well to coerce the Indians.

The process naturally generated ongoing conflicts, even among self-defined whites. Those who had opposed secession and the Confederacy and who were working assiduously to reconstruct the state in cooperation with the Radical Republican government drew particular ire, as did immigrants, particularly Germans, many of whom were also anti-secessionists.

Even more important over the long run, the large concerns that dominated the West could not have done so without violence. Cattle owners regularly used armed force to shape the economic opportunities of the cattle boom. The new Western Trail began in Texas at Kerrville, where smaller feeder trails brought cattle up from the valley of the Rio Grande. The trail continued north over the James, Llano, and San Saba Rivers and Brady Creek, before leaving the Hill Country at Cow Gap where feeder trails from Mason, San Saba, and Lampasas counties joined it. It continued north to Doan's Crossing of the Red River into the Indian Territory and beyond to Dodge City.

Although it has been described as the result of feuds, the violence that swept the West often reflected deep social conflicts and political tensions. Texas certainly experienced a bloodier and more multicultural version of the racial violence that swept the old Confederacy, but many of its white residents went at each other in a particularly systematic fashion. By the mid-1870s, old ethnic tensions fueled by beef exploded in Karnes and DeWitt counties, due south from Austin and about half of the way to the Gulf. Years before, the Anglos had tried to crowd out Mexican teamsters in Karnes County, leading to a "Cart War" on the eve of the Civil War. Throughout secession and the war to maintain black slavery, many of the local Anglos found the Mexicans insufficiently enthusiastic. Gunplay and lynching continued sporadically. With the arrival of the cattle business and the stockmen's decision to close the open range, the small ranchers found themselves with their backs to the wall. By 1875, small bands of them donned masks and began cutting fences in the night.[20]

In adjacent DeWitt County, a clan of particularly recalcitrant thugs called the Taylors murdered a number of black soldiers in 1866 and 1867, even adding a few white ones into the mix. The next year, a member of the clan lost his life resisting arrest by Deputy Sheriff William E. Sutton. More shootings followed and, though a former Confederate, Sutton joined the Texas State Police Force established by the Republican Reconstruction government, which had taken the place of the old Texas Rangers.[21]

The body count rose steadily after the Taylors brought John Wesley Hardin, an experienced killer and a fugitive from justice, into the fray. A few years before, at age fifteen, Hardin had gunned down his uncle's former slave, beginning a string of killings that made him a suitable thug for the Taylors. In the end, he and some of the Taylors gunned down Sutton as he tried to catch a steamboat to leave the area, and Hardin capped the celebration of his twenty-first birthday by gunning down Deputy Sheriff Charles Webb of Brown County. Terrified that the Taylors had gone out of control, a lynch mob broke into the jail and hanged several of them. With the end of the Reconstruction, the Democrats regained control of the state and, by 1876, their Texas Rangers had imposed a new order on the area, after the loss of only about forty lives.[22]

20 Henry D. and Frances T. McCallum, *The Wire that Fenced the West* (Norman: University of Oklahoma Press, 1965), 160–1.

21 C. L. Douglas, *Famous Texas Feuds*, 2nd ed. (Austin: State House Press, 1988), 61–103. See also Hays Day, *The Sutton-Taylor Feud* (San Antonio: Murray, 1937); Marjorie Burnett Hyatt, *Fuel for a Feud* (private printing, 1987); Napoleon Augustus Jennings, *A Texas Ranger* (New York: Scribner, 1899).

22 See also John Wesley Hardin, *The Life of John Wesley Hardin as Written by Himself* (Seguin, TX: Smith and Moore, 1896).

Whether the Reconstruction or Restoration regimes were in power, the state often had to assert its authority in the face of the weakness of local law enforcement. The resurrection of the Texas Rangers embodied this. Subsequent generations of Texans who remembered DeWitt County's "Taylor-Sutton Feud" demoted the Reconstruction official Sutton to a mere feudist, translating what had been a serious case of political violence into something more akin to a personal conflict.

Such conflicts could run far beyond the bloody issues of the late Civil War. The elites in Missouri learned to set aside their wartime conflicts in the interest of promoting economic development and the skewed prosperity the term implies. In the process, local officials in the North, South, and West sometimes ignored the results of voting in order to increase taxes and, their critics charged, their personal wealth. When the state assembly of 1871–2 simply ignored the pleas of the Legislative Farmers' Club, public suspicions that elected officeholders were being paid by corporations only heightened. Frustrated Pettis County petitioners sought to recall officeholders and talked of open resistance. At Macon, former Union and Confederate soldiers stormed the courthouse, which former officers of both sides defended.[23] In an age where corporate government has long been the unchallenged norm, it may be difficult to appreciate nineteenth-century anger at what seemed a crass violation of civic trust.

Citizens in southwestern Missouri found themselves governed by people they rarely knew or trusted, with minimal restraints on vigilantism. This went far beyond the racial patterns of such violence in the postwar South, as former Unionists sometimes targeted a former rebel guerrilla leader. On April 24, 1872, three officials indicted for fraud and scheduled for a May trial fled Harrisonville for Kansas City, only to be stopped by a barricade only twelve miles from town, near

23 David Thelen, *Paths of Resistance: Tradition and Dignity in Industrializing Missouri* (New York: Oxford University Press, 1986), 62–5; Buck, 194–5; William Earl Parrish, *A History of Missouri: Vol. III, 1860 to 1875* (Columbia: University of Missouri Press, 1973), 192–3, 198–200, 202–3, 209.

Gunn City. There, fifty masked men shot them before a supportive crowd of several hundred, who helped to riddle the corpses with bullets.[24]

Nobody ever determined who had initiated the crime. It may have represented the work of angry citizens. One must remember, however, that the failure of these officials to give testimony likely saved their superiors from prosecution or disgrace. Similarly, it remains unclear how a band of masked men who blew up furnaces and mills in nearby Jasper County were identified as desperate workers.

As the case of the Ingalls in Kansas demonstrated, the introduction of railroad interests and large-scale business became inseparable from the forcible displacement of the native peoples there. The brutalities of Indian dispossession created hard, brutal life on the open range.

The "open range" in turn provided a theoretically egalitarian economy in which anyone with cattle could graze them without hindrance on the unfenced prairies. Theories aside, this arrangement did not last any longer than it took the authorities to replicate the experience of the "enclosures" and closures that had swept the Old World.

The iconic cowboys emerged as the most sensitive element in this social universe. They emerged in the form they did after the Civil War, a rotating workforce of several thousand hands who managed the cattle drives. Few groups of laborers would prove to be as susceptible as the cowboys to the tiniest shifts in their industry and its fate.

As far as cowboys were concerned, the growth of the railroads reduced the need for overland freighters, stages, and wagon trains, as well as those long cattle drives. Development destroyed the massive buffalo herds and the Indians living beyond the control of the government. One cowboy later recalled how it became "increasingly difficult

24 On Gunn City, see Thelen, *Paths of Resistance*, 65–7, and F. A. North, ed., *The History of Jasper County, Missouri* (Des Moines, 1883), 214–15, 244. For vigilantism, see Parrish, *A History of Missouri*, 90–1. Despite contextual weaknesses, Mary Hartman and Elmo Ingenthron have penned an informative narrative as well: *Bald Knobbers: Vigilantes on the Ozark Frontier* (Gretna, LA: Pelican, 1988).

for the long-haired saddlemen, teamsters, and riflemen to make a living."[25]

Not surprisingly, cowboys began doing some unexpected things. Alexander L. Turner, a rural Texas boy of sixteen, helped drive a herd from Llano Texas to Dodge City around 1880.[26] The youngest member of the crew came to be called "Bud," which he readily accepted as a better alternative to "Alexander." He decided to stay in Kansas, working for various outfits. By 1882, he had found work with Hunter and Evans of the Comanche Pool.

Supposedly, the men decided to strike around the holiday season of 1882–3. Billy Blair, the general manager of the pool, "rode out to meet with the cowboys." Going to each man, he asked, "Are you striking?" If they said yes, he replied, "You've just lost your job with the Pool, so ride in for your time!" When Turner told him he would stick with his coworkers, Blair replied, "I'm sorry. I had a winter camp on the Mule Creek for you, but you'll have to go with the rest." The experience "cured" Turner of striking.

Unfortunately, Turner's account requires some interpretation and considerable caution. The strike may well have happened, but any cowboy would realize that the worst possible time to threaten to quit was the winter, when the bosses usually sent a sizeable portion of their workers home anyway.

We know of the strike only through what Turner told his daughter, Dulcie Sullivan, whose book simply compiled stories from old timers "recorded exactly as told to me." Turner ascribed the strike not to grievances but to "one of their cowboys, hoping to get a better job for himself," and "regarded strikes as an evil dish cooked up by the devil." For Sullivan's part, she dedicated her compilation to Jordan E. McAllister, the general manager of one of the companies most hostile to unionism in the Texas Panhandle.

25 "'Broncho John' Sullivan's Memories of Half a Century. As Told To, and Recorded By, His Son, John H. ('Texas Jack') Sullivan," Valparaiso, Indiana *Vidette-Messenger*, July 9, 1935, p. 8. See also *Vidette Messenger*, September 27, 1951, p. 2.

26 For his story, see Loula Grace Erdman, "Introduction," in Dulcie Sullivan, *The LS Brand: The Story of a Texas Panhandle Ranch* (Austin: University of Texas Press, 1968), 69–70.

Turner echoed the values of the dominant economic, social, and cultural institutions of society. First of all, government, the press, the pulpit, and the one-room schoolhouse insisted that hard work produced success, while villainy was ultimately thwarted. From their perspective—and that of their successors—citizens achieved freedom by responding naturally to market forces and economic opportunities. They scorned oppressive government actions that restricted or regulated their prerogatives or fettered their entrepreneurial ambitions. Ultimately, people who lacked wealth or power suffered only because of choices they themselves had made, as freely as had the cattle barons, the railroad tycoons, and the bankers.

Apologists for this system, then and now, have generally conceded that people who do not believe they are receiving fair treatment have the right to complain in a free America. A Bill of Rights guaranteed the right of those with little wealth and few resources to print what they wanted in the newspapers just as much as those with great wealth and resources. And, of course, the people had every right to organize themselves into unions, social movements, and genuinely oppositional parties.

Such may have been the intended subtext of television entertainment such as *Little House on the Prairie*, but history documents other little houses too. Only a little while after the Ingalls, the Benders turned up and established a much-needed way station to the north. John and his wife, son, and daughter offered food, lodging, and more to the weary traveler, and the women offered their services as spiritualists and healers. It later transpired that they often closed the night by bludgeoning their guests with a sledgehammer, dropping them through a trapdoor, and slitting their throats. After the guests bled out, the family planted them around back in the garden, and the son would take their horses and other property somewhere far away where they could be sold without attracting too much attention. Locals later found eleven corpses in the garden, but suspected that there had been many other victims. The Benders, they reasoned, would have most likely started burying bodies somewhere where they would be less likely to flavor the tomatoes. Most of us might see attacking guests and murdering all witnesses as questionable, but the Benders represented a point on a broad continuum of values to which the masters of their world adhered.

The Real West is under no obligation to offer mirages across the Great American Desert in order to vindicate the status quo. The mad barber Sweeney Todd did not require Fleet Street or the squalor of London. Neither did the various networks that challenged Gilded Age capitalism in America. In the West, one need not dig deeply to encounter class politics and class violence. And the precarious state of the cowboys represented the canary in that coal mine. It might be useful to see American history in this period as more than a simple process of westward expansion by an eastern, urban, industrial civilization. The general pioneering role of people in the post–Civil War West merits greater exploration.

ONE

Mysteries of the Heartland

The Emergence of Postwar Western Radicalism

In its later Texas incarnation, the Settlers' Alliance became an association of small farmers and stockgrowers. Where the great ranchers drove massive herds through Lampasas County on their way to the main course of the Western Trail, they often swept along the cattle of the smaller ranchers. So it was that the new organization made it the responsibility of the president in each sub-alliance to appoint two "Grand Smokeys" and to keep the identity of those appointees secret to protect both them and their families. While the official instructions of these Smokeys would be to "arrest, or cause arrest of anyone found stealing, or in possession of stolen stock," they resembled armed protectors of the alliance members.[1] Lines of power may have been clear enough, but they remained sufficiently contested where small ranchers arranged for their armed defense against their larger, more powerful, and ruthless neighbors backed by capital from the east and overseas and by the power of their own government at home.

1 "That particular provision didn't last long." Nelson A. Dunning was less forthcoming later about the "Grand Smokeys," writing that their identity remained "secret from all save the president. Their peculiar function has been forgotten." Dunning, *The Farmers' Alliance History and Agricultural Digest* (Washington, DC: The Alliance Publishing Company, 1891), 17–18.

Bound by familial and social ties to the countryside, a dedicated force of rural editors, village schoolteachers, county seat lawyers, and aspiring politicians built massive oppositional associations. Performing the role of what Antonio Gramsci termed the "organic intellectuals," they also built and sustained the largest third party movement since the antebellum emergence of the Republicans against the Whigs and Democrats. In part, developments in the West permitted them to reach beyond the sectional limits of the Republican North and the Democratic South, mobilizing support as readily in Texas as in Kansas, among ranchers as well as farmers, and hopeful of mobilizing the working classes—cowboys in the West as well as industrial workers in the East. In the end, though, these oppositional currents lacked the strength to keep influences beyond the region from cultivating a civic culture of electoral misdirection channelled by systemic political violence.

The Industrial Brotherhood

In the aftermath of the Civil War, small farmers organized an estimated 2 million Americans into the Patrons of Husbandry, also called "the Grange." Founded and promoted by civil servants, editors, schoolteachers, and professionals in farm towns, the Patrons won their initial membership in Minnesota but spread rapidly across the Midwest and beyond. The group consciously aimed to meet the social, economic, and cultural needs of white farmers and the communities with which they were associated by entirely avoiding any direct involvement in electoral politics.

Nevertheless, the National Grange had no end of trouble trying to contain the political impulses of many of the local Patrons. In 1873, farmers in Illinois secured the legislature's passage of their "Grange Laws" to regulate freight charges. However, the state's elected Supreme Court declared such regulation unconstitutional. In response, Stephen M. Smith, a Kewanee hog farmer, mobilized his angry neighbors into their own Peoples' Antimonopolist ticket, which overcame bipartisan opposition to bring down a State Justice. The victory inspired a State Farmers' Association to provide the political leadership the Grange would not.[2]

The new movement extolled and asserted the interests of farmers, but through farming communities. Its leaders were not isolated hayseeds but civically connected "producers" who regularly met in stores, town halls, clubs, and churches, as well as their own associations. There they found politicians, lawyers, clergymen, and sympathetic newspaper editors willing to explain their grievances and concerns, as best they understood them or as best suited them.

Schoolteachers such as Ohio-born and Indiana-raised Henry Asa Coffeen played a particularly vital role. Coffeen had studied science at Abingdon College—later Eureka College, the alma mater of Ronald Reagan—but he had a deep commitment to the well-being of the society around him. As the Grange and antimonopolist movements emerged, he eagerly joined them and helped refine their language and arguments.

Political concerns also moved farmers in neighboring Missouri, who organized large lodges of the Patrons near St. Louis as early as 1870. The following year, deputies of the Patrons' National Grange began organizing the state, establishing an impressive 245 local chapter with 2,000 members by May 1873. Less than a year later, in March 1874, the Grange in Missouri encompassed 2,000 clubs with 80,000 members. The groups had enough resources to sustain eighteen grain elevators and warehouses, eight gristmills, three meat packinghouses, and twenty-six factories producing everything from plows to cheese.[3]

Particularly vulnerable to the disappointing turmoil of Reconstruction politics, growing numbers of Missouri Patrons

2 Stephen L. Hanson, *The Making of the Third Party System: Voters and Parties in Illinois, 1850–1876* (Ann Arbor: UMI Research Press, 1980), 185–7, 189–90, 192.

3 Charles M. Gardner, *The Grange—Friend of the Farmer* (Washington, DC: The National Grange, 1949), 276; Solon Buck, *The Granger Movement: A Study of Agricultural Organization and Its Political, Economic, and Social Manifestations, 1870–1880* (Cambridge: Harvard University Press, 1913), 78, 58ff; D. Sven Nordin, *Rich Harvest: A History of the Grange, 1867–1900* (Jackson: University Press of Mississippi, 1974), 29, 146, who also noted that the loss of $20,000 through speculation by the state treasurer forced serious cutbacks in the cooperative plans for the year (p. 144).

thought the conflict opened all sorts of political possibilities. More specifically, they challenged the order's self-imposed race and class restrictions on membership. While the Patrons nationally accepted the exclusion of blacks to placate potential members among the Southern planters, Missouri leaders planned to organize African American farmers, albeit into separate lodges. At the same time, they desperately sought an alliance of "the producing classes" that would include the dynamic labor movement emerging from St. Louis. Its wartime Workingmen's Union of Missouri established a postwar *Industrial Advocate* that began to reach miners in the far southwest corner of the state.[4] Many Missouri Grangers wanted labor reformers of all sorts in their organization, whether or not they were farmers.

Andrew Warner St. John, a schoolteacher and farmer near Carthage, took up the Grangers' cause. The son of a Chautauqua County, New York, mechanic, he had grown up in the Wisconsin Territory and become a schoolteacher in Freeborn County, Minnesota. When war broke out, he had joined the Fifth Minnesota regiment, but he was eventually brought down in Mississippi by chronic dysentery, rheumatism, and lung disease. In the fall of 1867, St. John and his younger brother moved to Carthage; his first wife died and he remarried in 1870. In August 1872, he helped found a local Horticultural Society and joined the Grange.[5] A former Republican in a Democratic district, St. John retained the old Radical aspiration to unite all "producers," regardless of race or employment, particularly in terms of political action.

Yet St. John found an indispensable local ally in the Southerner who edited the local newspaper, Joshua A. Bodenhamer. The North Carolina–born son of a Methodist minister had gone to Iowa in 1860

4 On race, see Buck, *The Granger Movement*, 74 n1. In parts of Mississippi, the Ku Klux Klan reportedly used the Grange as a cover, but Nordin reports that some of the Louisiana lodges became integrated: Nordin, *Rich Harvest*, 32–3. On class, see Parrish, *A History of Missouri: Vol. III*, 218–19, 222–4.

5 North, *The History of Jasper County*, 369–70, 291, 249; Joel T. Livingston, *A History of Jasper County, Missouri and Its People* (Chicago: Lewis Publishing Co., 1912), 1: 352; Malcolm G. McGregor, *The Biographical Record of Jasper County, Missouri* (Chicago: Lewis Publishing Co., 1901), 443; Lucius F. Hubbard, "Narrative of the Fifth Regiment" in *Minnesota in the Civil and Indian Wars, 1861–1865* (St. Paul: Pioneer Press Co., 1891), 243–8.

and west during the war. He returned to become a newspaper printer in northwestern Missouri and Nebraska. After coming to Jasper County in 1871, he launched his *People's Press* in April 1872 (only days before the Gunn City incident). Although a militant Granger, Bodenhamer defined the goals of his paper as primarily "in the interest of the industrial and business classes."[6]

St. John and his comrades launched their own Industrial Brotherhood (IB) after the National Grange, gathering at St. Louis on February 4–12, 1874, where they flatly refused to expand its membership or reconsider its indifference to politics. Their new order naturally avoided direct conflict with the massive Patrons of Husbandry, instead emphasizing its similarities to the larger group. Like the Patrons, the IB admitted women: St. John insisted upon "the equality . . . of our mothers, wives, sisters and daughters" and another leader argued that without a "platform broad enough to let woman stand side by side with you," the group's members would "never be able to balance the mighty power of capital." The IB adopted a simplified version of the ritual and degree structure of the Grange and admitted blacks, along with all "honest, hard working men—mechanics and others." As the group's name implied, it oriented toward "the working classes" and explicitly excluded "wealthy merchants employing clerks" and "manufacturers employing many hands."[7]

It turned out that many leading Patrons in Illinois, Missouri, and Kansas shared these concerns and joined the IB though without leaving the Grange. By mid-March, the state lecturer of the Missouri Grange also spoke for and organized an IB in northern Missouri. Editors of pro-Grange newspapers in southwest Missouri and

6 North, *The History of Jasper County*, 205, 239, 259, 291, 323, 369–70.

7 "The Industrial Brotherhood" [from St. Louis *Democrat*] and "Sovereigns of Industry and Industrial Brotherhood" [from *Fort Scott Pioneer*], *People's Press*, Feb. 26, 1874, pp. 1, 2. From this last source, see "Origin, Objects and Plan of the Industrial Brotherhood," July 16, 1874. Mrs. L.C. Smith quoted in "Industrial Brotherhood," April 30, 1874, p. 2; "Origin, Objects and Plan of the Industrial Brotherhood." Buck, *The Granger Movement:*, 63–5, 78; Gardner, *The Grange— Friend of the Farmer*, 46–51; *Appleton's Cyclopedia for 1874* (New York: D. Appleton and Company, 1874), 799–80.

adjacent Kansas—such as the Lebanon *Anti-Monopolist*—began urging readers to form lodges of the IB.[8]

Some, such as Uzel Franklin Sargent, had experiences very similar to the founders of the order. Like St. John, Sargent had been born in New York, lived in Wisconsin and Minnesota, and taught school. However, he had studied law before going into journalism and coming to Kansas in 1873. He had just purchased the *Fort Scott Democrat* and renamed it the *Pioneer*. An advocate for temperance, he supported Greeley and the Liberal Republicans in 1872. Sargent reported applications for IB charters from Wisconsin and Kansas.[9]

The IB absorbed the efforts of veteran radicals, including Alcander Longley, one of several sons of Abner Longley, the southwest Ohio socialist pioneer. The family had passed through the earlier Owenite and Fourierist communitarian movements. In the midst of Reconstruction violence in Missouri, Alcander Longley established his self-described "Communist" Reunion Colony eleven miles west of Carthage near Minersville (now Oronogo). A similar group of social pioneers and freethinkers founded the nearby town of Liberal. Participants in these communities, such as N.T. Romain and Robert E. LaFetra, a disabled Union veteran, began to agitate for third party politics that lasted for decades along the Missouri-Kansas line.[10]

8 "Indorsements of the Industrial Brotherhood," *People's Press*, March 19, 1874, p. 3; "Indorsement of the I.B.," *People's Press*, March 26, 1874, p. 2, which also quotes Lemen and Oldham.

9 *The United States Biographical Dictionary, Kansas Volume* (Chicago and Kansas City: S. Lewis & Co., 1879), 526–7. "Sovereigns of Industry and Industrial Brotherhood" [from *Fort Scott Pioneer*], "The Industrial Brotherhood" [from St. Louis *Democrat*], and "The Industrial Brotherhood," *People's Press*, Feb. 26, 1874, pp. 1, 2, 3. For the claim of February 22 origins, see "Origin, Objects and Plan of the Industrial Brotherhood."

10 On Longley, see Robert S. Fogarty, *Dictionary of American Communal and Utopian History* (Westport, CT: Greenwood Press, 1980), 203; H. Roger Grant, "Missouri's Utopian Communities," *Missouri Historical Review*, LXVI (Oct. 1971), 39–40; Longley's letters to *The Socialist* are in the February 8 and 22, 1879, issues. A branch of Robert Ingersoll's Liberal League formed at Carthage according to the directory in *The Truth Seeker* for 1879–80. See also Edward K. Spann, *Brotherly Tomorrows: Movements for a Cooperative Society in America, 1820–1920* (New York: Columbia University Press, 1989), 122–3, 229; Robert S. Fogarty, *All Things New:*

St. John also courted the good will of W. H. Earle of the Sovereigns of Industry, the postwar venture of the Fourierists, who had been experimenting for over thirty years with cooperative "Protective Unions." St. John wanted "a union of the two orders," and his rejection prompted one of the veteran Sovereigns, John G. Drew, a veteran Fourierist and active Sovereign of Industry, to acknowledge frankly that the Sovereigns had pretty much resolved themselves into a successful business uninterested in politics. Already one of the politicized members of the Patrons, Drew found himself "riding two horses going opposite directions at the same time, and being too old to learn, I resolved to resign" from the Sovereigns and join the IB.[11]

The obscurity of the IB remains peculiar given its immense importance in American labor history. The National Labor Union (NLU) that had drawn together labor leaders and social reformers after the Civil War never provided much more than loosely structured annual gatherings. In 1872, even this had collapsed with a misdirected effort to launch a National Labor Reform Party (NLRP) behind a presidential bid by Judge David Davis. Labor officials met in 1873 and 1874 as an "Industrial Congress," even reverting to an antebellum name. In April 1874, representatives of the national labor organizations decided how best to foster the solidarity of "the producing classes."[12]

The leading body of the American labor movement narrowed its options to the Sovereigns of Industry or the IB. When St. John came

---

American Communes and Utopian Movements, 1860–1914 (Chicago: University of Chicago Press, 1990), 104–8; and Carl Guarneri, *The Utopian Alternative: Fourierism in Nineteenth-Century America* (Ithaca: Cornell University Press, 1991), 77, 195, 327–8, 389. For Romain, see his letters in *The Socialist*, June 7 and 21, 1879, and his listings as the secretary and resident agitator of the Urbana SLP. For LaFetra, see his letters in the issues of Oct. 5 and Nov. 9, 1878, May 3 and 24 and July 5, 1879, and service as a corporal in Company B of the Fortieth Ohio in *Official Roster of the Soldiers of the State of Ohio in the War of the Rebellion, 1861–1866*, comp. the Roster commission, vol. IV (Akron, 1886–95), 138.

11   Norman J. Ware, *The Labor Movement in the United States, 1860–1895: A Study in Democracy* (New York: Appleton, 1929), 15; "Sovereigns of Industry and Industrial Brotherhood" [from *Fort Scott Pioneer*], *People's Press*, Feb. 26, 1874; "Industrial Brotherhood and Sovereigns of Industry," *People's Press*, July 9, 1874, p. 4.

12   "Industrial Congress. Significant Meeting at Rochester. Reported by A. Briggs Davis," *Woodhull & Clafflin's Weekly*, May 9, 1874, p. 3, cols. 1–2.

west to address its gatherings, he spoke at Philadelphia and New York City to enthusiastic crowds. The Industrial Congress elected him its first vice president even as its president—NLU veteran Robert Schilling of the Coopers Union—declared "that he should caution industrial organizations against any connection with the S. of I."[13] In the end, the IB became the primary national organization of American labor between 1874 and 1878.

Alternatives to the IB might have provided the shell of a secret society, but not the kind of open-ended association capable of sustaining a broad movement that embraced trade unionism as a vital component of labor reform. IB members wanted a vehicle for cooperation, but not something so dogmatically exclusive in its focus as the Sovereigns.[14] Moreover, the IB left open the possibility of pursuing a variety of other strategic and tactical options.

Through the silent presence of the IB, the labor movement played a significant role in the subsequent national gatherings of 1875. In March, Howard H. Day got "representatives from all the labor organizations in New-York and Pennsylvania, including the Granges and retail coal dealers" to a Harrisburg convention around a much more sweeping range of issues. However, St. John, Smith, Boone, Schilling, and other IB leaders clung to the regular national Greenback organization that convened at Cleveland's Industrial Hall. The latter included an impressive array of old NLU and NLRP leaders like Troup, Richard

13   *Workingman's Advocate*, July 26, 1873; untitled notice and "Industrial Congress," *People's Press*, April 23, 1874, pp. 2, 4; "Industrial Brotherhood and Sovereigns of Industry," *People's Press*, July 9, 1874, p. 4. John R. Commons et al., *History of Labour in the United States*, vol. 2, 2nd ed. (New York: Macmillan, 1946), 162–4, 196; Ware, *The Labor Movement in the United States*, 15, 17, 60, 76; Philip S. Foner, *History of the Labor Movement in the United States: Vol. 1—From the Colonial Times to the Founding of the American Federation of Labor* (New York: International Publishers, 1947), 441; Foster Rhea Dulles, *Labor in America: A History*, 3rd ed. (Northbrook, IL: AHM Publishing, 1960), 111, 131; Samuel Bernstein, *The First International in America* (New York: A.M. Kelley, 1962), 59; Chester M. Destler, *American Radicalism, 1865–1901*, 2nd ed. (New London: Connecticut College Press, 1946), 60; David Montgomery treated the Industrial Congresses as essentially "a continuation of the N.L.U": *Beyond Equality: Labor and the Radical Republicans, 1862–1872* (New York: Knopf, 1967), 194–5.

14   Terrence V. Powderly, *Thirty Years of Labor* (Columbus, OH: Excelsior, 1889).

Trevellick, and J. H. Wright. Thomas Jefferson Durant, an antebellum Fourierist and wartime attorney general of Louisiana's Unionist
provisional government, presented credentials from the District of
Columbia.[15] They formally established the National or Independent
Party, soon more widely called the "Greenback Party."

A few years later, in 1878, the labor movement unsentimentally
abandoned the politically identified IB for the Knights of Labor, but
adopted the IB's strategy and platform. The Knights echoed the IB's
concerns about "the recent alarming development and aggression of
aggregated wealth, which, unless checked, will inevitably lead to the
pauperization and hopeless degradation of the toiling masses." It set
as its goal a "system adopted which will secure to the laborer the fruits
of his toil," and identified as the key to success the "co-operative
effort, of the power of the industrial classes; and we submit to the
world the objects sought to be accomplished by our organization,
calling upon all who believe in securing 'the greatest good to the greatest number' to aid and assist us."[16]

The specter of the order certainly haunted Alan Pinkerton, the
labor spy who hallucinated a "Universal Brotherhood" behind the
difficulties of capitalism. The IB's support for the equality of all workers regardless of craft, race, or gender offered implicit threats to the
social order. Most impressively, the eastern Knights of Labor reorganized itself to take up publicly the cooperative social vision of the IB,
which could embrace trade unionism without excluding other measures. Reflecting such continuities, Terrence V. Powderly became the

15 "The Anti-Monopoly Convention," *New York Daily Times*, March 4, 1875,
p. 1. Day's group followed with the "Cincinnati Conference of Mechanics and
Working-men" described in "The Working-men's Convention," Cincinnati *Daily
Enquirer*, Sept. 8, 1875, p. 8. "The Rag Men Come to the Surface," "Greenback
Men in Council at Cleveland, O.," Chicago *Daily Tribune*, March 11, 1875, p. 2,
and March 12, 1875, p. 2; "The Greenback Party," "Greenback Convention," "The
Greenback Party," Chicago *Daily Interocean*, March 11, 1875, p. 5; March 12,
1875, p. 5; March 13, 1875, p. 1; "More Greenbacks," "Greenback Enthusiasts,"
Chicago *Daily Times*, March 12, 1875, p. 3; March 13, 1875, p. 9.

16 Powderly, *Thirty Years of Labor*, 128–9. John R. Commons et al., eds., *A
Documentary History of American Industrial Society*, vol. 9 (Cleveland: Arthur H.
Clark Co., 1910–11), 43.

first head of the reorganized Knights, and Schilling remained active in the Knights and most other aspects of the movement well into the days of a national People's Party.[17]

Political Action and Alliances

The IB claimed agreement with the Grangers on politics: "That is they don't say anything about it unless they have a mind to." Unlike the Grange, though, the IB almost always *did* have a mind to speak politically. Already, the farmers' victory in Illinois had inspired angry voters to converge on the polls across the American heartland, brandishing independent ballots. In addition to the People's Party in Missouri, one could find Independent Parties in Illinois, Indiana, Nebraska, and Oregon; Independent Reform Parties in Kansas and Wisconsin; a Peoples' Independent Party in California; the National Reform Party in Michigan; and the Antimonopolist Party in Iowa. Interestingly, the dominant Republican Party responded differently in various states, blocking efforts to win Grange laws in Minnesota while saving similar legislation in Iowa and Wisconsin and, in Missouri, declining to divide anti-Democratic voters by running GOP candidates.[18] These

17   John R. Commons, *History of Labour in the United States*, vol. 2 (New York: Macmillan, 1918–35), 196; Alan Pinkerton, *Strikers, Communists, Tramps and Detectives* (New York: G. W. Carleton & Co., 1878), 88–9; Powderly, *Thirty Years of Labor*, 66, 67, 120; Craig Phelan, *Grand Master Workman: Terence Powderly and the Knights of Labor* (Westport, CT: Greenwood Press, 2000), 17–18, including efforts to establish a "Brotherhood of United Labor," 213, 229–30; Robert E. Weir, *Knights Unhorsed: Internal Conflict in a Gilded Age Social Movement* (Detroit: Wayne State University Press, 2000), 66–9. See Weir's *Beyond Labor's Veil: The Culture of the Knights of Labor* (University Park: Pennsylvania State University Press, 1996), and Kim Voss's *The Making of American Exceptionalism: The Knights of Labor and Class Formation in the Nineteenth Century* (Ithaca, NY: Cornell University Press, 1993). See also Britton A. Hill's *The Union of the Grangers and Working-men with the Greenback-men: Speech in Support of the Resolution* (St. Louis: n.p., 1877).

18   "The Industrial Brotherhood" and "Sovereigns of Industry and Industrial Brotherhood" [from *Fort Scott Pioneer*], *People's Press*, Feb. 26, 1874, p. 3; "Origin, Objects and Plan of the Industrial Brotherhood." Members included Mr. and Mrs. S. M. Smith, H. H. Day, John G. Drew, Dr. H. H. John, and J. M. Oldham.

third party movements groped toward a national issue that would leave the sectionalized two-party system incapacitated.

The Independent Reformers in Kansas continued to focus on state issues. They specifically complained about the bulldozing of home-steaders by the railroads, inspiring a convention at Topeka on May 27, 1874. A subsequent gathering on August 5 named candidates and declared that "equal and just laws, the rights of life, liberty and the pursuit of happiness shall be assured to all men, without distinction of race, color or nationality." It also declared, as part of its opposition to corruption and monopoly, "sympathy with the settlers on the Osage lands, and to homestead settlers whose titles are contested by railroad companies."[19]

Nevertheless, the panic that hit the economy in the fall of 1873 and the congressional passage of the Resumption Act had set a course whereby the country would replace the government-issued wartime paper "greenbacks" with specie, leaving the issuance of paper to banks. Not only was the paper currency widely identified with the prosperity of the late war years, but the inflationary expansion of the money supply had, in places, done much to free farmers from their tradi-tional, seasonal cycle of indebtedness. The government's planned contraction of the money supply seemed a reckless threat to the econ-omy and the standing of its vital middle class.

In response, by 1874, the Illinois and Indiana insurgents focused their appeal to "farmers, mechanics and other citizens" on the currency question. Initially these parties had hardly embraced that narrow focus. Indeed, the insurgent parties in Michigan and Kansas had explicitly declared themselves against such measures, as did a signifi-cant minority of the Illinois Independents. Nevertheless, on June 10, 1874, simultaneous conventions in Springfield and Indianapolis of state Independent Parties established "Greenbackism" as the corner-stone of a national program.[20]

19 For the Independent Reform Convention at Topeka, see Wilder, *Annals of Kansas*, 629, 641–3.

20 "The Rag-Men," Chicago *Daily Tribune*, November 26, 1874, p. 2; "More Money," Chicago *Daily Interocean*, November 26, 1874, p. 1; "The Independents" and "Meeting of Independent Politicians at Indianapolis," *People's Press*, December

Nevertheless, even as the national labor movement embraced the IB, the IB actively built a third party movement and led it toward Greenbackism. St. John and the IB were among the first to take up the cause of currency reform. The twenty-four-year-old schoolteacher Lewis Cass Tidball, a native of Zanesville, Ohio, who was then living with his parents who had moved west, took charge of the Jasper County IB.[21]

Moreover, the legacy of the IB passed on more than language to the Knights. Not only did St. John and other members quietly introduce issues beyond currency reform, but the very presence of IB leader C.W. Thompson, "a colored delegate, aged 18, from Richmond, Va.," who addressed the convention, provided another component of the group's platform. The convention cheered as Thompson hailed theirs as "a just movement" that "would result in the entire delivery of his race from the thralldom now surrounding it."

Most significantly, the Industrial Brotherhood, with its interracial membership, gained support in the South. The *Independent Workingman* of Nashville, Tennessee, heartily endorsed the project, particularly its rejection of a "too selfish" policy with regard to working women "where we have made the mistake all the time." "I am more than satisfied of the correctness of your opinion in regard to the necessity of an association to unite the laboring classes," added the *Valley Farmer* from Tuscumbia, Alabama. "There is no country under Heaven that needs reformation more than this part of the South." In Richmond, Virginia, black labor leader Charles Thompson helped establish and lead a large and powerful organization of tobacco workers under the auspices of the Brotherhood.[22]

3, 1874, pp. 2, 4; St. John, "Watchman, What of the Night?" *People's Press*, Nov. 19, 1874, p. 2; "Movement of Prominent Labor Reformers," *People's Press*, Nov. 26, 1874, p. 2.

21 Per Tidball's announcement in the *People's Press*, June 27, 1878, and material from the 1880 Census, which showed him at Leadville.

22 "Indorsements of the Industrial Brotherhood," *People's Press*, March 19, 1874, p. 3; Peter J. Rachleff, *Black Labor in the South: Richmond, Virginia, 1865–1890* (Philadelphia: Temple University Press, 1984), 75–8; Brooks in "Indorsement of the I.B.," March 26, 1874, p. 2. For the black Knights, see Phillip S. Foner, *Organized Labor and the Black Worker, 1619–1973* (New York: Praeger Publishers,

Across the state line from the developing Brotherhood in Missouri, D. G. Campbell in Kansas sought to foster the latest incarnation of the old Settlers' Alliance.[23] He sent material on the Alliance in Kansas back to New York. There it was absorbed by a man named Johnson. F. P. Root recalled that Rev. B. T. Roberts and the Cultivator of Albany took up the idea of organizing in February 1875. Over the next few years, a Farmers' Alliance flourished across upstate New York, periodically fielding its own candidates but often operating through the Greenback–Labor coalition. William Saunders, a founder of the Patrons, also took up the cause of the Alliance.

Then, the Farmers' Alliance of upstate New York—or the idea of an Alliance—drifted back west from upstate New York into Illinois. The *Western Rural* in Chicago formed the heart of what became a Northwest Alliance. Under the leadership of Marcus M. "Brick" Pomeroy, it became even more explicitly involved in electoral politics. Pomeroy's opposition to Republican hegemony in the upper Midwest predisposed him to support Democrats.

Even before the railroads, the alliance in Kansas naturally migrated along the lines of the cattle trails. Some of the participants in the old Settlers' Alliance headed to Texas. Campbell recalled "a man by the name of Tanner" who went south with "several families."

In 1874, the Tennessee-born John R. Allen arrived in Lampasas County, Texas. With Captain Lewis S. Chavose, he built what became the local schoohouse on Donaldson Creek, about halfway between the towns of Lampasas and Montvale. Reflecting the real economy of the area at that point, locals called the kind of rough-hewn lumber home he built "rawhide." Although the Confederacy—desperate for salt—had established works about eight miles away, where Saline

1974), 49. Melton A. McLaurin discussed the particular strength of the order at Richmond in *The Knights of Labor in the South* (Westport, CT: Greenwood Press, 1979), 40–2, 47–51, 64–7, 135–9, 142–7, 149–50, 169–70, 173–4, 184–5. See also Matthew Hild, *Greenbackers, Knights of Labor, and Populists: Farmer-Labor Insurgency in the Late-Nineteenth-Century South* (Athens: University of Georgia Press, 2007).

23 See Dunning, *The Farmers' Alliance History*, 11–12, 230–2, 233, 245.

Creek reached the Colorado River, Montvale hardly amounted to anything at this point, and that might be an exaggeration.[24]

These changes contributed to the decision of some in Lampasas County to organize themselves in 1875 to press for their own interests against the larger cattlemen and bankers. For a while, they called themselves the Knights of Reliance, taking up the grand and pretentious labels preferred by secret societies that flourished in American communities at the time.[25]

Several considerations explain the appearance of the Alliance in Lampasas County. Most overlooked is the Alliance's emergence from the local cattle industry that grew rapidly due to the shifting traffic of the cattle drives, which had blazed a new Western Trail that partly fueled the county. The organization owed its origins to cattle as much—or more—than to corn or wheat. It also represented a newly settled area, and the order grew alongside the Masons, Odd Fellows, Good Templars, Council of United Friends of Temperance, and other associations, with similar and overlapping membership. New buildings went up in the town square under the management of Thomas Horrell and other town fathers.[26]

Smokeys and the Range Wars

Violence framed the emergence of the Farmers' Alliance in Lampasas. On January 14, 1873, the Horrell brothers blocked the attempted arrest of two men by gunning down Sheriff Shadrick T. Denson. In response, the governor prohibited firearms in the county seat and sent

24 In the mid-1880s, the Gulf, Colorado, and Sante Fe Railroad built north from Temple, establishing a small depot there and inspiring the hopeful locals to rename their community Lometa, a bastardized spelling of "lomita" for the hill just east of Main Street. The town still has fewer than a thousand people.

25 S. O. Dawes and William L. Garvin, *History of the National Farmers' Alliance and Co-operative Union of America* (Jacksboro, TX: J. N. Rogers & Co., 1887), 14.

26 "Lampasas County" in "Texas Items," *Galveston Daily News*, December 15, 1874, p. 2, col. 5. See also "A Trip Through Lampasas, Coryell, Bosque, Hill, Johnson and Navarro Counties," *Galveston Daily News*, June 20, 1874, p. 1, col. 8.

a small squad of Texas State Police, a racially mixed armed force established in lieu of the white supremacist Texas Rangers, to enforce the prohibition.

On March 14, those Texas State Policemen arrested one of the Horrells, who asked to be permitted to go into Jerry Scott's saloon and inform his brothers of his arrest. When the men entered, the Horrells and Billy Bowen opened fire with their Winchesters, killing or wounding half of the law enforcement officers. The next day, Sheriff Denson and his posse began a five-day sweep of the area. The Texas Attorney General joined them with ten more state policemen, a company of the local militia and another company from Burnett County. They captured and locked up Jerry Scott and Mart Horrell.[27]

A few days later, the other Horrell brothers showed up and sprang the lot of them. Over the next several weeks, they and the authorities threw lead back and forth with inconclusive results. Early that summer, though, the Horrell boys turned up in the county seat. June 14 saw another gunfight in the streets of Lampasas, after which Sheriff Denson again called on the governor for assistance.[28]

With Texas turning up the heat, the Horrells lit out for Lincoln County in the New Mexico territory. There they cut a bloody swath among the Hispanic population, so much so that even the federal authorities took notice, and in short order, made the territory too hot for the brothers to stay.[29]

Meanwhile, the Democrats had returned to power back in Texas, so the Horrells decided to give Lampasas County another go. Locals

27 Bill O'Neal, *The Bloody Legacy of Pink Higgins: A Half Century of Violence in Texas* (Woodway, TX: Eakin Press, 1999), 30; Frederick Nolan, *Bad Blood: The Life and Times of the Horrell Brothers* (Stillwater, OK: Barbed Wire Press, 1994), 24–5; Claude L. Douglas, *Famous Texas Feuds* (Dallas: Turner, 1936), 130–3; C. L. Sonnichsen, *I'll Die Before I'll Run: The Story of the Great Feuds of Texas* (Albany, TX: Shackelford County Historical Survey Committee, 1974), 97–118.

28 "Texas Items" [from Lampasas Dispatch], *Houston Telegraph*, April 17, 1873, p. 8, col. 1, and "Untitled," *Dallas Daily Herald*, April 18, 1873, p. 1, col. 2; O'Neal, *The Bloody Legacy of Pink Higgins*, 29; Nolan, *Bad Blood*, 17–18.

29 Douglas, *Famous Texas Feuds*, 133–5; Frederick Nolan, *Tascosa: Its Life and Gaudy Times* (Lubbock: Texas Tech University Press, 2007), 103.

noted "the appearance in our streets of the wagons and families of the Horrells, who left this county last fall for New Mexico." If they expected a hero's welcome, they were in for a surprise, because the sheriff soon had his forces scouring Lampasas County, "aided by the minutemen of the country, as well as a large posse." By March 5, the sheriff's men began bringing in some of the Horrells though Mart and Tom Horrell remained at large.[30] Even as the first Alliance began organizing north of town, the county focused on carving out its niche in the cattle business, and that left no room for troublemakers.

Conditions no longer pit the Horrells against the hated Republicans, but against the Bourbon Democrats. John Pinkney Calhoun Higgins came to the fore in the effort to neutralize the Horrells. The former leader of the Ku Klux Klan, "Pink" Higgins had no sympathies for the old enemies of the Horrells, but this was about cattle, money, and the future development of the county.

Later, the authorities brought the two brothers in over a robbery at Meridan.[31] The jailer left when he got an urgent message about a sickness in his family. Within minutes, a crowd converged on the jail and blew away the last of the Horrells with their shotguns. Higgins always seemed the most likely suspect for this raid.

The killings continued. On June 7, 1877, Higgins came to town to post bond against murder charges, but called upon his relatives, the Mitchells, to protect him. In the town square, Tom Horrell waited with fifteen guns and seemed undismayed by the thirty-five that defended Higgins. After some heavy gunfire, Captain John Sparks of the Texas Rangers turned up and negotiated a ceasefire. The intransigent Horrells resisted the peace until Captain N.O. Reynold's detachment of Texas Rangers brought them into custody. Interestingly, though, Higgins took the last life in this conflict when he killed his

30 "Untitled," *Austin Weekly Democratic Statesman*, March 12, 1874, p. 1, col. 6. "Lampasas County" under "Texas Items," *Austin Weekly Democratic Statesman*, March 26, 1874, p. 2, col. 7, and "County Items" [from Lampasas Dispatch], *Dallas Weekly Herald*, March 28, 1873, p. 4, col. 3.

31 For this and the following paragraph, see Douglas, *Famous Texas Feuds*, 133–7, 137–42, 142–5.

partner, Bill Standifer, an old sympathizer of the Horrells, after the turn of the century.

The Higgins–Horrell feud framed the emergence of the Alliance, which incorporated the need for armed struggle into its very constitution. It directed presidents of the sub-alliances to appoint secret "Grand Smokeys" to protect the property of their members. None of this makes much sense without considering the nature of the cattle business at the time.

In September 1877, Allen, Chavose, Adolphus P. Hungate, and their neighbors reorganized as the Pleasant Valley Farmers' Alliance. From this point, the association spread like a prairie fire. In only a few weeks, Pleasant Valley was hosting a gathering of representatives from several new affiliates. On February 22, 1878, they established a Grand County Alliance, but the growth continued; on May 4, they started the Grand State Alliance. Soon they had established norms to be pursued by each affiliate, which came to be called a "sub-alliance." Peers across the region began organizing what became the Southern Farmers' Alliance.[32]

An important factor in the need for organization among the small farmers and ranchers was the expansion of something like low-level gang warfare around them. Across the state, the gentlemen of property raised their own little armies, and plenty of free companies and freelancers roamed the state trying to find a way to get into the game themselves. Texas Rangers, such as those under Leander H. McNelly, terrorized Indians, Mexicans, and blacks as a matter of course. McNelly's rangers regularly fought Juan Cortina and the armed Mexican nationalists across the border, not that the border meant that much to them. In 1875, McNelly invaded Mexico to take livestock at gunpoint, claiming that he acted in the lawful pursuit of stolen American cattle.

Violence flared just beyond the state capital at Austin. Calling themselves "notch cutters," an armed gang took up residence just to the southeast in Bastrop County. Disgusted with the ineffectiveness

---

32 Dawes and Garvin, *History of the National Farmers' Alliance and Co-operative Union*, 14; Dunning, *The Farmers' Alliance History*, 17.

of local law enforcement, citizens seized and hanged two of the outlaws in 1875, sparking a series of retaliatory killings. The following year, fifteen men attacked a ranch, killing two, burning the ranch house, and sparking more reprisals. Later, after several years of relative calm, the gunfights and beatings resumed, culminating in the murder of the deputy sheriff investigating them. A vigilante committee hanged a number of suspects, including three on Christmas Eve, leading to a Christmas shoot-out in the streets of McDade in front of a saloon. Three of the participants died, and all sides pulled back briefly from extralegal violence, though it sputtered on sporadically for another twenty years.[33]

The cattle bonanza touched off a series of notable conflicts in Duval County and across much of central Texas over these years. In general, the more persistent of these armed rivalries took place far enough from the easy control of official civic life, but close enough to influence it.

In 1875, the "Hood-doo War" erupted in Mason and Llano Counties. Large numbers of Germans settled in the area and resisted domination by the Democrats. During the war, a number of those Germans tried to reach the Mexican border in hopes of finding their way to the Union army, but were run down and butchered by local Anglos. The resentment festered as the first cattle drives organized by Anglo firms often tended to sweep up some of the beasts from the Germans' small herds. In 1872, the Germans elected John Clark as sheriff and Dan Hoerster as brand inspector. Captain Dan Roberts of the Texas Rangers saw Clark as "one of the blue hen's chicks," a former Union soldier.[34]

Clark's posse began catching some of the rustlers but had trouble proving the crime, which frustrated the Germans. On February 18, a large crowd of the Germans broke into the jail and seized five of the accused men, killing two and badly injuring another two before Clark

33 Sonnichsen, *I'll Die Before I'll Run*, 133–50.

34 Douglas, *Famous Texas Feuds*, 148–50. For more detailed accounts, see David Johnson, *The Mason County "Hoo Doo" War 1874–1902* (Denton: University of North Texas Press, 2006), and Glenn Hadeler, "The Mason County Hoo Doo Wars," 1998, available at texfiles.com/texashistory.

and Roberts arrived with a rescue party. In response, Tom Gamel, one of the stockmen, brought his own armed force into the town. Tensions built until March 24, when Gamel and Clark declared a truce, though several incidents took place through the summer. In early August, ex-Texas Ranger Scott Cooley assaulted and killed Deputy Sheriff Wohrle, using a knife to mutilate his body and take his scalp. This kind of violence drew in other desperados, including John Ringold, more generally known as Johnny Ringo. On August 19, the combatants had a shoot-out in John Keller's store that forced most of the county to take sides.

The state government responded by promising to send Texas Rangers. On September 24, Cooley's gang reappeared, engaging in a bit more gunplay, leaving a few more corpses, and settling themselves into Gamel's saloon. On the morning of September 28, when Hoerster and two others started up the street toward the saloon, the gang spread out and opened fire. The gunfight left Hoerster dead and Cooley's gang galloped through town, pistols blazing. That afternoon, Major John B. Jones's Frontier Ranger Battalion arrived and found Clark and a large number of Germans fortifying themselves in Keller's store. Jones's own men proved reluctant to bring in Cooley, a former Ranger himself. Remarkably, Jones offered his own men honorable discharges from the battalion if they chose not to enforce the law against one of their own.

In December, the authorities in Burnet County captured Cooley and Ringo, which removed a major reason for the persistent conflict. In January 1876, their colleague George Gladden organized the ambush and retaliatory killing of Peter Bader. Cooley and Ringo escaped from jail in Lampasas County and their band still remained active. That fall, though, Cooley suddenly died at the age of twenty-one, while others made their way to Lincoln County, New Mexico, and Ringo continued on to Tombstone and his ill-fated feud with the Earp brothers.

The same tensions that erupted in Mason County stirred passions to the north in San Saba County, where there was also considerable violence against African Americans and suspected anti-secessionist whites, particularly among the Germans. This continued beyond

Reconstruction, taking over two dozen lives. Supposedly, Texas Rangers ended the killing, but this was only after the Democrats had worked their will in the area. In several parts of the state, such as Shackleford County, west of Fort Worth, vigilantes seemed to run rampant.[35]

Such were the origins of the Farmers' Alliance, conceived amid the beef bonanza and an atmosphere of armed coercion. After engineering a series of mergers, it established the broad base and organizational foundations of what became the Populist or People's Party in the 1890s.

During these same years, developments in neighboring Arkansas clarified how the lingering violence of the war and Reconstruction extended almost seamlessly into later political conflicts. There, a strong Ku Klux Klan and its allies had been assaulting Republicans, including white officeholders as well as blacks, during the 1868 election. A new state militia restored order, but Republican arrangements over railroad bonds left the state increasingly indebted. Joseph Brooks—formerly a chaplain with a black regiment in the war—rallied Republican opposition within the party, with the support of most African Americans involved in the government. Marked by fraud and threats, the 1872 gubernatorial election reported a slim majority for Elisha Baxter over Brooks. When Brooks contested the result in January 1873, Baxter sought to broaden his own support by reaching out to former Confederates and fighting a delaying action in the courts. In March 1874, Baxter defied the railroads over funding their bond. On April 15, however, a county judge ruled the previous election fraudulent and swore in Brooks as governor. By the end of the day, a militia supporting Brooks seized the state capitol.

Both sides called out armed forces in the Brooks–Baxter War.[36]

---

35 Mike Cox, *The Texas Rangers: Wearing the Cinco Peso, 1821–1900* (New York: Forge, 2008), 439–41; Sonnichsen, *I'll Die Before I'll Run*, 164–85 and, on Shackelford County, 119–32. See also John R. Ross, "Lynching," *Handbook of Texas Online*, June 21, 2016, available at tshaonline.org/handbook/online/articles/jgl01.

36 John Harrell, *The Brooks and Baxter War* (St. Louis, MO: Slawson Printing Co., 1893).

Blacks took up arms on both sides under former Confederates. On May 3, Baxter's supporters hijacked a train out of Memphis and captured federal judges, reasoning that this would prevent the courts from ruling against them. What had degenerated into a simple struggle for power marked the beginning of the end for Republican rule in Arkansas and, with Louisiana, the eclipse of Reconstruction as a general policy across the South. More violent retaliation would follow.

How to Derail the Western Insurgency

Members of both the Industrial Brotherhood and the young Alliance participated in the efforts to shape a national third party from the various independent state parties. In Kansas, those who had helped to father the Republican Party twenty years earlier sought to repeat their achievement with the Greenbackers. In 1876, U. F. Sargent chaired the state committee of the Independent Reform, while he and others, such as La Fetra from Longley's community and Tidball from Jasper County, Missouri, almost simultaneously organized Greenback meetings and conventions.[37]

Despite the pitfalls, the project became essential to insurgents hoping to escape the dynamic of a sectionalized two-party system. Insurgents in places like Kansas, where the Republicans dominated, forged a seemingly natural, pragmatic alliance with the Democrats, while their comrades in Democratic Texas were drawn to the Republicans. With a presidential election looming, the new movement would have to demonstrate its independence or risk its general dissipation in one section or the other.

In May 1876, the national nominating convention gathered in the Academy of Music at Indianapolis. Delegates particularly hoped to

---

37 Wilder, *Annals of Kansas*, 712–13, 713–14. Through 1876, Sargent particularly fought the tendency of insurgents in that state to form coalitions with the Democrats, though he loyally supported Cooper for president after his nomination. *The United States Biographical Dictionary, Kansas Volume* (Chicago and Kansas City: S. Lewis & Co., 1879), 526–7.

field a ticket that would appeal to disaffected workingmen in the eastern cities. Unfortunately, they had none of the connections necessary to make a realistic effort to do so. At that point, a thirty-five-year-old New York–born politico named William A. A. Carsey appeared, one of those incorrigibly enigmatic characters who pop in through the back window at just the right point to change everything.

Carsey—a pioneer of political dirty tricks and dark ops—merits some attention. His parents, William Carsey and Mary McCarthy, had been born in, respectively, England and Ireland, but had married and settled in New York City before Mary gave birth to William Augustus Adolphus Carsey on October 16, 1841. William and Mary had Carsey baptized at Old St. Patrick's ten days later, so he most likely grew up a Catholic in the tough immigrant world of antebellum New York, where the gangs, political machines, and corruption were something of a given. By 1850, the family lived in Ward 17 of the city. How the Carseys made a living is difficult to determine, but they soon found themselves the subject of legal action by Charles Shields, the printer of drug labels, hinting that they sold patent medicines, such as snake oil. In late 1858, the high court of the city and county gave the Carseys notice to come forward in response to Shields's suit.[38] The Carseys, though, had left the city before that became necessary.

As the wheels of legal action ground against them back in Manhattan, the Carseys established themselves on the Fort Leavenworth Military Reserve, where a later census listed the elder William as a laborer. Although only twenty at the outbreak of the war, William A. Carsey enlisted in the First Kansas and, later, in the Eighth Kansas. He later told people that he had participated in Sherman's 1864 March to the Sea. While the Eighth fought with

38 The family appeared in the New York census records as "Carrey" or "Caffey," likely the result of a later transcription error, and the Charles Shields suit against the family is noted in an untitled item under "Supreme Court-City and County of New York," *New York Tribune*, December 3, 1858, p. 3, col. 4. William A. A. Carsey also used the names William A. Carsey and William Augustus Carsey; William Adolphus Carsey, who is mentioned in the 1858 lawsuit when he was only about sixteen, was probably a relative.

Sherman as far as Atlanta, they did not march with him to the sea at Savannah, but returned to Tennessee. However, documentation of Carsey's involvement in the Eighth Kansas remains a bit muddled.[39]

Once mustered out, Carsey likely stayed some time in Kansas, but, by 1870, he had made his way back to New York City. There, in that year, he married the sixteen-year-old Adele Z. Ostrander, and their first son was born two years later in the city.[40] Carsey seems to have found a job in the local construction trades. The Tweed Ring dominated Tammany Hall at that time and Tammany ran the Democratic Party, which controlled the city with a mixture of bribery and violence, to supplement what students of politics in the 1920s would call "identity politics" among white immigrants.

Carsey first came into the public eye as one of the rare younger American adherents of the International Workingmen's Association (IWA)—what came to be called the First International, which involved Karl Marx, Friedrich Engels, and Mikhail Bakunin. The local press described Carsey at the time as "a mason," though he described himself as both a bricklayer and a builder as well. At one point, for reasons that are utterly unclear, the IWA established an Industrial Workingmen's Party, which gained no real membership beyond the IWA. When the IWA realized this and walked away from it, Carsey remained and began presenting himself as the head of a powerful political force. Two years later, he still ran the organization, which now called itself an "'Independent Labor Party of New York." At an 1876 meeting, Carsey was elected president; he then, in his role as chairman of the parade committee, explained to the group why so few had participated in their parade. He then named fellow member of Tammany Hall James Gordon Bennett the editor of the *Herald*;

39 The 1865 Kansas Census and the 1870 federal census of the state clearly identified the household of the father William Carsey at Fort Leavenworth Military Reserve, along with the rest of the family. See also the obituary on "William A. Carsey," *Brooklyn Daily Eagle*, June 2, 1914, p. 2, col. 7.

40 Carsey and his wife had three children together. He then had one son from another relationship.

Bennett was "unanimously nominated as the workingmen's candidate for Mayor."[41]

In 1876, Gideon Tucker, Sanford Church, and other reform-minded Democrats sought to argue that their party was already pro-Greenback. The Democrats had nominated Horatio Seymour in 1868 and adopted Horace Greeley, candidate of the Liberal Republicans, in 1872. Therefore, argued some of these New Yorkers, the Democratic platform endorsed eight years earlier, which accepted government-printed paper money, was still in effect. "Greenback Democrats" had challenged the regular city delegation to the state Democratic convention, which decided in favor of the regulars. With the support of old-time Jacksonians like Peter Cooper, Carsey and Church hoped to appeal their exclusion to the national Democratic convention and had gone to the Midwest seeking allies for this internal Democratic dispute.[42] After attending the Democratic state convention, dropping in on the national Greenback convention was little more than an afterthought for the two men.

---

41   U.S. Congress, *Report of the Tariff Commission, Appointed Under Act of Congress Approved May 15, 1882*, vol. 1 (Washington: Government Printing Office, 1882), 341; 1900 United States Federal Census; see also "Cheap Transportation," *New York Daily Times*, Sept. 10, 1873, p. 8, and Sept. 11, pp. 1, 4–5. *The Socialist* discussed some of the prominent figures in the Industrial Workingmen's Party in "Christian Mayer," two pieces on the "Industrial Political Party" and one on "Political Action" in the issues on July 18 and 25, August 8, and September 26, 1874; "Independent Labor Party," *New York Evening Post*, 1876, p. 1, col. 4. See also Bernstein, *The First International in America*, 246. See Carsey's comment as an IWA spokesman in the Chicago *Daily Tribune*, Feb. 12, 1874, and "A Row Among the Nationalists," *New York Daily Times*, May 9, 1878, p. 5. "The Currency Question," *New York Daily Times*, July 29, 1875, p. 2; "Greenback Democrats," *New York Daily Times*, Feb. 20, 1876, p. 2; "The New York Inflationists," *New York Daily Times*, March 3, 1876, p. 2; "The Democratic Inflationists," *New York Daily Times*, March 15, 1876, pp. 1, 2; "Democratic Greenback Convention," *New York Daily Times*, March 22, 1876, p. 8; and "A Greenback Convention," *New York Daily Times*, March 25, 1876, p. 8.

42   *Appleton's Cyclopedia 1876*, 599–602. The Democratic convention adopted a national platform in 1868 which was not revised in 1872. Many continued to question the new party's emphasis on Greenbackism. Lincoln's former law partner and future biographer, William Herndon, had supported the independent farmers' tickets in Illinois but considered it a mistake to give currency the central role. David Donald, *Lincoln's Herndon* (New York: Knopf, 1948), 262–3, 286. So did Berkey in Michigan and Joshua King Ingalls, the old National Reform Association leader in New York.

Based on his later claims, Carsey also became "one of the founders" of the Knights of Labor in that he joined "the original assembly" among the goldbeaters and bricklayers of this city. He also explained the goal of the Knights as political and insisted that the order had nothing to do with strikes.[43] Later, he condemned the Knights for striking and echoed trade unionists in condemning the order for being insufficiently trade unionist.

During their trip to the Midwest, Carsey and Church discovered a national convention of largely rural Midwestern insurgents desperate to establish some connection with the labor movements of the big cities in the East. Carsey and Church offered them an almost instantaneous and serendipitous political connection—or the appearance of it. In the end, two minor Democratic functionaries from one of the most machine-ridden communities of a loyally two-party state found themselves in a position to shape the impact of the insurgent movement that had been building for two years.

In a remarkable double whammy, Church nominated Cooper for president and Carsey named U.S. Senator Newton Booth of California vice president. Oddly, this was acceptable to genuine insurgents like those in Missouri's delegation headed by Robert F. Wingate, the wartime attorney general and Radical Republican, himself a major vice presidential contender.[44] Later, when Booth declined, the Greenback leadership replaced him with Samuel F. Carey, a Cincinnati Democrat with no real credentials as an insurgent.

In short, Carsey and Church had nudged the Greenbackers to a remarkably self-destructive decision. They would offer their rural Midwestern constituencies with generally Republican

---

43 "Knights Badly Organized, Surplus of Labor the Cause of All Trouble. W. A. A. Carsey Describes the Knights as in a Chaotic Condition—Compulsory Arbitration," *New York Times*, February 13, 1887, p. 3.

44 "Rah for Rags," Chicago *Daily Times*, May 18, 1876, p. 3, and "Base and Bottomless," Chicago *Daily Times*, May 19, 1876, p. 3; "The Greenback Party," Chicago *Daily Interocean*, May 17, 1876, p. 5; "The Greenbackers," Chicago *Daily Interocean*, May 18, 1876, p. 5; "The Greenback Party," Chicago *Daily Interocean*, May 19, 1876, p. 5; and "Independents" in Buchanan's paper, the Indianapolis *Sun*, May 20, 1876, pp. 1–2, 5, with editorial on p. 3.

predispositions a septuagenarian urban Jacksonian, a philanthropist too elderly to wage an energetic campaign outside of New York who would win there only as many votes as Tammany and its rivals permitted. Not surprisingly, the 1876 Cooper–Carey campaign amounted to very little, winning only 81,740 votes nationally. The campaign's main achievement was the identification of a few irreconcilably insurgent localities, like Jasper County where St. John and his comrades had built a key third party stronghold that remained so for years.[45] The experiment might have ended there, had not sweeping events followed in the wake of the "Stolen Election" controversy between Republican Rutherford B. Hayes and Democrat Samuel J. Tilden.

Yet, history did not mark the Greenback cause for so simple an end. The deepening financial crisis and the unchecked power of the railroad bosses permitted them to survive the economic ills of the industry and continue to pay stock dividends to shareholders by simply slashing wages for their workers. The tiny railroad unions planned strikes but, painfully aware of their own weakness, kept postponing them. In July 1877, the B&O's announcement of yet another 10 percent pay cut for non-management employees sparked an open revolt that spread up and down the rail lines and moved workers at other railroad companies and in other industries to strike. Ignoring local officials, the federal authorities sent in troops at the request of the corporations. Cavalry, still laden with the dust of the Dakotas where they had been running down the Sioux in the wake of Little Big Horn, showed up to gun down Chicago workers. Local Greenbackers in places such as Toledo assumed leadership of the strike, as did socialists in St. Louis.

From the fall of 1877 to the fall of 1878, angry workers and genuinely concerned citizens began turning up at the polls and voting for candidates who represented their interests. Greenbackers and other independents swept into power. A new socialist party began electing people to office from New Haven to St. Louis and from Milwaukee to

45 *American Almanac and Treasury of Facts, Statistical, Financial, and Political, for the Year 1880*, ed. Ainsworth R. Spofford (New York and Washington, 1880), 281.

Covington in Kentucky. Following the Republican path to major party status seemed more plausible. In the course of this, the reorganized Knights of Labor began growing from 50,000 members to reach 700,000 by 1885.

Paradoxically, one place this did not happen was New York City. Press accounts regularly reported on candidates beyond those of the regular Democrats and Republicans. By 1880, these included independent Republicans, German Republicans, Tammany Democrats, Anti-Tammany Democrats based in the county, Taxpayers, Bread-Winners, and an anti-Customs House party. New parties of Greenbackers and socialists easily lost themselves in the crowd, particularly with the Anti-Tammany Democrats splitting in two, one hoping to end Tammany domination of the party and the other hoping to replace the Tammany leadership. The *New York Times* later attributed these many "small parties or factions outside of the two principal political parties" not only to genuine reform concerns but to deliberate ploys by the major parties to weaken the voting strength of their rivals and to "the self-seeking of a few individuals" eager to promote their own prospects within a major party.[46]

Carsey turned up in the leadership of one of the several currents claiming to represent Greenbackism in the city. Roughly half a dozen local Greenback factions were active in the fall of 1878 and, by 1880, about ten of these "third" parties were vying with each other. These included a Workingmen's Party, a Bread Winners' Party, a Greenback Party, an Independent Greenback Party, and a Greenback Labor Party, as well as Independents, Independent Democrats, Independent Republicans, German Republicans, and so on. The Socialistic Labor Party and the National Liberal League (so named because they were freethinkers on questions of religion) had their own organizations but ultimately opted to support the Greenback movement nationally.[47]

46   "Work Before Reformers," *New York Daily Times*, July 15, 1877, p. 6. See also "Trouble in City Politics," *New York Daily Times*, June 9, 1878, p. 12.

47   "The Nationals Organizing," *New York Times*, June 28, 1878, p. 5; "'Dick' Schell for Mayor," *New York Times*, October 4, 1878, p. 8; "The Greenbackers' Convention," *New York Times*, October 6, 1878, p. 1; and "W. A. A. Carsey's Convention," *New York Times*, October 11, 1878, p. 2.

Carsey's group became particularly adamant about denouncing "bogus" Greenback groups, though his included Theodore Tomplinson, former Congressman James E. Kerrigan, and future antimonopolist organizer Henry Nichols.

Upstate, the Greenbackers cooperated closely with a regional version of the Farmers' Alliance. Yet another Farmers' Alliance had formed and was organizing out of Chicago, this one largely sympathetic to the Democratic Party. The nascent Southern Alliance in Texas found itself torn between avoiding politics and pitching into the Greenback effort.

Meanwhile, the political orientation of the IB informed the 1878 reorganization of the Knights of Labor, which placed it on the road to becoming a mass organization. "In accepting the preamble of the Industrial Brotherhood," recalled Terrence Powderly, "the convention fully realized that for the most part the reforms which were asked for in that preamble must one day come through political agitation and action."[48]

The movement had such strength by 1880, that nothing could quite block its insurgent imperative. Former Union general and Iowa congressman James B. Weaver gained the nomination with Barzalai J. Chambers, a sixty-two-year-old, Kentucky-born Texan. The ticket enjoyed considerable coverage, though often more of a human interest sort. When Weaver took up the question of the white Democratic suppression of African American voting rights, the *Cincinnati Enquirer* published an exposé asserting that he was in the secret pay of the Republicans. Widely reprinted by other Democratic papers, the article provided justification for their decision to no longer cover more than one Republican candidate. So the Republicans stopped covering the Weaver campaign as well.[49] Electoral politics provided those who

48 Powderly, *Thirty Years of Labor*, 131.
49 I covered this amazing and neglected bid for the presidency in my *The Civil War's Last Campaign: James B. Weaver, the National Greenback-Labor Party and the Politics of Race and Section* (Lanham, MD: University Press of America, 2000). On Chambers, see *A Memorial and Biographical History of Johnson and Hill Counties, Texas* (Chicago: Lewis Publishing Co., 1892), 86–8, 116; A. J. Byrd, *History and Description of Johnson County and Its Principal Towns* (Marshall, TX: Jennings Bros.,

dominated the social and economic order a way to control the dialogue other than overt violent repression.

A kind of popular mythology assumes that American radicalism crystallized in the eastern cities—possibly imported there by immigrants with "foreign ideas"—to be dashed by the mythical egalitarian capitalism of the frontier. On one level, this mythology mirrors how contemporary literature ascribes conspiracies to corrupt and repressive societies. Eugène Sue's mid-nineteenth-century *Les Mystères de Paris* became a major literary model for Gothic melodrama on both sides of the Atlantic. Its success inspired Émile Zola's *Les Mystères de Marseille*, George Reynolds's *The Mysteries of London*, and a succession of other books on Lyons, Munich, Berlin, Hamburg, Amsterdam, and beyond. The American writer George Lippard's *Mysteries of Florence* used the structure and the title, though his *Monks of Monks Hall* provided an even better example. Ned Buntline wrote *The Mysteries of New York*, while others accorded similar treatment to Boston, Philadelphia, Chicago, St. Louis, New Orleans, San Francisco, and even Corpus Christi. The characters in these novels negotiate a shadowy maze of increasingly complex and unjust social realities through secret societies, often informed by implicitly occult wisdom. The genre both criticized and celebrated the exotic and worldly streets and back alleys of the new urban order.

In reality, the old practices replicated themselves in the West as much as possible. This involved the almost simultaneous processes of ethnic cleansing, ecological displacement, and imposition of a rigid social order, flagged as a sign of progress. As in similar settings, discontent became extensive, particularly among the farmers and

---

1879), 52–3, 53–4; "The Greenback Party's Ticket," *New York Daily Times*, June 12, 1880, p. 5. See also Alwyn Barr, "B.J. Chambers and the Greenback Party Split," *Midamerica* XLIX (1967), 276–84, and Chambers's own *The Great War of Monarchy versus Republicanism; or the Sovereignty of One Man or the Few Versus the Sovereignty, Equal Rights and Liberties of the People* ... (Cleburne, TX: Chronicle Job Office Print, 1888).

small producers pinched by expanding monopolies. Since the mechanisms of political, social, and cultural control remained relatively weak, popular hostility to the power structure in the West often seemed even closer to the surface than in the East. Indeed, some of the most explosive and massive radicalism of the period emerged in the American heartland and found itself reinterpreted and broken by the well-practiced mechanisms of urban machine politics.

After all, Sue himself drew much of his plot from James Fenimore Cooper's stories of the American frontier. Conversely, by the 1880s, any latter-day Natty Bumppo would find himself constrained by a social order that, in many ways, proved to be as rigid as that which Sue had chronicled.

TWO

The Wrong Side of the Tracks

The Dangerous Classes of the New American West

The railroad running up the middle of Main Street physically marked a social divide between the respectable citizens of a civilized bourgeois community that upheld law and order and the disreputable, largely transient denizens of the ramshackle dives on the wrong side of the tracks. In a Kansas cow town, being a "Texan" was a cultural designation, rather like being a "bohemian" in one of the major cities of the Western world. The term referred to persons beyond the pale of respectability and, perhaps, of law and civilization itself. While they herded riches into town, they remained "wild," inclined to behaviors that deviated from the acceptable rituals of middle-class life. Before they took on more romantic mythological trappings, they were called saddle tramps, saddle stickers, and saddle stiffs.[1] Crossing the tracks could have seemed like visiting another world.

1 A few references to western lore offer only erroneous definitions of "saddle tramp." The "Western Slang & Phrases" page on the *Legends of America* website implies laziness, defining "saddle tramp" as "a cowboy who spends most of his time in the chuck line" (legendsofamerica.com/we-slang-s.html). Cowboy Bob's Dictionary presents a thoroughly romanticized definition: "A cowboy with wanderlust, staying on a job just long enough to earn the 'road stake' needed to carry him over the next horizon" (lemen.com/dictionary-s.html). For background on cowboys, see Keri Leigh Merritt, *Masterless Men: Poor Whites and Slavery in the Antebellum South* (Cambridge: Cambridge University Press, 2017).

During the heyday of the cattle drives, the cowboys represented the most easily identifiable and volatile lowest echelons of civilized life. Their values and conduct might have raised questions about the extent to which the norms of "civilized" white settlements contributed as much to the violence as any residual frontier conditions. In a very short time, these new standards molded lives such as that of Billy the Kid. The process created Texas equivalents of the Kansas cow town, which had yet to build a railroad to separate civilization from the violent world of the cowboy and the six-shooter.

The Emergence of the Cowboy

By definition, cowboys made their living actually working with cattle, particularly on the drives north from Texas. They tended to be relatively young or, at least, were paid as though they were. Older workers had disproportionately easier access to permanent, year-round work on ranches, which usually involved more passive management of the herd. They and other workers had other duties—from looking after the horses and other work animals to riding the line—that took most of the attention, except during roundup.

Cowboys consisted of a tiny fraction of the agricultural workforce. Reasonable estimates suggested no more than a few thousand were regularly employed by the few hundred companies operating in the West, a number which might have doubled seasonally to handle the roundups and cattle drives. These mounted workers tapped into the romance of an older, upper-class equestrian tradition, still evident south of the border, and they certainly saw themselves as a cut above ordinary farm labor.

The explosive labor demands of the great beef bonanzas starting in the mid-1870s forged a polyglot workforce. It included Indians, Latinos, and African Americans, most of whom did not necessarily labor in mixed work groups. In some places, such as the Texas Panhandle, young Southern white boys fleeing defeat in the Civil War predominated and may well have been the least likely to engage in labor-related militancy.

Certainly, the Anglo "cowboy" may have understood that his very self-definition represented no more than a translation of "vaquero," which, along with "baquerro" and "buckaroo," came with the Spaniards to the New World. However, Anglo society had repeatedly warred against its Spanish-speaking neighbors to the south and west, and Latino cowboys more readily associated with Indian herdsmen. Very common—even predominant—in parts of the industry to the south, the Latinos remained grossly underrepresented in the newly settled Panhandle and the northern range.

Also underrepresented in the Panhandle were the black cowboys, who often dominated the cowboy workforce east of the Trinity River and in parts of the Rio Grande Valley. The wartime movement of vast numbers of slaves from across the South into Texas assured that large numbers would work in ranching, though putting a slave on horseback seemed a good way to lose both the rider and the mount. Still, some learned to carry out the work of a cowboy and predominated in parts of Texas. A few even turned up north along the trail, particularly in Kansas during the heavy migration of the "Exodusters" there in the late 1870s. Some, such as Bose Ikard, spent several years on cattle drives, but some of the Southern white cowboys harassed them mercilessly, in one case driving off a black cowboy in the middle of a drive.[2] The XIT ranch in the Panhandle kept Jim Perry, an otherwise talented cowboy, doing various jobs for twenty years without offering him even the modest advancement to cowpoke.

Women also did the work of cowboys, though the cowboys carrying out the strictest definition of a cowboy's duties in terms of the cattle drives were mostly men. Particularly when their families worked in the business, females might learn the work associated with ranch life, but few employers would have trusted their strength and stamina over the long weeks on a cattle drive. The overwhelmingly male settlements of the West had peculiarly mixed views on the rare women in

---

2 Sara R. Massey, *Black Cowboys of Texas* (College Station: Texas A&M University Press, 2000), on Jim Perry of the XIT Ranch, 207–12; on Mathew Bones Hooks, 219–41, a black cowboy who performed various jobs but was gradually confined to cooking. McCarty, *Maverick Town*, 109.

their society, generally according them only a few, well-defined niches that did not include the role of cowboy.

Long hours in the saddle gave anybody doing a cowboy's job an easily identifiable, bowlegged walk. Work in the sun or rain required a sturdy, wide-brim hat or a sombrero, as well as a bandanna usually worn at the collar of a checked shirt. Those strongly sewn and riveted denims introduced a generation earlier provided a functional pair of Levi's, protected by *armas* or *armitas* that quickly evolved into chaps or "chinks" (from *chigaderos*). Function rather than fashion shaped a cowboy's boots—called "mule ears" for how they stood when they were off his feet. Over his boots, he wore spurs. If he had the desire and the budget, he might wear a duster to protect his clothes, and some even had a yellow slicker, poncho, or serape in the event of rain.

The first statisticians of labor in the United States described the cowboy's 108-hour workweek.[3] Allowing for eight hours off per day, which had to have been spent mostly in sleep, this calculation meant that the cowboys worked sixteen hours a day, Monday through Saturday, with twelve hours of leisure on Sunday. Individualism proved incapable of managing massive herds of cattle, a process that encouraged teamwork and solidarity.

This incredibly intense and dangerous work was seasonal. It paid from twenty or twenty-five to forty dollars a month, though, most commonly, "thirty and found." Almost nobody could live for a year on what cowboys made during the time they were working. The more experience one had, the less one would willingly attempt it.

For many young men, working as a cowboy became something of a rite of passage, analogous to going to sea for the generations of young men in the coastal cities. Like military service in a later age, some who had worked as cowboys in their youth made the experience part of their identities throughout their lives, most likely out of nostalgia for a lost youth. Realistically, however, the romance and allure of the cowboy's life rarely lasted long, and those who returned

---

3 *Third Annual Report of the Commissioner of Labor, 1887: Strikes and Lockouts* (Washington: Government Printing Office, 1888), 580–1, 582–3.

for more the following season tended disproportionately to have no better options. Many drifted in and out of work on the trail, as need be. Labor as a cowboy, like other kinds of agricultural work, defied regularity.

Permanent work as a ranch hand proved hard to come by. It meant living on one of the large spreads that were too big to function on only the labor of the families who owned them. Although it meant that workers lived where they worked, subject to the beck and call of their employers, the work usually afforded the shelter of a bunkhouse, food of predictable edibility, and a nearby fire of some sort for the winter. J. Allen Evans complained bitterly of "the winter roundup," where the workers wandered unemployed from ranch to ranch, looking for work.[4]

In the early days, the ranchers and their regular hands did not necessarily view these visitations as a burden. Winter kept them all indoors for long stretches, and the arrival of someone new brought unheard stories and an extra hand in the kitchen or with other chores.

In April, as spring roundup approached, a ranch quickly expanded its workforce. In May 1880, for example, a Wyoming roundup employed 150 riders using 1,200 horses from eighteen outfits to bring in 5,000 to 6,000 cattle. The vaqueros to the south had their *hierra* or *yerra*, and gauchos in Latin America held the *llanero*. This involved rounding up the cattle in a designated district for the owners to sort out ownership, particularly of the new calves.

Roundups required many more horses than riders; the mounts had special skills and had to be relieved more regularly from their labors. Light horses, thoroughbreds, and quarter horses provided strong, trainable, and maneuverable mounts of 850 to 1,300 pounds. They usually had little need for smaller animals, such as ponies, and bred larger draft animals for strength to draw the wagons. In roundups, they relied on "cutting horses"—they called the best of them "whit-tlers"—to separate particular calves.

---

4   J. Allen Evans, letter from Trading, Wyoming Territory, January 14, 1885, "Wyoming Territory. Overstocked Labor Market. The Fate of the Cow Boys," *The Alarm*, February 7, 1885, p. 4, col. 3.

The roundup provided cowboys with an opportunity to demonstrate or learn almost all of the skills an experienced cowhand needed. Almost any horseman knew some of the etiquette, which included mounting on the left side of the horse—the other side was considered the "off-side" or "Indian side." Elementary horsemanship was essential to the work but insufficient for mastering it.

Special equipment and skills became necessary. South of the border, the vaqueros made their own saddles, but those in the United States bought manufactured products. Saddle styles varied, largely depending on the placement and number of the cinches (the strapping under the horse). Cowboys also needed to know how to handle the head gear or "tack"—the bridle, bit, and reins—in order to direct the mount, sometimes with a riding whip tied to the reins. A cowboy concerned about the horse's well-being would avoid painful bits and whips and made sure to keep the horse groomed, avoiding tangles in the mane—the so-called "witch's bridle."

Cowboys kept miscellaneous items of personal property as their "plunder" in a "war bag" or "war sack"—what lumberjacks called a yannigan bag—tied behind the saddle. This included a pan, flour, and some grub for when they were far away from the chuck wagon. The well-supplied cowboy also carried "makins"—tobacco and papers.

One could rope horses or calves on foot—a tricky proposition—but rope work from horseback required staying firmly in the saddle while using both hands. The cowboy would secure the rope on the saddle horn with a Texas tie, using a lariat, sometimes made of rawhide and horsehair, from south of the border—the word "lasso" came from the Spanish *lazo*. A skilled roper heeled the calf with the rope and leapt from the saddle to "wrestle" it to the ground, while one had to "bulldog" a steer. The most skilled could throw the hollihan from over their heads, getting the rope where they wanted it on one try.[5]

A cowboy could also make mistakes that would make everybody else's day. After all, even the best of horses had minds of their own and

---

5 These activities can be demonstrated more easily than described. A number of skilled rodeo workers have uploaded videos that demonstrate these tricks to YouTube.

sometimes made their riders well aware of it. Cowboys used steam-boat lingo to describe the saddle on a bucking horse as "the hurricane deck." The great temptation then would be to grasp the saddlehorn or the pommel; this was called "squeezing the biscuit," "squeezing Lizzie," "chucking the horn," or "clasping the leather." It offered the illusion of something secure to hold the cowboy in the saddle, but it also narrowed the base of gravity. An experienced hand almost always approached an animal from the left rear and used the rope to the right side of the horse, but if you wound the rope clockwise over the saddle horn—what the old hands called "coffee grinding"—you had the rope with a possibly volatile animal on the other end looping danger-ously near the inner side of your upper right thigh. Such errors could follow a cowboy around for days or even seasons.

Once the cowboy had separated, roped, and restrained the animal, he would have to brand it. Older methods used knives to earmark the beasts or put wattle marks on their necks or jaws. Shortly after state-hood, Texas began requiring registered brands. The use of off-centered or tilted letters gave rise to descriptions of them as "tumbling," "rock-ing," "flying," "running," or "lazy." The brand was usually made on the left hip so that a right-handed roper approaching from the rear could easily see it. Branding the animal too deeply would raise the skin, which was called warting. A tallyman kept count of the animals processed.

After the spring roundup, the ranchers might have no further work for such large numbers of cowboys. There might be another roundup in September or even as late as December on the Southern plains. As a general rule, though, the cattle would lose weight if you kept moving them from place to place, so ranchers avoided doing so when they could.

However, after 1866, it became evident that there were great profits to be made by moving cattle across the country to markets where they could fetch much better prices. So the spring roundup in Texas became a prelude to the cattle drive. Initially, these drives involved longhorn or twisthorn cattle, products of the open range that prevailed into the mid-1880s, but increasingly the more docile and easily herded "open-faced" or white-faced Hereford cattle prevailed.

This represented a massive managerial undertaking. The trail boss ran the entire operation with crew foremen supervising small groups of workmen, who shared a chuck wagon run by a cook and possibly an assistant. The division of labor included a brush popper to keep the way clear ahead, often through dense shrubs, and tailer or tail riders to keep the stragglers moving forward. Along the edges worked line riders and outriders, the mobile versions of the fence riders.

When the sun began to go down, the team stopped and posted "night guards" on two- to four-hour shifts to keep the cattle from straying. This fueled the practice of cowboys singing to lull the cattle and help quiet them to sleep. At this most vulnerable part of the day, though, a quick thunderstorm coming up could create a disaster. Panic could spread quickly through large numbers of cattle, particularly the longhorns. A stampede could cost equipment and lives and always cost time, scattering the herds across miles; this would require a massive and unplanned reorganization on the trail.

Chuck wagons provided remarkably good food for a workforce on the move, though their menus did not vary much. They started as rebuilt army supply wagons, with iron axles replacing the wood. Drawn by six oxen, each chuck wagon carried a full complement of iron kettles, a dutch oven, a large coffee pot capable of holding three to five gallons of liquid, and a wagon box on the back for more storage. The cook—called a grub slinger, grub worm, or pot rustler—could stash enough food to keep a crew of sixteen to twenty men fed for five to six weeks.

The nature of the work required the chuck wagon to maintain a constant supply of readily drinkable coffee. Before the end of the Civil War, retailers sold green coffee that the consumer would then roast. Then, John and Charles Arbuckle of Pittsburgh began toasting coffee beans for sale. Cowboys needed it very strong and consumed enough, observers said, to float a horseshoe.

Of course, most of the food walked alongside them in the form of fresh beef. The cook regularly made a brown gravy called "Texas butter" or "sop" for use with biscuits. Deer, buffalo, or other game supplemented this dish. A Louisiana wagon boss horrified his crew during one meal by giving the cook time off and cooking crawdads found along the trail.[6] Cowboys usually grabbed a snack to take with them between meals, such as dried beef. Mexican cowhands kept raw beef and cold tortillas on hand.

Surviving records indicate that cowboys also made soda biscuits and carried corn, tomatoes, molasses, biscuits, potatoes, and beans ("whistle berries"), as well as canned fruit and vegetables as they became more common. Bread and jam became more common over time, though eggs, bacon, ham, and light loaf bread, called a "wasp nest," were all generally rare. Butter—axle grease, cow grease, cow salve—was eaten quickly when they had it, partly because it could not be kept in large amounts over time.

Some of the food also served as a test for newcomers. All sorts of unsavory castoffs from the cattle butcher went into a general pot. Cowboys called it "son of a bitch stew." Then, too, the selective castration of some of the young cattle at branding time made available the roundup delicacies known as mountain oysters, prairie oysters, or calf fries.

For the young men and boys who worked these jobs, the cattle drive provided a great adventure and a test of their stamina. They changed horses several times in order to spend twelve to sixteen hours a day in the saddle. They worked terribly hard and took consolation where they could.

Life as a Cowboy

One commonly reprinted description of life among the cowboys describes them as "composed of two general classes: those born to the business and those who are exported west by relatives who have wearied of them and their gay and tumultuous practices of doing nothing but spending money and accumulating bad habits." Native Westerners "can neither read nor write, are grave of mien, and hard men when trouble comes on." The transplant would be "drunk

6 Sullivan, *The LS Brand*, 71–2.

whenever possible, but he is otherwise pleasing to the eye and harm-less enough. The educated ones read the newspapers to their Brethren on subjects of national interest."[7] This gross oversimplification flies in the face of reality.

In reality, cowboys were as complicated and mixed a lot as any. Saddle tramps shared a world generally deprived of life's niceties. Those who did not read passed their time inventing and telling tall tales. Like war veterans or others in stressful jobs, cowboys spun stories that eased their plight by making light of it.

One native Westerner, John Harrington Sullivan, became one of the few working cowboys to leave much in writing about their lives and experiences. He claimed to have been born in 1859 in Wyoming. He grew up "in the companionship of wild creatures. I loved wild animals." He "began life among men at about six years of age," going to work "among the uncivilized, the wildest and most severest of man, beast and climate; also among the greatest of good men, such as explorers, army officers, missionaries, great Indian chiefs and nature's beauties." Sullivan developed an early dislike for the dominant civili-zation, when he came to have "great sympathy for the outlawed pony, especially when he was made so by cruel masters." By the age of eight, he came to be called "Broncho John."[8]

Sullivan "started out alone, with the exception of two first-class Oregon horses" at the age of twelve, around 1871. When some pros-pectors threatened to take the horses, Sullivan demonstrated his shooting skills to provide them with "a good feast of prairie chickens."

7 *Waterloo Courier*, April 1, 1891, p. 2; *Sioux County Herald* Newspaper Archive, April 8, 1891, p. 6; *Malvern Leader* [Iowa], April 9, 1891, p. 2; *The Jackson Hustler*, April 17, 1891; *Topeka State Journal*, April 25, 1891, p. 6; *The Hutchinson News*, May 1, 1891, p. 1; "A Cowboy Strike: The Strange Pranks of a Lot of Unruly Ranchmen," *Lawrence Democrat*, May 1, 1891, p. 1; "[Untitled]," *Bill Barlow's Budget*, May 6, 1891, p. 7; "[Untitled]," *Middletown Daily Press* [New York], June 27, 1892, p. 1.

8 "He donned the sombrero and spurs when he was 12 years old," and "fifteen years . . . have passed since then": "Cowboys on the Alert," *The Sun*, February 21, 1886, p. 3. Records also exist of a "Broncho John" Sullivan with a ranch in Wyoming. The quotations in the text are taken from Broncho John H. Sullivan's *Life and Adventures of Broncho John: His First Trip Up the Trail* (Valparaiso, IN: J. H. Sullivan, 1896).

One of them asked him directly if he would use his weapons on them "and I told him to try me once." Continuing south on his own, he passed through "many little Mexican settlements," where he fell in "with the Mexican and half-breed boys. I liked them all because they were kind and honest." In New Mexico, he joined several old cowboys on their way to San Antonio. From there, Sullivan joined a cattle drive that consisted of "eight Northern white cow boys and six Mexicans, all long haired men and a boy, 'myself,'" joined later by an Indian named Prairie Fox.[9]

Cowboys—and those who actually knew them—understood that the value of their work ran deeper than their abysmal pay indicated. The *Las Vegas Daily Gazette* offered a more independent and honest assessment of the situation.

It would be hard to imagine any other class of employees who can more completely control the situation than the Texas cowboys. Their places cannot be well supplied, at least, in a short time. It takes men who know the country, and who are trained to the ranges, to be efficient in the business.

A good cowboy, the *Gazette* explained, "must know the landmarks, mesas, patches of timber, peaks and outlines of the landscape." He had to know "the location of water holes, springs and the course and distances of the streams," and, of course, be prepared to live in the outdoors "with nothing but his blanket." "The superior cowboy," the *Gazette* wrote, "or the 'Pride of the Panhandle' as he is styled, is no slouch, and a stranger cannot take his place simply for the lack of the technical knowledge of the profession."[10] The same paper sagely noted that a neophyte "is more liable to wander estray [sic] himself and be forever lost on the boundless plains, than to find stray cattle."[11] New

9   Sullivan, *Life and Adventures of Broncho John.*

10   "[Untitled]," *Las Vegas Daily Gazette*, March 28, 1883, p. 4, with the same piece in Westermeier, *Trailing the Cowboy*, 124–5, "Cow Boys," *Trinidad Weekly Advertiser*, March 30, 1883, cited in Westermeier, *Trailing the Cowboy*, 150n29.

11   "[Untitled]," *Las Vegas Daily Gazette*, March 28, 1883, p. 4; "The Panhandle Trouble," *Las Vegas Daily Gazette*, April 19, 1883, p. 4.

men, reasoned the paper, would be of no use without old hands to direct their work.

One only learned these skills the hard way. Stalked by gangs of rustlers and unidentified Indian war parties, the cowboys assigned Sullivan to learn scouting from Prairie Fox, who at one point was wounded and cornered by a Commanchie war party. Sullivan used firepower to break the encirclement and "managed to get the wounded scout to camp," though the Indian did not survive. At thirteen, Sullivan found himself saddled with the responsibilities of "a full fledged scout and guide." With no other options, he piloted the cattle drive past bands of white rustlers, Pawnee and Sioux. Added Sullivan, "They did no damage and I don't think we did either."[12]

Once they arrived at a Kansas cow town, cowboys like Sullivan found the railroad's division of the community an undeniable manifestation of the restrictions enforced by the respectable classes. However, the shrewd cowboy learned that he and his comrades could get cleaned up and stroll through the best parts of town. With a steady job and some luck, a few of them could even take up residence there.

Though Sullivan and others learned how to cross over and behave credibly, however, the tracks remained firmly fixed. The traffic went both ways. Coffeyville's neighborhood for the huddled and transient masses yearning to blow off steam centered on Twelfth Street, also known as "Red Hot Street." There, in 1872, a woman of ill repute shot Coffeyville's marshal in her hotel room, and a passerby responded by killing her instantly. A later mayor ordered local law enforcement to sweep the area and arrest anyone caught gambling in the town, an operation that netted not a single cowboy but brought in most members of his town council.[13]

On what had been designated as his side of the tracks, the cowboy's options remained limited. Aside from those statistical few who found their way into regular year-round employment as

12 Sullivan, *Life and Adventures of Broncho John.*
13 Dary, *Cowboy Culture*, 206.

ranch hands, cowboys in general could escape into prospecting, mining, working on the railroad, and other forms of skilled and unskilled labor. More rarely, they might make a living by the gun on either side of the law, or even try their hand at gambling. Some even overcame formidable cultural barriers to herd sheep or farm.

In practical terms, getting out of the cowboy life became less a matter of individual ambition than absolute necessity. An aging hand accumulated a great deal of know-how at the price of declining stamina and the wisdom to see the work as an innately transitory pursuit for young men. Conversely, while one or two old-timers who knew the job and the trail could be of great practical use to a crew, more would just weigh it down. A properly motivated eighteen-year-old might even find it rewarding to rise to the challenge of a sixteen-hour workday, finding compensation in the confidence gained from meeting that challenge (rather than in the pathetic pay). This became more difficult, though, as cowboys aged, needed more sleep and considered what awaited them in the next stage of life. By 35 or 40, anyone who had not yet found a less draining occupation would have been looking for one. As the older men drifted off, newcomers eager to learn the business turned up.

From the respectable side of Main Street, these transient young cowboys seemed to exist on the margins of respectable society. To a great extent, the cowboys tended to reciprocate the sentiment. They called farmers "plow chasers" and shepherds "scab herders," the latter far removed from the respectable and manly labor performed from horseback.

Long hours among mute and uncomprehending beasts cultivated a taste for profanity and swearing, including highly refined curses. Certainly, the gritty realism of cowboys' language has remained one of the most evocative aspects of the culture. Ab Owen, for instance, raved on a particularly bad day along the trail, "I hope it starts to rain right this minute, and keeps on raining until everybody drowns! I hope it rains some more and the world sinks and I'll be the last man standing on the highest peak to see the mess go down!" Spellbound by this tirade, one admiring cowboy turned to another, smiled, and commented simply, "That ole' Ab, he just don't give a damn, does he?"[14]

Cowboy life deepened a militantly unsentimental and pragmatic secularism. Given the paltry amount of leisure time cowboys enjoyed, religion seemed to offer very little practical return for the investment of time and attention it demanded. The literary scholar Jack Weston reasonably described most cowboys as "hostile to Christianity, indeed all religions."[15]

Having very little time for a life of their own beyond work, the young cowboys had to pack a lot into their off-hours. Coming off the dry trail into the cow towns, they made a beeline for the saloons (also called, in Spanish, *bodegas, cantinas*, and *pulperías*) Beer became more common later in the century, but the thirsty cowboy usually threw down "bitters" bourbon, rye, or corn. Cowboys referred to whiskey as "Kansas sheep-dip," pop skull, Taos lightning, firewater, coffin varnish, bug juice, tonsil paint, tornado juice, and tarantula juice. Ordering two drinks at once made a "pair of overalls."[16]

Cowboys engaged in other recreational activities that allowed them a great deal of discretion as to when they could end the activity. They loved games of chance such as poker and referred to decks of cards as California prayer books. Recently paid cowboys were pursued by sex workers—described, among many colorful phrases, as "girls of the line" and "soiled doves"—who produced a steady income for the brothels in town or for the "cat wagons" that periodically turned up to greet cowboys on the trail. Cowboys wrote and sang songs like "The Whorehouse Bells Were Ringing," satirizing the Victorianism of the upstanding middle-class people on the respectable side of the tracks.

The nature of the business encouraged cowboys to pack iron. Firearms became so critical to their lives that they even referred to old-fashioned ranches as "cap and ball outfits." (A generation before,

14   Sullivan, *The LS Brand*, 68.

15   Jack Weston, *The Real American Cowboy* (New York: Schocken Books, 1985), 80.

16   One of the men regularly mentioned in histories of Tascosa was the hard-drinking "Catfish Kid," often identified as "John B. Gough." This was almost surely not his real name, as "John B. Gough" was a well-known lecturer on temperance.

the outbreak of the Mexican War had saved the Colt company.) Hip holsters, tied to the leg at the appropriate level for drawing, became common; some kitted up for cross drawing. Usually, cowboys kept "five beans in the wheel": five shots in the revolver cylinder with one empty for safety. They also carried Winchester rifles—"the gun that won the West."

Gunplay became common enough, though it rarely a resembled a cinematic showdown. David Dary notes that there were forty-five reported homicides in Abilene, Wichita, Ellison, Dodge City, and Caldwell collectively from 1870 to 1885; in only fifteen had the victims had a chance to return gunfire.[17] No wonder so many landed in the "calaboose" (from the Spanish *calaboza*).

Reformers in most cow towns found the cowboy as worthy of their efforts as the "fallen women" associated with them. Some of them published a document by an alleged cowboy association near Helena, the members of which had resolved to reform themselves, save money, take only "a small amount of red liquor," and avoid gambling and the "siren sisters."[18]

People widely took it upon themselves to do "the right thing" or support others who did so. The old song "Buffalo Skinners" told a tale of the bossman Grego, who hired a group of young cowboys to hunt and skin buffalo in the summer of 1883. After a hot, miserable, flesh-bespattered, and bloody summer, the boss told the work crew that they "had been extravagant, [and] was in debt to him that day." The crew members argued and pleaded, but Grego refused to bend. Finally, "We left old Grego's bones to bleach on the range of the buffalo."

Western communities often lacked the civilizing influence of abject deference to their social betters. The capitalist who hired Bat Masterson to grade the Main Street in Dodge City never paid him. Masterson heard that this capitalist had been flashing a large wad of bills and would soon be passing through town. When the locomotive reached Dodge, Masterson boarded the train and forced his former employer

17 Dary, *More True Tales*, 104, 110.
18 "A Cowboy Association," Peach Springs, Mohave County, *The Arizona Champion*, March 27, 1886, p. 4, col. 2.

outside at the point of a six-gun. When the man protested that he was being robbed, Masterson insisted that he wanted only the $300 owed him. Reluctantly, the boss removed the wad of bills and peeled off what he owed to the cheers of the approving crowd that had gathered.[19]

A successful cowboy understood the importance of teamwork and cooperation. Individualism, rugged or otherwise, could leave the hired man's bones lying out in the sun with old bossman Grego.

Surviving in the Panhandle

Not surprisingly, as the cattle business developed, it forced cowboys to struggle harder and harder to get out from under financial insecurity. They had traditionally done so by taking in unfenced and unbranded mavericks—cattle or horses—on the open range that clearly belonged to nobody. It seemed an easy and perfectly legitimate way to build up a small herd of one's own, and, after acquiring some land as a base, to set oneself up as one's own master. Some ranchers even arranged to pay cowboys partly in calves and brand mavericks and allowed their workers to graze their own small herds on their land.[20]

All of this changed as ranchers began to operate on a larger scale, fencing the open range and actively discouraging even the smallest competitors. Then, too, access to mavericks provided an ongoing distraction for the workforce. New ranch owners, interested in expanding their holdings and increasing their profits, insisted that the hands work only for wages and claimed mavericks as their own, using their influence in the government to crack down on what they now redefined as "rustling."

Finally, law enforcement remained entirely in the hands of the ranchers, who arranged to pass measures that only benefited themselves, such as Wyoming's Maverick Law. Backed by the law, the road

---

19 Vestal, *Queen of Cowtowns*, 8–9.
20 Weston, *The Real American Cowboy*, 90–1.

agents actively pushed small homesteaders and ranchers from the area. The courts and the press remained under what Sullivan called "the terrorist *regime* of the ranchers." Over time, "small settlers, robbed of their little stock, become cowboys and the wage-slaves of the ranchers, who are all staunch upholders of the sacred rights of property."[21]

The decision of the owners to criminalize what had been common practice deprived cowboys of the only vital perquisite of the job: an opportunity to escape from it as one grew too old for its rigors. Cowboys responded by continuing to practice maverick work as a fair supplement to their poor wages. For this reason, "the name 'rustler' was synonymous with 'settler' in the days when Jack Flagg was in his prime." Rustling was soon designated a capital crime and rustlers were sometimes subject to extralegal violence, as in 1878 when Nebraskans removed two men suspected of rustling from a Custer county jail, tied them to a tree, and burned them to death.[22]

The harder employers pressed, the more naturally cowboys moved to do something about their wages. Some had always filled the few empty hours on the trail with reading. Some wrote, though mostly (and understandably so) short pieces. Joseph R. Buchanan's Denver *Labor Enquirer* appeared in September 1882; despite a low print run and poor circulation, it soon began getting letters from cowboys, such as "Maverick." "The cowboys have evidently been reading the new papers," noted the Cheyenne *Transporter*, "hence they follow the steps of the Knights of Labor."[23] Awareness grew of the efforts of that successor to the Industrial Brotherhood to bring all workers into a common organization.

Perhaps this crisis in the cattle business manifested most sharply in the Texas Panhandle, where the big spreads appeared almost

21 Eleanor Marx-Aveling and Edward Aveling, *The Working-Class Movement in America* (London: Swan Sonnenschein & Co., 1888), 163–5.

22 "The Passing of 'Jack' Flagg," "A Mob Burns Two Men to Death," *Cheyenne Daily Leader*, December 13, 1878, 1.

23 "[Untitled]," Cheyenne *Transporter*, May 12, 1886, p. 1, cited in Weston, *The Real American Cowboy*, 93–4, which calls the paper the *Labor Inquirer*.

overnight. Boston entrepreneurs ranching in Colorado left that crowded range to start the LX Ranch in the Panhandle. Between 1882 and 1884, the operation expanded into a ranch of nearly 190,000 acres across from Palo Duro Canyon to the drift fence near present-day Dumas in Moore County, taking in the entire eastern half of Amarillo's Potter County.[24]

Investments from Leavenworth and beyond backed W. M. D. Lee and Lucien B. Scott in their LS Ranch, a massive spread that got about 35,000 acres in the Panhandle in late 1880 and quickly absorbed other ranches. It maintained satellite operations on adjacent areas on the Canadian River in New Mexico, at Leavenworth, and near the Yellowstone River in Montana.[25]

In contrast, those who came to dominate this brave new order saw their rapid enclosures in the American West as signs of progress. By the spring, the partnership of three men had fenced in around 240,000 acres, one of the first extensive fencing operations in the area. That fall, its owners began using the T-Anchor brand, which they had already employed on their ranch in the Indian Territory.[26] In the summer of 1882, the T-Anchor organized the largest single drive in history, with so many cattle that it took a mounted cowboy over an hour to ride around them at a fast trot.

The life of the ordinary cowboy took a bleak turn. When Broncho John began his career, the trail hand could have ridden the hundreds of miles of the cattle drive alongside the owner of the cattle and planned his own future as a landowner. In what seemed like the blink of an eye, he found himself tied to a more permanent workforce bunked in with others on an isolated ranch to

24   Laura V. Hamner, *Short Grass and Longhorns* (Norman: University of Oklahoma Press, 1943); Della Tyler Key, *In the Cattle Country: History of Potter County, 1887–1966* (Amarillo: Tyler-Berkley, 1961).

25   Alvin H. Sanders, *The Story of the Herefords* (Chicago: Breeder's Gazette, 1914); Donald F. Schofield, *Indians, Cattle, Ships, and Oil: The Story of W. M. D. Lee* (Austin: University of Texas Press, 1985). See also Dulcie Sullivan's particularly useful book.

26   Pauline D. and R. L. Robertson, *Cowman's Country: Fifty Frontier Ranches in the Texas Panhandle, 1876–1887* (Amarillo: Paramount, 1981).

labor directly under an exploited and hopeless workforce of cowboys.

The large landowners cooperated to organize Oldham County in 1880, only a few years after the collapse of Reconstruction in Texas. Although the state paid pensions to only five Confederate veterans in the county, its founders named the new county for a Confederate senator. The XIT Ranch already claimed most of the county's land, though the headquarters of the LIT, located near Tascosa, played a major role in the organization of the county's government.[27] Nevertheless, the severity of the following winter left the area in severe need of new investments and the Prairie Cattle Company—a British syndicate—bought the LIT for $253,000.

Even though the big ranches competed viciously, they pooled their efforts to establish the "drift fence" spanning the Panhandle from west to east, unaware that it would also keep cattle from getting to water and from moving south away from the cold. Meanwhile, the largest ranches became embroiled in a wave of lawsuits centered in particular around the LS Ranch, which filed countercharges of its own, mostly challenging cattle ownership.[28]

The rise of these massive ranches marked the beginning of the end for the open-range cattle industry. During the 1880s, new owners representing eastern and European investment companies gained control of the ranching industry and introduced innovations that directly threatened the well-being of many of their employees. Not surprisingly, repression became increasingly overt.

---

27 On the night of the county's first election, Dudley Pannell and another cowboy named Phillips stayed late in Tascosa to collect the returns. While riding back to the ranch, the two men began shooting into the air in the spirit of celebration. When a careless shot from Phillips's pistol grazed Pannell's head, Pannell's horse suddenly shied and jumped, throwing Pannell to the ground, with his foot still stuck in the stirrup. The terrified horse then dragged him to death. Pannell was buried on a knoll near the LIT headquarters.

28 Sullivan, *The LS Brand*, 63–4, 78–9.

Beyond the Law

This crisis in the vital beef bonanza coincided with the end of federal Reconstruction across the South, but the "feuds" or "range wars" continued, reflecting deep social tensions just beneath the surface of the West. After 1876–7, the authority of the restored Democratic Party backed by the Texas Rangers strutted confidently across Texas into New Mexico. However, the Republican Party dominated the national government and most territorial appointments. These conflicts almost invariably involved issues of race as well as class.

For years, the regional population of Native Americans and Latinos had drawn from the salt lakes near Sierra Diablo on the western slopes of the Guadalupe Mountains, about ninety miles southeast of El Paso.[29] Then, in 1877, Charles Howard, a Virginia-born ex-Confederate Missouri lawyer, became a district judge at El Paso, from which position he ruled that the saltworks were in the public domain and therefore open to a claim by citizen-entrepreneurs. And at the head of that line stood the good judge himself.

That fall, two local Mexican leaders in San Elizario, about twenty miles down the Rio Grande from El Paso, announced that they would take their salt without paying Howard, who ordered their arrest based on their "intentions." About sixty armed Chicanos—some reportedly from south of the Rio Grande—stormed the jail and freed the two men. The authorities then took Howard and his partner into custody for their own protection and later claimed that they had negotiated a deal that recognized Howard's proprietorship but required him to leave the area. However, when Howard became convinced that Louis Cardis, an Italian-born Democratic boss among the Mexicans, had betrayed his interests, he returned from New Mexico with his own body of armed men.

---

29   For the San Elizario Salt War, see Paul Cool, *Salt Warriors: Insurgency on the Rio Grande* (College Station: Texas A&M University Press, 2008), and C. L. Sonnichsen, *The El Paso Salt War of 1877* (El Paso: Carl Hertzog and the Texas Western Press, 1961), as well as Douglas, *Famous Texas Feuds*, 108–25, and Sonnichsen, *I'll Die Before I'll Run*, 95.

By December 12, Howard arrived in San Elizario with not only his own armed escort but also the Texas Rangers under Lieutenant J. B. Tays. Meanwhile, larger numbers of irate Chicanos poured into the community. Around 10 p.m., Charles Ellis, one of Howard's allies, sauntered over to the crowd with a revolver in his boot to disperse it. Someone gave a shout and a lasso cast from horseback dropped over Ellis, immediately dragging him several hundred yards out of the village, where he was stabbed and his throat cut. Unaware of this incident, Tays and his boys arrived to find several hundred armed Chicanos. Asked what could preserve the peace, the insurgents replied that they wanted an end to Howard's attempts to monopolize the community's salt. Almost instinctively, everybody knew that there was only one way to accomplish this, so the Rangers scurried back to fortify their quarters.

Tensions mounted throughout the chilly night. Gunfire broke out around 9 a.m. and continued through the day until around 4 p.m. At that point, the Mexicans demanded the surrender of Howard. Tays and Sheriff John Atkinson ventured out under a flag of truce to negotiate terms. Tays later said that Atkinson agreed to surrender the garrison in return for his own security and $11,000, though the Ranger claimed that a Mexican priest had sent a note declaring: "Kill all the gringos. I will absolve you." Although they have since been called "a mob," the victors behaved with remarkable discipline, forming ranks and using firing squads to dispatch Howard, Atkinson, and one of the salt agents.[30] The Texas Rangers left unscathed, save in reputation.

Such upheavals in the far west of Texas more resembled conditions in the New Mexico Territory than central Texas, where Republicans with federal patronage were as likely to be wielding power as local Democratic rings of cattlemen and other migrants from Texas. Republicans proved just as willing to raise their own private armies that fought Indians and each other. Over the previous decades, the authorities had granted speculators vast tracts of land, such as in the Beaubien-Miranda Grant, which reached about 1.7 million acres. An

---

30 In February 1878, U.S. and Texas authorities demanded that the Mexican officials return those who had taken refuge in San Elizario.

American, Lucien Bonaparte Maxwell, had married into the Beaubien family and became their heir after the U.S. conquest and the sole proprietor of the largest privately owned real estate property in the country by 1864. A few years later, Maxwell began selling off parts of the grant to speculators, who resold it to others, though large numbers of settlers already occupied the lands through arrangements with Maxwell or simply as squatters. When squatters refused to pay rent, the company referred their collection to the territory's attorney general, himself in business with the speculators. Rioting followed at Elizabethtown.[31]

The "Colfax County War" began when the federal government reversed itself, declaring the grant to be public domain, even as the company defaulted on paying its property taxes. An associate of the attorney general bought the property for around $16,500 in back taxes, with plans to pass it on to Catron for $20,000. The Dutch owners then redeemed the property. However, the plan exposed the well-connected Republican "Santa Fe Ring." The next year, Frank Springer, a lawyer and pioneering Western paleontologist, launched the *Cimarron News and Elizabeth City Railway Press and Telegraph* in opposition to the Ring.[32]

One of the Ring's henchmen, Francisco Griego, got into an altercation over a card game that ended when he murdered two soldiers. When the Republican cabal kept Griego from getting indicted, Franklin J. Tolby wrote an exposé for the *New York Sun*. In September 1875, gunmen ambushed and killed him outside of Pascoe.

Reverend Oscar Patrick McMains, outraged by the murder of Tolby, a fellow Methodist circuit rider, joined forces with the gunman Clay Allison to organize the vigilantes who began running down the guilty parties on their own. Matters escalated until the killing of Cruz Vega.

The Ring retaliated. Pancho Griego tried to get the jump on Allison in Cimarron's St. James Hotel, while the authorities used the law to

31   Maria E. Montoya, *Translating Property: The Maxwell Land Grant and the Conflict over Land in the American West, 1840–1900* (Berkeley: University of California Press, 2002).

32   Morris F. Taylor, *O.P. McMains and the Maxwell Land Grant Conflict* (Tucson: University of Arizona Press, 1979), 35–8, 39–46, 47–55.

indict McMains for inciting a riot. Although Springer defended him, the jury convicted McMains of a fifth-degree felony and fined him $300. Clashes over the dominance of the Ring continued for years, but mostly through the courts.

The Sante Fe Ring's reliance on violence to maintain power exploded most famously in nearby Lincoln County. There, Major Lawrence C. Murphy and his mob confronted a number of would-be rivals, including John Henry Tunstall, backed by his attorney and partner Alexander A. McSween, as well as John Chisum, who had come into the area from the Panhandle.

The most remembered participant in the Lincoln County War of 1878, William Henry Bonney ("Billy the Kid") came from the most humble of its ranks.[33] Not only did Bonney leave little consistent information about his past, but the man who killed him wrote Bonney's first biography. It has taken a century for scholars to cobble together a plausible account of his background, during which time he has been referred to as Antrim and McCarthy in addition to Bonney.

The latest accounts seem to indicate that William Henry Bonney's mother, Catherine Devine, married one William Harrison Bonney, who had gone to Kansas, apparently on his own, and died in 1862 in what became Coffeyville. Other versions have her married to a man named McCarty, with whom she had two sons: Joseph in 1854 and Billy in 1860 or 1861, though his killers claimed he was born in 1859, making him twenty-one at the time they killed him rather than only nineteen. Some time after 1862, Devine took her children to Indianapolis.[34] By 1870, she had taken up with William Antrim, who brought the entire family with him to Kansas. Different accounts place them in Coffeyville and Wichita. It seems likely that, with two

33 Robert M. Utley, *High Noon in Lincoln: Violence on the Western Frontier* (Albequerque: University of New Mexico Press, 1987), 15, 20, 25.

34 Another possible father, William McCarthy, enlisted in the 88th New York and was killed at Antietam. The address 210 Greene Street was within walking distance of the Church of St. Peter. 1860 United States Federal Census for New York City, Manhattan First Ward, enumerated by Assistant Marshal Edward Hogan on June 26, 1860, p. 176.

Williams in the family, the stepson came to be called "Henry," his middle name. As a result, some later accounts give his name as "Henry McCarty."

Soon after the family reached Kansas, Catherine contracted tuberculosis, and they headed to the drier climate of Santa Fe. There, in 1873, she and Antrim married with her sons as witnesses, after which they continued on to Silver City. Antrim went prospecting for work elsewhere and expressed less interest in the family, though Billy sometimes carried the surname "Antrim" and established an early reputation as "Kid Antrim." In 1874, Devine died in Silver City and Antrim headed into Arizona, leaving the stepsons behind.

Then only about fourteen, Billy took up residence in a local boardinghouse, earning his own way by working as a dishwasher and waiter. He was punished periodically for stealing food. Then he got caught with a bundle of stolen laundry that he claimed to be holding for a friend. Breaking out of custody, he fled to Arizona in hopes of seeking shelter with his stepfather, who, after 1875, refused to have anything to do with him.

Left to his own devices, Bonney fell in with an ex-cavalryman running a horse-thieving gang. Locals referred to him as "the kid" because of his youth and frail physique. The summer of 1877, which brought violence across the region, also saw Bonney's first fatal altercation, in which he shot a blacksmith who had been bullying him. Although taken into custody, he once more made his escape.

So it was that he returned to New Mexico, initially recruited by the Murphy gang allied to the Santa Fe Ring to rustle from Tunstall. Caught red-handed, he accepted Tunstall's offer of a second chance. Always personally loyal to a fault, Bonney became an active and ruthless partisan, particularly after Tunstall's murder by law enforcement officers in the pay of the Murphy gang in February 1878. Revenge killing continued for a year until newly appointed Governor Lew Wallace helped arrange a truce.

After Chisum shifted away from Lincoln County and others set aside their vendettas, Bonney looked for a way to make his own living, taking about 125 horses into the Panhandle near Tascosa. John Middleton, an old outlaw in his forties, Henry Brown, and Fred

Waite, a Chickasaw cowboy who later became future governor of that nation in the Indian Territory, set off on their own from Tascosa. When they turned up in Tascosa, the big ranchers brought Bonney in and told him he could remain as long as he behaved himself, which he did. He became particularly close friends with Dr. Henry C. Hoyt, the local surgeon.[35] Thereafter, "the Kid" turned up regularly in town.

The line between what was lawful and what was not at Tascosa had always been muddled. In 1879, William C. Moore took over the management of one of the large ranches in the Panhandle, after having held similar positions in Wyoming. However, the law there wanted him for murder, as they did in California. The men called him "Outlaw Bill" Moore. Shortly after, his company sent people to run down and kill accused outlaws, including "Dirty Dave" Rudabaugh and Tom Pickett, two former law enforcement officers from Las Vegas.

In March 1880, the big ranchers sought to make amends with each other through a common Panhandle Cattlemen's Association at Mobeetie.[36] That fall, one of their shared objectives became an expedition against the Kid and his presumed gang. They put together a force that included Frank Stewart, a detective of LIT, Kid Dobbs, Lon Chambers and Lee Hall of the LX, Charley Reasor of LIT, Pat Garrett Moore of LX, Charles Siringo, Cal Polk, Jim East, Tom Emory, George Williams, Louis Bousman, Rob Robinson, Frank Weldon and a Mexican cook.

The operation became one of the great dramas in the history of the West though, at the time, Bonney hardly had a gang. After going back to New Mexico, he and O'Folliard had fallen in with Charles Bowdre, Billy Wilson, Rudabaugh, and Pickett, the lawmen from Las Vegas. On December 19, they played poker in a small adobe building as Garrett and his lot approached. Bushwhackers put two slugs into O'Folliard and brought him in to die, which he did while cursing

35   McCarty, *Maverick Town*, 77–9, 79–80, 80–1.

36   On the Panhandle involvement, see McCarty, *Maverick Town*, 82–3, 84–6, 87–8, 88–9, 89, 90–1. On Tom Pickett, see Earle R. Forrest, *Arizona's Dark and Bloody Ground: An Authentic Account of the Sanguinary Pleasant Valley Vendetta that Swept Through Arizona's Cattleland in the Latter Eighteen-Eightes—the Graham-Tewksbury Feud* (London: Andrew Melrose, 1953), 182–3.

Garrett. The next day, they found Rudabaugh's horse dead twelve miles distant.

The other unconvicted accused had slipped through their fingers. Cold and hungry, the posse sent Siringo into town with money from the Panhandle ranchers. He spent $100 of it and came back with nothing for the group to eat, after which he and Robinson refused to continue the pursuit and went into winter camp at White Oak. Garrett continued with Chambers, Hall, East, and Emory, locating their elusive prey at Stinking Springs on December 23. Garrett went forward with Emory, Chambers, Hall, and East, leaving Stewart, Bousman, and Williams with horses. They surrounded the place, killed Bowdrie, and continued their pursuit of the others.

Three days later, Garrett brought his captives into Las Vegas on their way to Santa Fe. Some of the locals nearly rioted when the lawmen tried to move their prisoners to the capital. They particularly wanted to get their hands on Rudabaugh, who had made many enemies while wearing a badge there.

The posse had kidnapped men without a warrant against them, and some of Bonney's friends were therefore released. On April 28, 1881, Bonney himself made another of his daring and inexplicable escapes. Over in Texas, the Panhandle Cattlemen's Association sent John William Poe to aid Garrett. In July 1881, Poe and the Texans learned of Bonney's presence on the Maxwell place. It had probably been no accident that, of all the lawyers, lawmen, businessmen, speculators, and politicians who fueled and benefited from the Lincoln County War, the only victim of official justice was an orphaned legal minor.

Violent Tensions in the Panhandle

Carving out any niche for yourself independent of the big spreads was not easy, but Jesse R. Jenkins had the grit to try. His father, Jonathan Jenkins, had brought the entire family to Texas from Alabama, though most of the Jenkins family lore seems unlikely.

They claimed to have arrived around 1851 when Jonathan surveyed what became the town of Cleburne, though the town was not incorporated for another twenty years. The Jenkins family also claimed that Jonathan had been a colonel in the Confederate army who returned home after his health had broken; no records exist of this. After Jonathan's death, his widow remarried a farmer and Methodist minister in Dallas County, who brought eight children from an earlier marriage and had little use for his stepchildren, particularly the youngest of them, Jesse.[37] At a fairly early age, they packed him off to live with an older brother.

Charles Harroway Jenkins had been sent out earlier. He had studied law in Dallas, where he took charge of the county's surveying office and then became the city engineer under the Reconstruction government. In 1877, he moved to Brownwood just ahead of the railroad, serving in various municipal capacities, including as mayor. One visitor later described the town as an oddity, where church members and reform-minded locals forbade liquor and prostitution and—to Owen Wister's horror—required people to dispose of their trash in refuse bins rather than simply throwing it into the street. One of these chronic do-gooders, Charles H. Jenkins, had already become a founder of the Greenback movement in Texas and would cling to the hope of launching a genuine party of the people for years.[38] Though he became increasingly focused on horsemanship to the exclusion of other interests, Jesse remained close to Charles throughout these years, periodically turning to him for political and legal help.

In 1881, at the age of eighteen, Jesse headed north to join his eldest brother. Two years older than Charles, William Alonzo Jenkins had come of age in time to participate in the great buffalo slaughters around Mobeetie. "Lon" made himself a fairly indispensible

37 On the Jenkins brothers, see Frederick Nolan, *Tascosa: Its Life and Gaudy Times* (Lubbock: Texas Tech University Press, 2007), 218–21, 222–3, 227. Lon Jenkins's wife was a niece of P.T. Barnum and had been a snake girl in the circus. At this point, at least, Charles was not a "staunch Democrat."

38 Fanny Kemble Wister, ed., *Owen Wister Out West: His Journals and Letters* (Chicago: University of Chicago Press, 1958), 115–16.

entrepreneur in those parts, performing odd jobs around the fort, working freight and building saloons. Jesse not only helped with these tasks but, finding himself at the end of the telegraph wire, began making good money running messages to more far-flung businesses. Lon, meanwhile, realized that the cattle trails had shifted west and headed in that direction to set up shop in Tascosa, running a freighting business up to Dodge and operating a saloon in town. Eventually, Lon would go into partnership with Pat Garrett in Roswell, New Mexico.

In 1881, young Jesse Jenkins turned up to help Lon in Tascosa. Over time, a natural division of labor between him and Lon left him running the saloon. He provided the booze, girls, gambling, and other services that the locals needed. Interested in business development in the West and directly connected to the founders of the optimistic Greenback current in Texas politics, Jenkins also began functioning as the fixer for the little town and its hinterland.

Yet, features of the Panhandle economy placed many problems beyond an easy fix. Conditions revitalized a feudal sense of nobility and masculinity. Those unready to appear deferential could find themselves in a lethal clash over honor or manhood.

In August 1881, Frederick Leigh, a thirty-four-year-old, English-born cowhand, sought relief from the summer heat in Tascosa. Most likely he, like his brother-in-law Robert Mitchell, had participated in the Higgins–Horrell violence in Lampasas County before deciding to escape to the north. On August 8, Leigh was drinking in a saloon and began to amuse himself by taking potshots at the ducks that regularly played in a ditch of water standing in what hopeful locals liked to call a street. Sheriff Cape Willingham asked for his gun, but Leigh replied that he would have to "take it out of cold hands." Leigh's Hestonesque posturing failed to impress the sheriff, who popped into a nearby store, emerged with a shotgun, and came back across the street to the saloon. It was hard to discern later what had happened when Willingham repeated his demands and Leigh reached for his gun. Some claimed that Leigh did so to hand over his revolver as asked, but when he reached for it, Willingham blasted him, even as others arrived to support him. Mitchell contributed

$50 to Leigh's burial, according him the dubious honor of being the second man buried in the town's new "boot hill."[39]

The voters—mostly cowboys—tended to see Willingham as more of a bully than a hero. In 1882, they sent him packing and elected Jim East, one of the heroes of the hunt for the Kid.[40] East proved to be less than universally popular, however.

At about this time, Bill Gatlin, a Texas-raised native of Alabama, turned up in Tascosa.[41] The 1880 census revealed that his real name was Dan Bogan and that he resided in Hamilton County, and a later newspaper account reported that he had two older brothers, both horse thieves. One had been killed by a sheriff while trying to escape, and the other had been sent to the penitentiary in Texas.

Near his twenty-first birthday, Bogan had gone barhopping through Hamilton with his friend Dave Kemp. As they moved between saloons, they encountered F. A. "Doll" Smith, who had words with Bogan, who pulled his gun at close quarters. When the drunken youngster tried, Smith landed a blow to his chin that knocked him down, then stepped on his arm to wrench away the pistol. Kemp reportedly began striking Smith with his revolver, and when Smith turned with Bogan's revolver, Kemp tried to blast him, but the hammer failed to detonate the bullet twice. Bogan then rose up and hit Smith just as Kemp got his bullets working. As Smith fell, he threw the revolver at Kemp, hitting him in the head. When Sheriff G. N. Gentry arrived on the scene from the nearby courthouse, Kemp supposedly aimed and pulled the trigger again, only to strike another "squib."

A bystander grabbed Kemp and the crowd soon carted him and Bogan to the jail. Later, the grand jury indicted both as "actively engaged" in Smith's murder. Defended by Eidson and Mills, two of the best lawyers in Hamilton County, the two obtained a change of

39　Nolan, *Tascosa*, 102–3, 103–4.

40　McCarty, *Maverick Town*, 109.

41　On Gatlin and his activities, see Robert K. DeArment, *Deadly Dozen: Twelve Forgotten Gunfighters of the Old West* (Norman: University of Oklahoma Press, 2003), 152, 152–3, 155–6, 228n1 (not to be confused with his *Deadly Dozen: Forgotten Gunfighters of the Old West* or his 2010 *Deadly Dozen*).

venue to Coryell County, and the trial started on June 11 in Gatesville. The jury convicted both of them and the judge sentenced them to death, but one of the defendants nabbed a gun from a careless guard and both men leapt through a second-story window. Kemp broke his leg, but Bogan got to a horse and made his getaway. Kemp managed to challenge the sentence and got his sentence down to 25 years.

"Gatlin" washed up in Tascosa, along with many other men with shadowy pasts who found security there, even after their pasts became widely known. Siringo later described Bogan as a decent and likable fellow. He fit a world where "Outlaw Bill" managed the ranch despite at least two warrants for murder.

Yet, once placed on the wrong side of the law, suspicion always seemed to cling to Brogan. After he began to go by the name of Gatlin, he escaped the wrath of local law enforcement by signing on for a cattle drive. A later account suggested that when gunplay took place in the cow town at the end of the line, he must have been involved.[42]

Honor and reputation carried great weight among the cowboys. Employers relied heavily on hired men to manage affairs in their absence. The LIT's best-known cowboys were Gene Watkins and W. H. "Harry" Ingerton, who came into the area as employees of the large firm to build the line camps and corrals and round up strays during the severe winter of 1881.

The twenty-eight-year-old Louis Phillip Bousman—known as "the Animal" to his friends— hoped to avoid the blighted life of an aging cowboy by becoming a gambler. It is likely that he never thought of himself as a prize liar, but men in that world habitually spun stories to while away the long nights. Bousman described himself as the Virginia-born grandson of a powerful slaveowner. His father, he said, had come to Lafayette County, Missouri, joined Sterling Price's Confederate army, and got mustered out on the Red River. Actually, Bousman's father was likely Joseph Bousman, who joined the Fortieth Missouri of the Union army in August 1864 to fight against Sterling Price.

Bousman, too, had a connection with Lampasas County. His father-in-law, Tom Cruce, who may have been an African American,

---

42 DeArment, *Deadly Dozen*, 156.

lived with a Choctaw who went by the name Katherine Rutledge and ran a brothel as "Indian Kate." A Thomas Owen Cruce joined the Second Florida of the Confederate army in July 1862, but got discharged August 1, joined the U.S. forces, and was later thought to be living in Florida. Tom and Kate's daughter, "Swayback Mag"— apparently Sarah Eldora "Sally" Cruce—married Bousman in 1878.[43]

In the fall of 1882—hardly a year after the killing of Leigh—a cowboy named Bob Gibson rode into town early in the morning and proceeded to drink his way through the day and into the evening, getting unapologetically ripped to the gills. He ended up in the upstairs room of Sally Emory, a "soiled dove" employed by the brothel that, along with a gambling hall, was housed under the same roof as the aptly named Hog Town Dance Hall. Gibson had passed out. As the night wore on, a gunshot was heard but the sound was common enough that nobody investigated.

The next day, Gibson was missing. A search party found him in Sally's room, where he had been robbed. Suspicion fell on her and the bartender, Johnny Maley. Sheriff East investigated but months went by with no arrest.

In response, Ed Norwood showed up in the Hog Town Dance Hall, flashing a large bankroll and ready to drink. He ended up in Sally Emory's, where he let her fall asleep, drew his revolver, and waited. The night ended with Maley dead and Norwood revealed as Gibson's long-lost brother. Sheriff East arrested him reluctantly but, in the night, a sympathetic crowd of locals sprang "Norwood", who lit out of town, never to be seen there again.

Through the rest of the 1880s, nothing stemmed the rise of capitalist development. The larger landowners gobbled up the smaller ones,

43 Nolan, *Tascosa*, 197–8. Edward Cruce and John Cruse were enlisted, respectively, in the Eighteenth U.S. Colored Infantry raised in Missouri and the Fifty-First U.S. Colored Infantry of Mississippi volunteers.

particularly in the cattle business. Larger enterprises strung barbed wire to close the old open-range system of grazing.

A contemporary later wrote of "many labor strikes on the range," their number, scale, and successes naturally minimized by employers. A recent scholar reasonably suggested that, though under-documented, the conditions fostered "slowdowns, threats, intimidating behavior, and collective defiance among cowboys."[44]

Tascosa was ripe for such an innovation.

---

44 Gene M. Gressley, *Bankers and Cattlemen: The Stocks-and-Bonds, Havana Cigar, Mahogany-and-Leather Side of the Cowboy Era. Politics, Investors, Operators from 1870 to 1900* (Lincoln: University of Nebraska Press, 1971), 124.

THREE

The Panhandle Strike of 1883

An Appropriately Rough Interrogation of the Sources

The general manager on one big ranch later recalled the behavior of his discontented cowboys. His hired men, he complained, chose to take action at "a trying moment, because we had a herd of beef just about ready to start to market." When the boss refused their terms, "they turned their horses, gave a cowboy yell, waved their Stetsons in the air and made a bee-line for the headquarters." That night, the boss claimed that he heard "a good deal of talk about lynching or licking or tar and feathering, and, as a prelude they fired off their revolvers." After "a bit of a pow-wow" in the morning, the cowboys in the other outfits rode off. In this case, the manager described himself as being "at a disadvantage, work had to be shoved forward, they were obliged to brand their calves and gather beef, and as they had no time to get more men, were obliged to comply with the demands of the strikers and restore their wages."[1]

In early 1883, cowboys in the Texas Panhandle went on strike. A contemporary observer recalled that it had not been "directly" related to wider range wars, but "in almost every respect tied in with the struggle between big and little men that went on over a period of years on the Western range." Contemporary newspapers naturally

---

1 Quoted in Weston, *The Real American Cowboy*, 96, 97–8.

tended to describe this development—so distant from their presses—based on information supplied by employers. Nevertheless, enough of the muddied course of the strike can be unraveled to reveal a great deal about the dynamics of power in the West.

The Making of a Strike

In the first weeks of 1883, the owners of the big spreads in the Panhandle began planning for the spring roundup and the lucrative cattle drive to Dodge City. The cattlemen enjoyed soaring profits from herds of record size and increased their margin of control by unilaterally throttling their men's customary access to mavericks.

Perhaps nobody understood these developments as clearly as the wagon bosses. These generally constituted the more experienced, reliable, and highly paid cowboys who coordinated the work crews operating out of particular chuck wagons. These foremen regularly dealt with all the men and understood the changes in class relations from both sides.

In March 1883, Thomas B. Harris, an Alabama-born Texan, decided the time had come to exercise the power of the foremen. Harris may have brought more skill to this task than his employers expected: records show that an Alabama-born man named Thomas B. Harris, the nephew of the Honorable A. J. Harris, had gained admission the year before to the bar in Belton, Texas. The 1880 census listed a Thomas Harris, likely our cowboy living in San Miguel County, New Mexico, not far from the Texas line. As a foreman at the LS Ranch, he carried real weight both with the men and the bosses. He earned an exceptionally high wage of $100 a month, which makes his course all the more admirable.[2]

Two other wagon bosses agreed with Harris and decided that it was worth sticking their necks out as well. We know little about Roy

2 Austin *Weekly Democratic Statesman*, April 20, 1882, p. 4, col. 5; Sullivan, *The LS Brand*, 65; DeArment, *Deadly Dozen*, 156–7; McCarty, *Maverick Town*, 110. Twenty-six-year-old Thomas B. Harris also married Nancy Alice Nichols on August 9, 1883, in San Saba County, Texas, one of the more violent centers of range warfare. Nolan, *Tascosa*, 149, 143.

Griffin of the LX. He appeared in the 1880 census as a resident of Runnels County, a cowboy born in Texas to an Irish immigrant and a Georgia woman.

The other, Waddy Peacock of the LIT, was surely the J. W. Peacock signing the original strike call. Of the several individuals with these initials in Texas at this time, one of the two Georgia-born laborers, then in their early or mid-thirties, had been farming in Hunt county a few years earlier.[3]

These men served as intermediaries between the bosses and their hired men. They had been making the case about static wage levels for some time by early March when the strikers acted. "Cowboys have some knowledge of the immense profits cattle owners are making," wrote the *Caldwell Commercial*, "and it should not be at all surprising if they asked fair wages for what is the hardest kind of hard work."[4]

In the end, Harris, Griffin, and Peacock persuaded nearly two dozen cowboys to sign a written agreement that left no doubt as to what they wanted. They agreed to a mass meeting on April 1, giving their employers until March 31 to agree to the terms. Generally treated as a strike call, the agreement survives with about two dozen signatories.[5]

When someone finally got around to interviewing Dave Lard in 1937, he made no bones about his opinion of his friend Tom Harris

3   The 1880 U.S. census for Texas shows a James W. Peacock, a thirty-year-old farmer (born around 1850) living in Precinct 4, Hunt County.

4   Clifford P. Westermeier, *Trailing the Cowboy* (Caldwell, ID: Caxton Printers, 1955), 124, 150n28.

5   McCarty, *Maverick Town*, 109; DeArment, *Deadly Dozen*, 156–7; Robert E. Zeigler, "Cowboy Strike of 1883: Its Causes and Meaning," in Bruce A. Glasrud and James C. Maroney, eds., *Texas Labor History* (College Station: Texas A&M University, 2013), said to be reprinted from *West Texas Historical Association Yearbook* 47 (1971): 32–46, and used as Texas State Historical Association, "The Cowboy Strike of 1883," June 12, 2010, Handbook of Texas Online, available at tshaonline.org/handbook/online/articles/oec02. For the statement, see McCarthy, *Maverick Town*, 110; Nolan, *Tascosa*, 143–4. Signatures on McCarty, *Maverick Town*, 110, and Nolan, *Tascosa*, 144. Bob Wheatly and Jim Gover, associated with Harris's activities after the strike and with the Tabletop brand of Gatlin, were almost surely among the strikers. Nolan, *Tascosa*, 223.

or the strikers he had led over half a century earlier. Harris, he insisted, had been

> in the right, really. Them companies moved in there [as] cold blooded as a bunch of damned snakes and they wouldn't allow people to have cattle or state land or nothing. Peons, that's what we were. I may get the devil for saying this but I always was in sympathy with them.

Of the strikers, he said, "A whole bunch of the best cowpunchers and men was in with that outfit and I tell you they was a damned sight better men than some of the cowmen that brought that on."[6]

Some can actually be traced to individuals who made a mark on the historical records. Two had seemingly Latino surnames: W. B. Borina brought into the Panhandle a surname unique to the New Mexico and Arizona Territories. Based on the census records, the most likely Juan A. Gomez was a forty-year-old Juan Antonio Gomez, a Pueblo Indian from the Taos Agency.

The written document provides a test of the accuracy and origins of contemporary press accounts. The statement specifically declared that the cowboys wanted a minimum monthly wage of $50 for the hands and $75 for wagon bosses. Remarkably, the Federal Commissioner of Labor actually obtained and later printed solid information on the strike to incorporate into its statistical view of "Strikes and Lockouts" in those years.[7] The compilers of these accounts often had ties to workers and reform associations and regularly acknowledged that they could not know the precise details of the strikes; modern scholars can assume that what they did publish was factual.

Although they were the lowest rung of society—so marginalized that they were, in some ways, hardly part of it—the most transient of

---

6 Quoted in Nolan, *Tascosa*, 148.

7 Strike for wage increase, no organization, seven employers. March 23 to April 4, 1883. Won, employers lost 3,835. 328 strikers, earning $1.18 per day at start, attained $1.68 per day. Work week ran to 105 hours. *Third Annual Report of the Commissioner of Labor, 1887: Strikes and Lockouts* (Washington: Government Printing Office, 1888), 580–1, 582–3.

the cowboys insisted upon an almost unparalleled wage increase—40 percent, from $30 to $50 for most cowhands.

Contemporary press accounts offered generally accurate information about the goals of these strikes, though they were not necessarily consistent about the wages cowboys received. In all likelihood, the $30 in monthly pay attributed to cowboys in most sources was accurate, particularly on the larger spreads, but some newspapers reported $20 or even $40. In all likelihood, the papers printed what they heard from various agents of the big ranchers, who regularly visited the more populous towns to purchase supplies.[8]

None of them seemed to have anticipated the intelligence and strategic sensibility of the cowboys in acting when they did. Ranchers had a very small window of time in which to organize, begin their spring roundup, and get their cattle drives underway. The later they delivered their cattle to market, the less they could get for them, but leaving too soon risked not finding enough forage and running into flooded fords along the way. This was the point at which the cowboys would have their best hold over the bosses, and it would have to be quick.

In short, the cowboys' timing could not have been better. "This is a very critical time for such trouble," wrote the *Leadville Daily Herald*, "as preparations for the season's drive are at hand, and efforts are being made to compromise matters." As another newspaper reported, the cowboys had chosen "the beginning of the spring round-up," which was "a very critical time for such trouble, as preparations for the season's drive are at hand."

The actual timing of the strike remains more than a bit muddled. The press, which likely did not have the strikers' statement, reported that the cowboys "will have a meeting on April 1st and decide their

---

8 "[Untitled]," Medicine Lodge KS *Barbour County Index*, March 30, 1883, p. 1; Westermeier, *Trailing the Cowboy*, 124, 125; "[Untitled]," *Fort Collins Courier*, April 12, 1883, cited in Westermeier, *Trailing the Cowboy*, 150n30; "Cowboys' Cunning," *Denver Republican*, March 27, 1883, cited in Westermeier, *Trailing the Cowboy*, 150n27. A New Mexico paper muddled what was at stake, printing that the bosses had offered to compromise on $13 but the cow punchers held out for $30. "The Panhandle Trouble," *Las Vegas Daily Gazette*, April 19, 1883, p. 4.

programme."[9] On the face of it, then, the hired men had given their employers until March 31 to head off the strike.

Nevertheless, many cowboys seemed to have already stopped work prior to the date of the meeting. Indeed, the Commissioner of Labor describes the action as starting on March 23. An account from Fort Worth the following day said that the cowboys had already "struck for a raise of salary." A report from St. Louis on March 26 declared that "an extensive strike among the cowboys in the Panhandle of Texas is progressing, and trouble is apprehended." The *Fort Collins Courier* reported that "the novelty of the strike is that the men have struck before work has begun, and the serious feature is that it is in anticipation of the spring work, or the regular annual roundup which can not go on without them."[10]

The confusion most likely reflected the character of the cowboys' work. The roundup, requiring larger amounts of manpower than usual, had been scheduled for April 1, but a great deal of preliminary work took place at the ranches among those regularly employed. Men who would otherwise be lining up for work on the roundup were likely not doing so.

The cowboys had taken the employers by surprise to the extent that the bosses had no coherent response to them. The existing historical accounts are entirely dependent on the employers on each of the big spreads for accounts of their specific responses; allowances must be made for self-aggrandizement and bravado. The owners of the LE claimed that they had fired all of the cowboys on the spot.[11] However, it remains unclear when or if this took place; the owners would have

9 "A Cowboy Strike [from *Texas Live Stock Journal*]," *Fort Worth Daily Gazette*, March 29, 1883, p. 6.

10 "Trouble with the Cowboys," *Sacramento Daily Union*, March 26, 1883, p. 4; "Cowboys on a Strike," *Leadville Daily Herald*, March 27, 1883, p. 1; Westermeier, *Trailing the Cowboy*, 125; "[Untitled]," *Fort Collins Courier*, April 12, 1883, cited in Westermeier, *Trailing the Cowboy*, 150n30. Newspapers from as far away as Colorado covered the dispute. Zeigler, "Cowboy Strike of 1883."

11 Sullivan, *The LS Brand*, 65–6; McCarty, *Maverick Town*, 112; Nolan, *Tascosa*, 144. Zeigler reported that officials at the T-Anchor and the LE fired striking employees on the spot. The LS and the LIT offered a slight increase in wages and fired workers if they refused. Zeigler, "Cowboy Strike of 1883."

had to make arrangements beforehand with enough men to keep the ranch functioning.

Accounts exist from the management of the larger ranches.[12] Roy Griffin's crews on the LX ranch stood firm enough. Their management later reported that they had chosen to wait and see what happened; several of the large ranches, in fact, seem to have done the same, holding back until the even larger ones took action.

The management at the massive old LIT recounts that one of their number, Bob Robinson, rode out to negotiate with the strikers, offering Waddy Peacock and the boys a compromise: the LIT would pay $35 a month and $65 to wagon bosses. When the men refused, the management retrieved their horses out from under the men riding company mounts, leaving the strikers on foot.

Accounts from the T-Anchor center on the owners' expectations of violence. The management stocked up on buffalo guns. When they heard that the strikers planned on attacking the ranch, they rigged a keg of gunpowder in the blacksmith shop and sent one of the few black workers in the local industry to detonate it when the hired men showed up. Plans of intentional homicide aside, the bosses there seem to have had no viable plans to deal with the strike.

The strike at the time likely centered on the LS ranch, where the two owners—W. M. D. Lee and Lucien B. Scott—were out of town, leaving Jordan McAllister to deal on his own with the eighty to ninety cowboys already on the payroll. McAllister hoped to act moderately but sent word to Lee, who immediately boarded a train at Leavenworth for Dodge City, where he rented a rig and pressed on. Thirty-six hours leaving Leavenworth, he barged in on McAllister, demanding to know why he had not just fired everybody. "Why don't you meet their demands, and keep 'em at work? I can bring in all the men we'll ever need at my own price, then I'll fire every LS man that's in this strike." "Settle it to suit yourself," McAllister responded.

---

12 Sullivan, *The LS Brand*, 65, 66–7; Nolan, *Tascosa*, 144, 145; McCarthy, *Maverick Town*, 111, 112–13. Gus Lee was "the faithful and later famous Negro cook" who lit the bomb prepared for strikers. McCarty, *Maverick Town*, 113.

Lee called in Harris to discuss the matter. He later claimed that Harris took with him five or six armed strikers and "some of the men fired their guns." However, the content of the discussion, if accurately conveyed by Lee, certainly precluded the presence of others. Lee reminded Harris that he already got $100 a month, but Harris pleaded the case for the cowboys as a whole. Lee said that he then "offered to pay $50 to every man you recommend as a top hand if they'll stay on the job." Likely recognizing a liar when he saw one, Harris refused. "You're fired!" Lee countered, "and cut them off at the LS chuck line."

Although most accounts report that the strike took place on only five ranches, the federal authorities knew of seven firms hit, with a collective loss of $3,835.[13]

No organization moved the cowboys to strike, according to the Commissioner of Labor, but the strikers proved to be well organized. "In anticipation of the strike," recalled one observer, "the participants had been saving their money earned." Harris reportedly mandated that the workers set aside some of their pay for a small strike fund. Moreover, the cowboys made their way to the Alamocitos Creek near Tascosa after leaving the job, where they "set up a new camp" and "propose[d] to hold the fort if it takes until next winter." This placed them near the headquarters of the LS. They held their April 1 gathering at Juan Dominguez Canyon, west of Mitchell Canyon.[14] Having given the employers fair warning and received their responses, the strikers showed no signs of weakening in their resolve.

By all accounts, Jesse Jenkins's saloon took up much of the organizational slack left by the absence of a union. With his Greenback connections, Jenkins viewed the big spreads and their power with great suspicion. He had deep ties to the cowboys, including a large group of Mexicans, who frequented his business. Jenkins also had a

13 Zeigler, "Cowboy Strike of 1883."

14 "The Panhandle Trouble," *Las Vegas Daily Gazette*, April 19, 1883, p. 4; John Arnot in Nolan, *Tascosa*, 143, citing manuscript 296n15; Sullivan, *The LS Brand*, 67; also Pauline D. and R. L. Robertson, *Cowman's Country: Fifty Frontier Ranches in the Texas Panhandle, 1876–1887* (Amarillo: Paramount, 1981). On the April 1 meeting, see McCarthy, *Maverick Town*, 111.

strong friendship with Harris, even marrying one of his sisters, Molly, in 1886. Inseparable from this event, though, was Harris's trial as an accused horse thief, in which he was ably defended by Jesse's brother, Charles H. Jenkins, the prominent Greenbacker.[15]

Tall Tales

Thanks to the ongoing digitization of contemporary American newspapers, we know that the press from Kentucky to California began carrying accounts of the strikes on March 26, most of them reprinted articles attributed to a regional source. However, the regional sources themselves were located far away from the strikes. What was said to be Amarillo's first newspaper, the *Livestock Champion*, was not printed until 1887, when that town was founded forty miles south of where the cowboys went on strike.

Coverage in the major Texas papers initially reflected that isolation.[16] They merely reported "difficulties between cowmen and cowboys in regard to rates of pay. Particulars beyond the bare facts of the existence of the trouble have not been ascertained owing to quarantine from small-pox at Mobeetie." The paper admitted to lacking information, declaring it "useless to make further remark," but then did so, warning that under "threats of lawlessness, the adjustment of difficulties can only be difficult."

As with most labor coverage, the newspapers—employers themselves—tended to favor the owners. The *Texas Live Stock Journal* postured as reasonable and impartial, because "the sooner this business is amicably settled, the better it will be for all parties interested." It thought cowboys "entitled to all ranchmen can afford to pay," but added that the cowboys had been "hereto for [sic] paid on merits." In an unconscious admission of bias, the *Journal* claimed that employers

15   Nolan, *Tascosa*, 223, 224, 149–50.
16   "A Cowboy Strike," *Texas Live Stock Journal*, March 12, 1883, p. 6, and "A Cowboy Strike [from *Texas Live Stock Journal*]," *Fort Worth Daily Gazette*, March 29, 1883, p. 6 in Westermeier, *Trailing the Cowboy*, 123–4, 150n26; Nolan, *Tascosa*, 146.

alone should decide on appropriate wages for the cowboys, whom they described "as workmen . . . not worth the horses and calves they kill."

In the end, the *Journal* reported that merely planning for a strike carried implicit "threats of lawlessness." "The Texas cowboys threaten to go on a strike," quipped the *Leadville Daily Herald*. "This is a form of deviltry of which the cowboys has [sic] hitherto been innocent."[17]

A Kansas paper defended the right of the cowboys to strike. "If the boys think their wages are not renumerated well enough," it suggested, "they should apply peaceably for a raise and if it is not granted, then quit." It continued, though, that workers could "not resort to unlawful and desperate means to compel their employers to grant their request."[18] Having created a workforce on the edge of the law and redefined its work as illegal, the paper warned of the workforce's need to remain within the law.

Beyond the class bias of the newspapers, any real news that managed to reach the printing presses rarely originated with a striking cowboy joyriding hundreds of miles from the job. Employers regularly sent their representatives to visit the rail heads and larger cities, making arrangements for transporting and selling their cattle or purchasing necessary supplies. "A cattle rancher of the Texas panhandle arrived from Tascosa yesterday and reports a big strike among the cowboys," declared a New Mexico paper.[19] In almost every case, printed information came from the same sources.

---

17   "[Untitled]," *Leadville Daily Herald*, March 28, 1883, p. 2; "A Cowboy Strike [from *Texas Live Stock Journal*]," *Fort Worth Daily Gazette*, March 29, 1883, p. 6; Zeigler, "Cowboy Strike of 1883." See also Weston, *The Real American Cowboy*, 99–104; McCarty, *Maverick Town*, 109–14; Ruth Alice Allen, *Chapters in the History of Organized Labor in Texas* (Austin: University of Texas Press, 1941); B. Byron Price, "Community of Individualists: The Panhandle Stock Association, 1881–1891," in John R. Wunder, ed., *At Home on the Range* (Westport, CT: Greenwood, 1985); Donald F. Schofield, *Indians, Cattle, Ships, and Oil: The Story of W. M. D. Lee* (Austin: University of Texas Press, 1985).

18   "[Untitled]," Medicine Lodge KS, *Barbour County Index*, March 30, 1883, p. 1.

19   "The Panhandle Trouble," *Las Vegas Daily Gazette*, April 19, 1883, p. 4.

This gave the employers a virtually unchecked monopoly on documenting the strike, an advantage they exercised by generating deliberately muddy fictions. Reports in the *Live Stock Journal* that "the talk is of range burning, and wire-fence cutting if their demand is not granted" drew only on conversations that excluded strikers.[20]

There were exceptions. Papers not explicitly and overtly opposed to the strikers were said to be favorable to them. The *Trinidad Weekly Advertiser* took a peculiar position after repeating the bosses' story. The strikers, it wrote,

> propose to burn the ranches, confiscate the cattle and kill the owners in that particular part of the world called the Panhandle, which was recently sold by the state of Texas to a Chicago syndicate and transferred by them to an English company. With the country the English millionaires have bought a hard constituency, as they are in a fair way to find out. An ordinary cowboy is as explosive as a nitro-glycerine bomb, and a good deal more dangerous. We shall watch the war with interest, not caring much which side whips or gets whipped.

In short, it disliked the foreign ownership of western ranches.[21]

The bosses reported two mutually exclusive versions of the strike. The first revisited the ancient morality tale of the dumb peasant forgetting his place in the world and failing to show sufficient deference to his lords and masters. "With money in their pockets, killing time became monotonous, so the crowd rode to Tascosa for a little fun," it recounted. "This proved to be a mistake. For several days Hogtown enjoyed a bonanza, then the boys were broke, and the strike was over." Lewis Nordyke's history of the range repeated the tale. The striking cowboys had "a little pile of money" for the strike fund, but spent it all quickly on women and whiskey, while the bosses had no

20 "A Cowboy Strike," *Texas Live Stock Journal*, March 12, 1883, p. 6, cited in Westermeier, *Trailing the Cowboy*, 123–4, 150n26.

21 "The Latest News," *Trinidad Weekly Advertiser*, April 25, 1883; "The Striking Cowboys," *Texas Live Stock Journal*, April 28, 1883, p. 8, cited in Westermeier, *Trailing the Cowboy*, 127, 129–30, 150n33, 150n35.

problem hiring strikebreakers and getting along with them.[22] At the end, the shortsighted, ungrateful strikers went crawling back to their employers, only to find their jobs taken by others.

Other bosses told a story of a long, vicious strike, dragged out by the stubbornness of the strikers—"an extensive strike," according to the *Denver Republican*. Most historians describe it as a two-and-a-half-month conflict.[23]

This version of the strike includes mention of large numbers of strikebreakers. Press reports of employers' plans to recruit enough scabs to replace the strikers quickly turned into accounts that they had done so. In fact, there exists no indication that the ranches advertised for or recruited those new hands. Certainly, "some of the better cowboys continued to work for the ranch." Nevertheless, as the *Las Vegas Daily Gazette* noted, "A new man is no good on earth and is more liable to wander estray [sic] himself and be forever lost on the boundless plains, than to find stray cattle."[24] Without experienced hands to teach them, the newcomers would be useless.

That said, large numbers of strikebreakers became essential to the employers' portrayal of the cowboys as armed bullies. The *Gazette*, for example, reported that "if stockowners do not accede to their demand, they will quit work and prevent others from taking their positions." These tactics were

> unlawful means to compel their employers to grant their request. These strikes, no matter what industry is involved[,] always result in much evil and no good, and it is generally the case that those who strike come out at the little end of the horn.[25]

---

22 Sullivan, *The LS Brand*, 67; Lewis Nordyke, *Great Roundup: The Story of Texas and Southwestern Cowmen* (New York: William Morrow, 1955), 110–11, addressed in Weston, *The Real American Cowboy*, 99–100; Robert E. Zeigler, "Cowboy Strike of 1883."

23 "Cowboys' Cunning," *Denver Republican*, March 27, 1883, cited in Westermeier, *Trailing the Cowboy*, 124, 150n27.

24 "[Untitled]," *Las Vegas Daily Gazette*, March 28, 1883, p. 4; on old hands staying at work, McCarty, *Maverick Town*, 111–12. Owners and managers continued with roundup plans by hiring replacement workers at temporarily increased wages. Many of the replacement workers were in fact strikers who had asked to return to work. Zeigler, "Cowboy Strike of 1883."

25 "Threatened Cowboy's Strike," *Las Vegas Daily Gazette*, March 18, 1883, p. 3.

One story reported that the bosses "imported a lot of men from the east, but the cowboys surrounded the newcomers and will not allow them to work." The bosses or their sympathizers told the *Fort Collins Courier* of strikers "armed with Winchester rifles and six-shooters and the lives of all who attempt to work for less than the amount demanded, are in great danger." "The most vicious strike that has been organized," shrieked the rural Kentucky *Semi-weekly Interior Journal*. The cowboys, it warned, "will not work themselves and they promise to murder anybody who take [*sic*] their place."[26]

Alleged threats to fictitious strikebreakers essentially humanized a more tangible concern of the employers. The Western Associated Press at Chicago echoed the warning from Fort Worth that "well armed" strikers not only planned to kill strikebreakers but "to fire ranches and work general trouble." Ever sensitive to this vital concern, the *Texas Live Stock Journal* also assured its readers that the strikers would "burn the ranches and run off the stock."[27]

Strikers were specifically charged with planning to engage in "range burning, and wire-fence-cutting if their demand is not granted," as well as the "indiscriminate killing of cattle" and other attacks on private property.[28] The "fence-cutting" accusation attempted to link the strike to a practice that had already involved local and state law enforcement in a series of violent range wars across parts of Texas.

26 "Cowboys on a Strike," *Leadville Daily Herald*, March 27, 1883, p. 1; "[Untitled]," Stanford KY *Semi-weekly Interior Journal*, April 27, 1883, p. 2; Westermeier, *Trailing the Cowboy*, 125; "[Untitled]," *Fort Collins Courier*, April 12, 1883, cited in Westermeier, *Trailing the Cowboy*, 150n30.

27 "Cowboys Strike [from Western Associated Press], April 19," *Las Vegas Daily Gazette*, April 20, 1883, p. 1, repeated in: "Cowboy's Strike," Omaha *Daily Bee*, April 20, 1883, p. 1; "Cowboy's Strike," St. Paul *Daily Globe*, April 26, 1883, p. 3; "The Striking Cowboys," *Texas Live Stock Journal*, April 28, 1883, p. 8, cited in Westermeier, *Trailing the Cowboy*, 129–30, 150n35.

28 "A Cowboy Strike [from *Texas Live Stock Journal*]," *Fort Worth Daily Gazette*, March 29, 1883, p. 6; "Trouble with the Cowboys," *Sacramento Daily Union*, March 26, 1883, p. 4; "[Untitled]," *Fort Collins Courier*, April 12, 1883; "Cowboys on a Strike," *Leadville Daily Herald*, March 27, 1883, p. 1; "Cowboys Strike," *Las Vegas Daily Gazette*, April 20, 1883, p. 1.

Other newspapers suggested that strikers had tried to intimidate Billy Edwards of the *Panhandle* in Amarillo, reporting that he had received anonymous notes from strikers with illustrations of skulls. Evidence for such a tactic, reasons that the strikers would have chosen to employ it, and indications that this paper was being printed at Amarillo in the first place are nonexistent.[29]

What some scholars of the strike have called the only instance of attempted intimidation was aimed at Kid Dobbs on the LS. After only ten days on the job, Dobbs reported, "Harris sent a man to him with this message: 'If you want to keep a whole hide, and know what's good for you, quit the LS at once.'" Dobbs sent the messenger back with a defiant response. Later, when Dobbs and Ed King encountered Harris on the range, the strike leader "staged a friendly act," so Dobbs let the matter drop.[30] Only Dobbs's account exists of this series of events.

Harris himself wrote to the *Texas Live Stock Journal* in response to charges of threatened violence.[31] He explicitly declared that "it is not the intention of the cowboys to resort to any violence or unlawful acts to get adequate compensation for their services, but to do so by all fair and legal means in their power."

The *Live Stock Journal* responded at length. "Cowboys have [a] perfect right to ask for a proper remuneration for their services," it conceded, adding,

> They also have the right to leave work in a body, unless satisfied; they assert their manhood in so doing. They may benefit themselves by such combined action, but directly they make threats of damage to property of others, they laid themselves open to suspicion, and the good among them, the law abiding element, are likely to suffer from the acts and words of those who do their best to bring into dispute the interests they are apparently trying to advance.

29 "He Don't Scare," *Texas Live Stock Journal*, April 28, 1883, p. 8, cited in Westermeier, *Trailing the Cowboy*, 128–9, 150n34.

30 Sullivan, *The LS Brand*, 68; McCarty, *Maverick Town*, 112–13.

31 For this exchange, see "The Cow-Boy Strike," *Texas Live Stock Journal*, April 21, 1883, p. 6, cited in Westermeier, *Trailing the Cowboy*, 125–6, 150n31.

As fair-minded as ever, though, the paper insisted that "we know of a certainty that men who have connected themselves with the strike have made these threats coupled without others to shoot down cattle, to overpower ranchmen and disarm them." It described the striker as a "a kind of cross of the desperado, ready and willing to join any movement, showing a promise of revolution and disorder, and who rejoice in a general chaos in all kinds of business." It then quoted an earlier accusation it had made against the strike, and declared that the story, "now verified, still remains that threats have been made and openly made by some strikers."

Beneath the snow of newsprint lies a bedrock of hard truth. Certainly, all of the strikers were armed. Yet, in spite of the fact—or perhaps because of it—there seems to have been not a single case of violence associated with the strike. Even the later history of the LS Ranch acknowledged that "none of the cowboys used force."[32]

In the end, the press's record for veracity during the strike could hardly have been worse, though it had the immense disadvantage of a predisposition simply to repeat what the employers told them. And some of the leaders among the owners, such as Lee, had already decided on a strategy of deception, according to the people closest to him.

What Actually Happened

Employers' persistent charges of violence against strikebreakers, destruction of property, and fence-cutting represented an intentional strategy on their part, which laid the foundations for involving the armed power of the state. Even as Harris brought attention to the essentially peaceful methods of the strikers, the *Live Stock Journal* noted the presence of Captain John Hoffer's Texas Rangers engaged nearby in operations with the Indians. It also suggested that the new Tombstone rangers who had been deployed against a rumored Indian attack on San Carlos could "transfer their operation

---

32 Sullivan, *The LS Brand*, 66.

to the Panhandle and make a clean job of it"[33] and that "the cattle-owners will call upon the state forces to protect them if their own means fail."[34] In the event of violence, "the cattle owners will call upon the State forces."[35]

On this point, too, the press distorted what little information it seemed to have. Someone from the owners' side seems to have told the press that, if they could not protect their property and their new strikebreaking employees, they would "secure United States troops and Texas rangers" to break the strike.[36] In short order, this became a report of a request for assistance: "Many of the ranchmen have asked for aid from the troops."

Word reached Las Vegas that the area was about to be invaded by the militia. The *Gazette* reported:

> Governor Roberts has been appealed to and has ordered out the state militia which will probably be a rich graft for the 200 cowboys. They are a hard class to tackle and Governor Roberts should have had a higher regard for his militia people.[37]

In fact, though, Governor Oran M. Roberts had left office in January, replaced by another Democrat, Governor John Ireland. Neither sent troops.

33 "The Striking Cowboys," *Texas Live Stock Journal*, April 28, 1883, p. 8, cited in Westermeier, *Trailing the Cowboy*, 129–30, 150n35.

34 "Cowboys on a Strike," *Leadville Daily Herald*, March 27, 1883, p. 1.

35 "Cowboys' Cunning," *Denver Republican*, March 27, 1883, cited in Westermeier, *Trailing the Cowboy*, 124, 150n27.

36 "Trouble with the Cowboys," *Sacramento Daily Union*, March 26, 1883, p. 4; "A Cowboy Strike [from *Texas Live Stock Journal*]," *Fort Worth Daily Gazette*, March 29, 1883, p. 6; "Cowboys on a Strike," *Leadville Daily Herald*, March 27, 1883, p. 1; "Cowboys Strike," *Las Vegas Daily Gazette*, April 20, 1883, p. 1, essentially repeated in "Cowboy's Strike," Omaha *Daily Bee*, April 20, 1883, p. 1; "Cowboy's Strike," St. Paul *Daily Globe*, April 26, 1883, p. 3. Also: "[Untitled]," Stanford KY *Semi-weekly Interior Journal*, April 27, 1883, p. 2; and, on Governor Roberts, "The Panhandle Trouble," *Las Vegas Daily Gazette*, April 19, 1883, p. 4; Zeigler, "Cowboy Strike of 1883;" "[Untitled]," Stanford KY *Semi-weekly Interior Journal*, April 27, 1883, p. 2.

37 "The Panhandle Trouble," *Las Vegas Daily Gazette*, April 19, 1883, p. 4.

Notwithstanding their exaggerations of the threat posed by strikers, the newspapers almost always understated the number of participants, often referring to the list of attendees on a meeting call as a strike agreement. At one point, the *Texas Live Stock Journal* insisted that the the core of strikers actually "only amounts to some forty or fifty." As early as mid-March, though, the *Las Vegas Daily Gazette* passed on a rumor from the *Panhandle* "that 100 cowboys near Tascosa have signed an agreement."[38]

Toward the end of the month—on the eve of the April 1 meeting—a Kansas newspaper reported "that one hundred and sixty cowboys near Tascosa have signed an agreement to strike for a raise." By then, the *Live Stock Journal* placed the number at 200. Even earlier, the *Sacramento Daily Union* reported that "the strikers number about 200," though, with its general penchant for error, it located the action "at Pasca [meaning the town of Tascosa in Oldham] county, near the New Mexican line, where a meeting will be held the first of April."[39]

After attendees of the April 1 meeting opted to expand and continue the strike, the numbers reported in the press froze. The *Las Vegas Daily Gazette*, the *Fort Collins Courier*, and other papers continued to write that about 200 cowboys had gone on strike.[40]

Already, though, a Fort Worth account for the Western Associated Press reported "between two hundred to three hundred cowboys on the ranches in the panhandle are on strike." Shortly after, the *Texas Live Stock Journal* printed its diatribes against several hundred strikers. The most thorough researcher of the strike conceded that the

38 "The Striking Cowboys," *Texas Live Stock Journal*, April 28, 1883, p. 8, cited in Westermeier, *Trailing the Cowboy*, 129, 150n35; "Threatened Cowboy's Strike," *Las Vegas Daily Gazette*, March 18, 1883, p. 3.

39 "[Untitled]," Medicine Lodge KS *Barbour County Index*, March 30, 1883, p. 1; "Trouble with the Cowboys," *Sacramento Daily Union*, March 26, 1883, p. 4; "A Cowboy Strike [from *Texas Live Stock Journal*]," *Fort Worth Daily Gazette*, March 29, 1883, p. 6.

40 "The Panhandle Trouble," *Las Vegas Daily Gazette*, April 19, 1883, p. 4; "[Untitled]," *Fort Collins Courier*, April 12, 1883, cited in Westermeier, *Trailing the Cowboy*, 125, 150n30.

number of strikers might have grown as large as 325, and the Federal Commissioner of Labor recorded 328 strikes.[41]

Such numbers represent the equivalent of about three-quarters of the voting population of Oldham County, Texas, going on strike—indication that something more than a curio of local history had occurred.

The strikers also enjoyed considerable support in the town of Tascosa itself, where the small businesses had grievances of their own against the big companies. Harris's brother-in-law, a saloonkeeper named Jesse Jenkins, proved to be very supportive. His defiance made him lifelong enemies among the big ranches.

The federal report also documented that the strike ran from March 23 to April 4 against seven of the big ranches, which reportedly lost nearly $4,000 by refusing to settle.[42] The strike lasted a matter of days rather than the two and a half months that employers were telling the press.

The most important point employers wanted made in the papers, which the owners of those papers helped to emphasize, was the dire consequences of going on strike, hoping to warn any cowboys away from repeating the job action.

However, it is quite clear that the strikers won, though only a few accounts at the time said so and few directly contradicted stories of the strike's alleged defeat. "The cowboys['] strike in the Panhandle may be regarded as a success," reported the *Austin Weekly Statesman*. "Away out there none will dare attempt to take their places." A correspondent at Fort Dodge spoke to someone just up from Texas, who reported the cowboy strike "pretty well settled, and the boys have compromised on $42.50 a month."[43]

41 "Cowboys Strike," *Las Vegas Daily Gazette*, April 20, 1883, p. 1, essentially repeated in "Cowboy's Strike," Omaha *Daily Bee*, April 20, 1883, p. 1; "Cowboy's Strike," St. Paul *Daily Globe*, April 26, 1883, p. 3; Westermeier, *Trailing the Cowboy*, 129–30; "The Striking Cowboys," *Texas Live Stock Journal*, April 28, 1883, p. 8, cited in Westermeier, *Trailing the Cowboy*, 150n35; Zeigler, "Cowboy Strike of 1883"; McCarty, *Maverick Town*, 113–14.

42 *Third Annual Report of the Commissioner of Labor, 1887: Strikes and Lockouts* (Washington: Government Printing Office, 1888), 580–1, 582–3.

43 "[Untitled]," *Austin Weekly Statesman*, April 26, 1883, p. 4; "The Cowboy," *Fort Worth Daily Democrat*, May 14, 1883, p. 2, col. 1.

In short, the most easily available sources present a cautionary version of events, deeply influenced by employers' accounts and incorrect about a long, painfully drawn-out, and bloody defeat. In reality, the strike was so well planned, well timed, and well executed that it won a quick victory and seems to have inspired a wave of strike activity that continued to shape labor relations in the more isolated corners of the American West for years. As great an authority as the U.S. Commissioner of Labor confirmed the strike as a victory for the workers, and offered a persuasively detailed breakdown of their raise in daily earnings from $1.18 to $1.68—a pay increase of more than 42 percent. Historian Robert Zeigler expressed doubts regarding the veracity of the commissioner's report, suggesting that it was "derived from newspaper accounts and interviews by government representatives." However, none of the commissioner's specific information comes from the newspapers, which generally describe a long defeat.[44]

The victorious strikers returned to work and some of the ranchers moved their herds up the trail toward Mobeetie.[45] Indeed, on April 25, the *Denver Republican* noted that should the Panhandle strikers cause any more difficulty, Hoffer, "with a company of frontier battalion Texas rangers" stationed near Mobeetie, would be "in the center of the troubled district, and will do everything possible to preserve order." Had Mobeetie been near the center of any possible conflicts, the cowboys that concerned them would have already been cowpunching for days up the trail.

However short it had been, the strike had clearly knocked the employers off their game such that they postponed the roundup for weeks. The Denver press noted that the stockmen in the Panhandle "at their recent meeting decided to begin the spring roundup of cattle in the Canadian and Wichita Rivers and Wolfe Creek districts on May 10 and in the Salt Park and Red River districts May 20. If there

---

44 "[Untitled]," *Austin Weekly Statesman*, April 26, 1883, p. 4; Zeigler, "Cowboy Strike of 1883."

45 On these threats against the strikers, see "Texas Round-Up," *Denver Republican*, April 25, 1883, cited in Westermeier, *Trailing the Cowboy*, 127, 150n32.

be any trouble with the striking cowboys it will develop at these roundups."

Indeed, the last mention of the strike in the contemporary press was in the *Dodge City Times* on May 10. That final account read: "The cowboys['] strike in the Panhandle has been a failure." Kid Dobbs also reported that the strikers were defeated and scattered.[46] This was, after all, the employers' line in later years. The paper in distant Dodge City, however, may well have been simply mistaken, and the appearance of the account at the very end of the cattle trail indicates that the cowboys had gone back to work.

There seems to exist only one obvious hint about a longer strike. While the Dodge paper was reporting the collapse of a strike to the south in the Panhandle, the *Dallas Weekly Herald* reprinted accounts of a strike telegraphed from Fort Supply in the Indian Territory. This was 200 miles northeast of Tascosa in the general direction of the Kansas railheads. On April 23, several weeks after the victory in the Panhandle, it reported the strike at Fort Supply "ended, and some of the strikers have gone to work at former wages."[47] The timing rather suggests that successful strikers rode north through the area and that word of mouth inspired additional strikes, indicating that whatever happened along the cattle drive was part of a movement larger than the Tascosa area.

Most importantly, while the cowboys seemed to think that the strike ended with the settlement, but the bosses never ended their operations against them. In some respects, the devious strategy proposed by the LS owner, Lee, seems to have been generally adopted. Although the owners agreed to the pay increase, they never made their peace with the new wages, the strikers who promulgated it, or even the idea of collective bargaining. The big ranchers did not accept the victory of the hired men in good faith.

Indeed, their allies in the press found the violent predispositions attributed by the bosses to their hired hands a useful aspect of the

---

46 "[Untitled]," *Dodge City Times*, May 10, 1883, p. 1; Nolan, *Tascosa*, 146.

47 "Sherman. The Cowboy's Strike About Over—Those Horse Thieves—Light Frost," *Dallas Daily Herald*, April 26, 1883, p. 1, and *Dallas Weekly Herald*, April 26, 1883, p. 7.

turmoil that formed a background to life in Texas at the time. On April 27, eighteen-year-old Lewis Miller entered the freight office of the Dallas and Texas Central Railroad in Hutchins and forced the clerks at gunpoint to open the safe. The Montana paper that reported this made a point of asserting that he "had just returned from the cowboy strike in the Panhandle district."[48]

The summer of 1883 brought a severe drought, increasing the impact of the legislated control of the big cattlemen over access to water. That fall, the American Pastoral Company of London acquired a large share of the LX ranch, a sign that the big ranchers would continue to grow and become more well-connected.

On the ground, the big spreads made changes. After hiring an expanded workforce for the roundups and cattle drives, they did not even have to fire the strikers. Once roundup season ended, the jobs of most of the victorious strikers ended as well and the big ranchers needed only to avoid bringing back the same men. As to strikers among their permanent workforce, the bosses could easily make their working situation increasingly unpleasant.

The official history of the LS Ranch frankly states that "the big ranches refused to hire men who had participated in the strike." The *Dodge City Times* also reported of the strike's veterans "that a number of the most prominent and violent ones have been refused work on the range and have been forced to abandon the country to secure employment."[49]

Certainly, by the time of the next spring roundup, the LS had replaced all of its wagon bosses. Jim May took over what had been Harris's wagon and Dunk Cage, Sam Buford, and Tobe Robinson took other outfits. Kid Dobbs was hired to boss a fifth wagon. The owners paid each of them $75 a month.[50]

Bud Turner, who later told his daughter that he had been soured on strikes while in Kansas, arrived at the LS Ranch in the spring of 1884.

48 "Entering a Depot and Forcing the Agent to Hand over the Contents of the Safe," Benton MT *Weekly Record*, May 19, 1883, p. 1.

49 Sullivan, *The LS Brand*, 67; "[Untitled]," *Dodge City Times*, May 10, 1883, p. 1; Zeigler, "Cowboy Strike of 1883."

50 Sullivan, *The LS Brand*, 67; McCarty, *Maverick Town*, 111–12; Nolan, *Tascosa*, 145.

He joined the crew under the Mississippi Cage, who had come west with his sickly brother Hays. Both had a good education and the former, an experienced newspaperman, also wrote articles for the *Louisiana Gazette*.[51]

As to the strikers, "many left the country to seek work elsewhere," the official history of the LS declared, "but some stayed in and around Tascosa, and succeeded in bringing a hornet's nest about the ears of the ranch owners." It continued: "Angry over the outcome of the strike, the disgruntled men retaliated by rustling." After the walkout, wrote Zeigler, the Panhandle was plagued with an outbreak of rustling that the employers blamed on frustrated strikers.[52] These reports and the definition of "rustling" itself came directly from the employers, of course. The cowboys may have been following standard practice in branding mavericks, though the bosses insisted that calves belonged to whomever owned the mother.

The big bosses' determination to dictate terms without being challenged did nothing to quiet widespread predispositions in Tascosa toward gunplay. On March 24, 1884, Gene Watkins and Julián Martínez shot and killed each other, allegedly over a game of monte in a Tascosa saloon. The resulting melee also took the life of Dave Martínez, Julián's brother.[53]

At the same time, Tom Harris gathered some of those former strikers who, like himself, had trouble working for the large spreads. The cooperative that resulted was variously called "W.A. Cattle Company," "The System," and "The Get Even Cattle Company" and became associated with the Tabletop brand of Gatlin. Perhaps to avoid the big firms, the group operated along the Trujillo Creek near what became Endee, New Mexico.[54]

Without mentioning Harris by name, his former employers snarled that he was "a man with more brains than the easy marks who accepted his orders." Harris, they claimed, now ran a band of outlaws and

51   Sullivan, *The LS Brand*, 69.

52   Ibid., 67; Zeigler, "Cowboy Strike of 1883."

53   *Amarillo Sunday News-Globe*, August 14, 1938; J. Evetts Haley, *George W. Littlefield, Texan* (Norman: University of Oklahoma Press, 1943). Pauline D. and R. L. Robertson, *Cowman's Country*.

54   Nolan, *Tascosa*, 146, 223.

"instructed his gang to ruin Lee and Scott by rustling their cattle. The grudge ended in bloodshed."[55]

The bosses regarded the entire operation as a rustling ring, assuming that the gang included Jesse Jenkins, Tom Harris, Louis "The Animal" Bousman, Lem Woodruff, "Poker" Tom Emory, his brother Charley, and John Gough, also known as "The Catfish Kid."

On a larger scale, the state legislature responded to the wishes of the big operators by cracking down on the armed fence-cutters, with whom the employers sought to link the strikers. Calling themselves Owls, Javelinas, and Blue Devils, these armed men rode through the countryside cutting fences, fully prepared to use their firearms if they encountered owners or their employees. The resulting gunfire took several lives. By the fall, the authorities estimated the damage in Texas at $20 million, with some of the press guessing that the troubles had undercut tax values by $30 million. Certainly, the Fence-Cutter War discouraged farming and settlement.

Governor John Ireland called the legislature into a special session in January 1884. Amid great controversy, it made fence-cutting a felony punishable by one to five years in prison and malicious pasture-burning by two to five, an innovation that certainly interested the big ranchers. As a sop to the small owners, fencing public lands or lands belonging to others without permission became a misdemeanor, requiring the removal of wrongfully placed fences within six months. Big ranchers who fenced a public road had to place a gate every three miles and keep it in good condition.[56]

All of this made it much harder for the smaller operations to remain competitive, and placed the hope of holding property even farther from the reach of the working cowboy.

55 Sullivan, *The LS Brand*, 67.

56 McCallum and McCallum, *The Wire that Fenced the West*, 163–4; Hans Peter Nielsen Gammel, *Laws of Texas, 1822–1897* (Austin: Gammel, 1898); Wayne Gard, "The Fence-Cutters," *Southwestern Historical Quarterly* 51 (July 1947); Roy D. Holt, "The Introduction of Barbed Wire into Texas and the Fence Cutting War," *West Texas Historical Association Year Book*, 6 (1930); Henry D. McCallum, "Barbed Wire in Texas," *Southwestern Historical Quarterly* 61 (October 1957): 207–19.

The big ranchers may have lost the strike of 1883, but they rightly believed themselves authorized by the state, with a great deal of latitude, to take lethal action against fence-cutters and rustlers. In the Panhandle, the big firms privately staffed the various enforcement bodies that acted with the authority of the state behind them.[57] As they had under Pat Garrett, the big spreads took it upon themselves to enforce the law however they wanted.

The bosses in Oldham County put Ed King in charge of the local enforcers. Their own accounts describe him as an arrogant, quarrelsome bully, particularly when he drank, which tended to be often. He would also resort to violence at the slightest excuse. Meanwhile, in town, Jenkins heard and passed on rumors that the bosses had compiled a "death list" of troublemakers.

57 Zeigler seems to have erred in asserting that the owners won the strike because they "found effective means of dealing with the strikers that required no force." Zeigler, "Cowboy Strike of 1883." Jack Weston instinctively rebelled against the idea that the struggle in the Panhandle over better pay had been a fiasco or a farce, but accepted the idea that the employers prevailed, though he suggested that the strike may have had larger, positive implications. *The Real American Cowboy,* 102–3.

FOUR

The Cowboy Strike Wave, 1884–6

*Worker Persistence, Employer Responses,
and the Political Implications*

News of the victory of the Panhandle strikers needed no newspapers to spread across the West. Those who pursued this seasonally migratory occupation carried the story with them. After the cattle drives from the Panhandle broke up in the early summer of 1883, those 328 successful strikers shared their experiences with residents of Kansas and the Indian Territory. While some stayed there, others moved off individually and in small groups into Colorado, Nebraska, the Dakotas, Wyoming, and Montana. Soon, those with whom they worked after the strike would be aware of and discussing it as well.

The cowboys generally won these strikes because they knew just when the employers most needed their labor and acted quickly. Without established union organizations to protect them, strikers often found themselves victimized after work resumed. Matters became even more desperate as the strike movement spread into the newly opened northern cattle range, partly due to a wave of preemptive extralegal executions. The strikes and the violent repression that followed gave rise to a clear strain of cowboy radicalism. The repression both reflected and intensified the earlier explosive political insurgencies across the West. The new political movements around the ideas of Henry George aimed to change society radically without actually reversing the relations of power, and the national appearance of an Antimonopolist Party hailed a new kind of protest voting that aimed at expressing a concern rather than building a new political party.

The Strike Movement Spreads, 1884–6

Won or lost, strikes, like wars, often continue beyond the surrender. The cowboys apparently sought to repeat their success by going on strike again in 1884. Bill Gatlin was identified as one of their leaders. The results are uncertain, though the outcome hints that they suffered no great defeats.

Employers likely had an active blacklist during the aftermath of such a strike. Generally well liked by his coworkers—and even by those gunning for him—Gatlin briefly joined Tom Harris's outfit.[1] While there, he registered two brands: the K-Triangle and, with Wade Wood, the "Tabletop." The latter, a rectangle with legs, represented an excellent "maverick " brand, to which, complained the large ranchers, many of their own brands could be changed.

The community generally did not see the independent cowboys as rustlers the way the regulators and bosses did. A deputized group from the LS and LIT Ranches took and butchered thirty-five head of cattle with Gatlin's brand, selling much of the meat before he could act. Gatlin convinced H. H. Wallace to take the state and county officials to court. Realizing that their deputies had far exceeded their authority, officials agreed to pay $25,000 in damages, and the county settled for $800.

The LS and the big ranchers set about bringing large numbers of newcomers into the Panhandle.[2] At about this time, the LS employed 150 ranch hands. With an expanded workforce for the drive, it got 10,000 calves and 5,000 mixed cattle to Dodge, moving them in two herds. Each herd got its own annual roundup:

1 DeArment, *Deadly Dozen*, 157, 156, 158.
2 Sullivan, *The LS Brand*, 68, 69, 79, 67; DeArment, *Deadly Dozen*, 157, 158.

one near the New Mexico line in the west and the other near Mobeetie in the east. These became so massive that they employed groups of cowboys from Colorado, New Mexico, the Indian Territory, and even Kansas.

Labor conflicts continued "for the next several years," though the owners often reported it as rustling and other illegal activities by their hired men. In response, the employers brought Pat Garrett, the killer of Billy the Kid, back into the Panhandle and placed him at the head of a company of regulators, paid, armed, and supplied by the big ranchers. Garrett and his men believed that the former strikers were rustlers and that their job was to kill them. They also functioned implicitly as an arm of the "Redeemer" Democratic restored to Texas to sustain the old racial order.

The fall of 1884 found Garrett and an armed posse brandishing 159 indictments and planning to make "a sweep of the Canadian River valley." He and the posse made no secret of their whereabouts, hoping that the subjects of the indictment would simply leave the area, freeing them from having to prove anything in court.[3] Those who would not, however, might well face the worst that passed for law in the Panhandle.

The indictments that the owners gave Garrett aimed to decapitate the strike movement. The numbers alone placed a significant portion of the adult male population beyond the law. Garrett and Oldham County Sheriff Jim East learned that three of the holdouts, those who refused to leave the Panhandle, were hiding out with strike leader Tom Harris at the headquarters of his little operation near the border. From there, wrote one local historian, they caused "a more serious problem for the big cowmen than Billy the Kid had in his day."[4]

In February 1885, that inimitable company man Kid Dobbs led the regulators through a nighttime snowstorm to the rock house that served as a base for Harris's cooperative.[5] As they approached, they

---

3 DeArment, *Deadly Dozen*, 158–9.
4 McCarty, *Maverick Town*, 125.
5 On this confrontation, see DeArment, *Deadly Dozen*, 158–9.

saw Bob Bassett outside gathering firewood. Spotting a large group of armed men approaching, Bassett hurried inside and alerted the others, who apparently grabbed their six-guns.

As the armed band got closer, Harris stepped forward and asked Garrett what his business was. Garrett replied that he had warrants for Gatlin, Wad Woods, and Charles Thompson, and had no wish to bother anyone else. Harris said that Woods was not present, though Gatlin and Thompson were. After a brief consultation, Harris led eight others from the house, explaining to the posse that Thompson and Gatlin did not trust the regulators and stayed behind.

It made sense for the two holdouts to distrust the man who had bushwhacked Billy the Kid and for the posse to move slowly and cautiously when the shooting began. During a lull, they talked Thompson into coming out and surrendering, but Gatlin still refused. Finally, the posse advanced close enough to begin dismantling part of the roof supports, which would leave Gatlin exposed. Three members of the posse had already been wounded, but the regulators wanted to make a final effort to take Gatlin into custody. Sheriff Jim East pointed out that Gatlin would surely shoot Garrett if he had the chance, so East grabbed his Winchester, announced that he was coming in to talk, and went inside.

The confrontation ended remarkably well. Garrett and East got Thompson and Gatlin into custody and prepared to incarcerate them at Tascosa, which had no jail. They chained the men to the floor of an adobe building in town. At some point in the night, sympathizers of the cowboys—likely Harris and his friends operating out of Jenkins's saloon—got in and released them.

Garrett left a few weeks later, and his quasi-official body of regulators supposedly disbanded. In fact, many of them went to work as a security force with the LS and other large ranches. They continued to function as pseudo-lawmen for months thereafter.

Another strike broke out in the Panhandle in 1885—the third year of strikes in a row—which "deferred spring work considerably."[6] This

---

6 Gressley, *Bankers and Cattlemen*, 124, quoted in Weston, *The Real American Cowboy*, 91; "[Untitled]," *Cheyenne Transporter*, May 12, 1886, p. 1.

also seems the best explanation for why the employers began a new concerted effort in the early summer to blacklist the former strikers, label those who remained "rustlers," and use gangs of armed thugs to deal with them.

After slipping away from Tascosa, Gatlin found it safest to leave the area, signing on as a drover for the Worsham R-2 Ranch on a cattle drive to Dodge City. Another cowboy, T. J. Burkett, later recalled a thunderstorm that caused a general stampede, during which Gatlin singlehandedly calmed 600 head of cattle and kept them from running. When he passed through Dodge, the town marshal Jack Bridges and his deputies ran the hard-drinking, feisty cowboys out of town, killing John Briley, who later got planted on the local boot hill. Some speculation as to Gatlin's involvement followed.[7] But it would have been smartest for Gatlin, a man wanted in Texas and in a community with plenty of Texans, to keep his head down.

The persistence of the hired hands in the Panhandle helped inspire similar movements in New Mexico. Years later, John J. Dickey's account of a cowboy strike in that territory appeared in the virulently anti-labor *Chicago Tribune*, from which it was widely circulated and reprinted across the country.[8] Indeed, no contemporary article on cowboy strikes ever matched its circulation.

Despite its popularity, however, the article's sources are exceedingly tenuous. Dickey wrote his account based on what he had been told by Dan Quin. "When I was in New Mexico eight or nine years ago," said Quin, "I saw a singular labor strike." This was inaccurate: Quin got the story from the bookkeeper of the Triangle Dot Ranch, described as a Colonel Small, left in charge by the regular manager who had gone to Chicago on business.

---

7 DeArment, *Deadly Dozen*, 157.

8 *Waterloo Courier*, April 1, 1891, p. 2; *Sioux County Herald*, April 8, 1891, p. 6; Malvern [IA] *Leader*, April 9, 1891, p. 2; *The Jackson Hustler*, April 17, 1891; *Topeka State Journal*, April 25, 1891, p. 6; *The Hutchinson News*, May 1, 1891, p. 1; "A Cowboy Strike: The Strange Pranks of a Lot of Unruly Ranchmen," *Lawrence* [TN] *Democrat*, May 1, 1891, p. 1; "A Strike on the Ranch," Douglas WY *Bill Barlow's Budget*, May 6, 1891, p. 7; "A Cowboy Strike. Strange Pranks of a Lot of Unruly Ranchmen," Middletown [NY] *Daily Press*, June 27, 1892, p. 1.

Quin/Small described "Jackson, the agitator" as "contentious and much given to argument. He had been reading reports of labor troubles in the east to the men." One night, the cowboys "fell into discussing their wrongs," though "it happened that Jackson, the agitator, was out riding herd with some of the others." Deciding to act without him, the cowboys decided to strike, selecting "one, Kelley, popularly know as 'Texas' Kelley, as chairman."

They approached Small in a group. He, in turn, quoted Texas Kelley: "You see, Col. Small, we has become dead tired of filling the coffers of Chicago plutocrats. We are free-born Americans, an' no Chicago packin house prince has got title to us." Small asked what he could do to address their grievances.

Since the men had none, Small explained, they

withdrew to formulate their statement of hardships and presently returned. "We has, after a due an' deliberate considerin, decided on this, Col. Small: We is gittin' too much fresh beef, an' too little salt hoss, an' we strikes for that reason."

The bookkeeper ran through the sums quickly in his head. As salt pork was worth only $6.50 per hundred and beef, even on the range, sold for up to eighteen cents a pound, Small seized upon the solution:

I ought to have thought of this before and I will start the wagons for the ranch to-night for two barrels of pork and 500 pounds of bacon. As long as I'm running things you men shall have what you want.

The story, as presented, strains credulity. One would have to believe that any group of workers would decide to strike without the input of their key agitator, the "anarchist" Jackson, that they failed to have a set of grievances to present, and that they did not know the price of meat. It did, of course, confirm the stories that employers told themselves about the small-minded ignorance of their rural workers.

Meanwhile, the appearance of labor strife broke out on the more recently developed northern range. No sooner did white settlement begin than there developed a tension between developers and the settlers they brought in to make the area commercially profitable.

Entrepreneurs there not only sought the extermination of the buffalo, but also convinced the government to place bounties of $1, then $2 a head on the wolves. The new "wolfers" slaughtered thousands of wolves and coyotes every year, though the big ranchers grumbled that they often failed to kill the pups in order to ensure their future income.[9]

The trade spawned others, and hamlets such as Rocky Point developed disturbingly beyond the control of the masters of the market economy. In short order, these masters began to regard those brought in to eliminate four-legged pests as two-legged pests themselves. In the wide open spaces of the region, large concerns regularly lost significant numbers of cattle and horses. They attributed this to well-organized conspiracies, complaining to the authorities that rustlers alone accounted for a 5 percent loss of stock. One historian of the state acknowledged that his information came exclusively from "the memoirs of old-timers" and "the newspaper reports of their attacks." The state ignored demands to establish a rigorous and expensive process of inspecting the livestock being taken from Montana.

Theodore Roosevelt arrived in the midst of these conflicts. Only a couple of years older than Tom Harris, Jack Flagg, John Sullivan, and Billy the Kid, he shared nothing with them apart from age. He had embraced early on the strenuous life to deal with a debilitating level of childhood asthma, and survived to graduate from Harvard in 1880. He entered the New York State Assembly in 1882 and became the minority leader the following year, but lost the nomination for Speaker. In September 1883, he went on a twelve-day getaway to the northern range. Once back east, tragedy struck on February 12, 1884,

---

9 Joseph Kinsey Howard, *Montana: High, Wide, and Handsome* (New Haven: Yale University Press, 1943), 121–4, 125, 126.

when he lost both his mother and his first wife within eleven hours of each other.[10]

Saying that the light had gone out of his life, Roosevelt headed west and bought a ranch called "The Maltese Cross Ranch," which Roosevelt came to call the "Chimney Butte Ranch," seven miles south of Medora, North Dakota, on the banks of the Little Missouri. There he worked on his multivolume *The Winning of the West*, which covered colonial and early American history, though clearly with an eye to what was transpiring around him.

At the same time, Roosevelt established close ties to other entrepreneurs of the upper West and the lawmen who protected them. He met Seth Bullock, the famous sheriff from Deadwood, and became involved with cattle merchant Marquis de Mores, a French nobleman with a packing plant in Medora who had been introduced to the West by, among others, Broncho John Sullivan. Another of their peers was Russell Benjamin Harrison, great-grandson of President William Henry Harrison and son of future president Benjamin Harrison. Granville Stuart helped galvanize such figures, who elected him the first president of the Montana Stockgrower's Association.[11]

The Montana Stockgrowers' Association pressed the state to regulate livestock being taken from the territory. When the authorities naturally balked, and the association's members opted to take matters into their own hands. Stuart later recalled that when the association met in the spring of 1884, Roosevelt called for waging a war and "cleaning the rustlers out." Stuart supposedly persuaded them to act not as the association but as individuals. A month later, they met at Stuart's ranch along with some detectives and trusted company men to form what Stuart called a "Vigilance Committee" of fourteen

---

10   Roger L. Di Silvestro, *Theodore Roosevelt in the Badlands: A Young Politician's Quest for Recovery in the American West* (New York: Walker & Co., 2011).

11   William S. Reese, "Granville Stuart of the DHS Ranch, 1879–1887," *Montana: The Magazine of Western History* 31 (Summer 1981): 14–27; Clyde A. Milner II and Carol A. O'Connor, *As Big as the West: The Pioneer Life of Granville Stuart* (Oxford, UK: Oxford University Press, 2009). On Sullivan's relationship with de Mores, see "The Tale of Medora," St. Paul *Daily Globe*, September 24, 1887, p. 1.

members, though it came to be known more popularly as "Stuart's Stranglers."[12]

Roosevelt became even more involved with his peers as his career back in New York continued to fall apart. As the Republican National Convention approached that summer, he joined the "Mugwump" faction that tried in vain to shape the Republican nomination. Around the same time, he purchased more cattle and bought a new spread, the Ellkhorn Ranch, fifty-six miles north of Medora.

The cleansing he advocated—called "the Horse Thief War"—began almost immediately.[13] Within days of the meeting of Stuart's Stranglers, one of the participants went after two men for rustling, killing one of them (who had allegedly fired on him) and putting the other behind bars. A supposedly spontaneous mob seized the jailed rustler and hanged him, pinning a card on his coat that read, "Horse Thief." Six days later, other members of the Vigilance Committee captured Sam McKenzie, a mixed-race former wolfer, and dealt him similar fate. On Independence Day, they shot to death "Rattlesnake Jake" Fallon and "Long-haired" Owens in Lewistown.

The vigilantes later claimed that their victims had been armed and drunk, reacting "like many a rebel and anarchist westerner" by assaulting a resident dressed as Uncle Sam. Shortly after, they cornered an alleged army of rustlers led by a man named John Stringer in a cabin at a woodyard on Bates' Point on the Missouri River, east of Mussellshell. Most of those in the cabin died, either shot or burned alive when the vigilantes torched the cabin. The U.S. Army caught the few who escaped and turned them over to a duly

---

12 Granville Stuart, *Forty Years on the Frontier As Seen In the Journals and Reminiscences of Granville Stuart, Gold-Miner, Trader, Merchant, Rancher and Politician* (Lincoln : University of Nebraska Press, 2004[1925]), 197; T. A. Clay, "A Call to Order: Law, Violence, and the Development of Montana's Early Stockmen's Organizations," *Montana: The Magazine of Western History* 58 (Autumn 2008): 48–63, 95–6; Oscar O. Mueller, "Rustlers, Renegade and Stranglers—Ridding the Range of Renegades," in Michael S. Kennedy, *Cowboys and Cattlemen: A Roundup from* Montana:The Magazine of Western History (New York: Hastings House, 1964), 240–52. See also Howard, *Montana*, 126, 127–8.

13 For the Horse Thief War, see Howard, *Montana*, 128–33, 135–6, 137.

deputized group of Stuart's Stranglers, who strung them up. The killings continued into August, with some estimating as many as seventy-five victims.

The conduct of the Stranglers proved to be notoriously brutal. At one point, they captured a mixed-race boy who could fiddle and forced him to entertain them for the evening. The next day, they killed him. "His being a fiddler hadn't nothing to do with his being a horse thief," one said.

Although these developments caused some controversy in the Canadian press, the U.S. press seemed to ignore them. In the fall of 1884, James Fergus, one of Stuart's neighbors and a Republican running for the legislature, quipped that Stuart, a Democrat, had been doing him the favor of lynching Democrats to reduce their majority in his district. Stuart and the newspapers complained that the comment was in bad taste, but the perpetrators had no fear of any investigation or prosecution.

These perpetrators included the founders of the state of Montana. Their "3-7-77" warning—said to notify targets to buy the $3 ticket to the 7 a.m. stage to take the 77-mile trip from the area—remains part of the insignia of the state's highway patrol.[14] The Stranglers claimed to be acting in response to the failures of the legislature to pass the desired legislation, but they described their targets as rustlers—that is, outlaws. Had the evidence existed of their wrong-doing, there would have been no excuse not to bring them to trial, but the real goal had been to inflict extralegal terror on the inhabitants of Montana.

While illegal killings could be lionized, the press tended to deal with strikes by ignoring them as much as possible. In 1886, for example, the *Cheyenne Transporter* reprinted the account of a New Mexico strike, writing, "This is the first instance, save once of the kind that has ever occurred on the range, as there is hardly business of any kind

14 Frederick Allen, *Decent, Orderly Lynching: The Montana Vigilantes* (Norman: University of Oklahoma Press, 2005); Rex C. Myers, "The Fateful Numbers 3-7-77: A Re-Examination," *Montana: The Magazine of Western History* 24 (Autumn 1974): 67–70.

that prices are so well known as that of a cowboy."[15] By then, the cowboys had been going on strike regularly in the Wyoming Territory for several years.

One of the ranch managers, John Clay, made no bones about it in his book *My Life on the Range*.[16] In the spring of 1884, he worked on the lower Powder River, where "half a dozen or more outfits met." There, "the cowpunchers . . . struck for higher wages. They had said nothing when engaged or on leaving for the meeting point." The bosses in Wyoming caved rather quickly and "granted the demands of the boys."

Late that September, Clay headed for home in the Sweetwater Valley. A committee of three men approached him, bypassing the foremen. The cowboys

> wanted their wages till the end of December instead of being paid off as was the custom when the fall work closed. If the request was not granted, they would quit at once. It was rather a trying moment, because we had a herd of beef just about ready to start to market.

Clay refused. The cowboys then

> turned their horses, gave a cowboy yell, waved their Stetsons in the air and made a bee-line for the headquarters. One by one the other boys, except two, came up, made the same demand and promptly galloped off to the ranch. Eight of them, I think, resigned in this manner.

Sensitive to such things, Clay noted that, in the evening, he heard threats about violence. The next morning, the cowboys returned for a

---

15 "[Untitled]," Cheyenne *Transporter*, May 12, 1886, p. 1.

16 John Clay, *My Life on the Range* (Chicago: n.p., 1924), 123–4, 124–6. Clay names one of his foreman as Gatlin, but his was John Gatlin, not Bill Gatlin, which was the alias of the leader of the earlier cowboy strike in Texas and a man known to work in Wyoming at times.

while and left only three strikebreakers staying behind.[17] In the end, Clay noted, the employers had to capitulate.

Cowboy Radicalism

Young, seasonally employed and grossly underpaid, cowboys often remained footloose and rootless in the communities that relied upon their labor, fitting the classic anarchist profile almost perfectly. One ranch manager talked of "Jackson, the agitator," describing him as a Yale-educated radical who gave "anarchistic speeches" that sparked a strike. Some cowboys did correspond with Joseph R. Buchanan's *Labor Enquirer* in Denver.[18]

As cowboy discontent was spreading, political action had faltered even on the far socialist left. Americans had built postwar sections of the International Workingmen's Association (IWA), launched in London by an odd collection of radicals, including Karl Marx and Friedrich Engels. A decade before the cowboy strikes began in the West, these sections began breaking along ethnic lines, with many turning toward the construction of a new social democratic party similar to the movement building in Germany. However, most of the new American movement had thrown its weight behind the Greenback-Labor effort.

Adherents of the old IWA in San Francisco seem to have inspired a local lawyer, Burnette G. Haskell, to attempt its revival, launching a newspaper called *The Truth* in 1882. By 1883, Haskell had begun to construct one of the most intricate secret societies of the age. Members carried red cards while leaders—who openly described themselves as socialists—had white ones. The organization's structure divided the continent into Pacific Coast, Rocky Mountain, Mississippi Valley, Eastern, and Mexican divisions, each managed by officers with

---

17 Quoted in Weston, *The Real American Cowboy*, 97.
18 On "Maverick," *LE*, October 27, 1883, cited in Weston, *The Real American Cowboy*, 93–4; and, on Sullivan, *Labor Enquirer*, May 1, 1885, p. 1, c. 3, cited in Weston, *The Real American Cowboy*, 92–3.

alphanumeric descriptions, such as F-11 and N-91.[19] The reality proved to be much more mundane.

While the so-called "Red International" had various newspaper affiliates across the country, it had substantive strength only in the West. The IWA had a strong center of nineteen groups in San Francisco, as well as two groups in Oakland, two in Berkeley, and others in San Rafael and San Jose. In addition to affiliates in Eureka to the north, there were groups in Stanislaus and Tulare Counties as well as Healdsburg, Stockton, and Sacramento. The order also had outposts in Denver and Honolulu.[20]

A "Black International" of anarchists also vied with the "Red International." Furious at the fraud and intimidation that met electoral efforts in the late 1870s—and the ban on a successful socialist electoral movement in Germany—many radicals in New York and Chicago turned to anarchism. Their definitions of anarchism varied, but they did establish an International Working People's Association (IWPA). This "Black International" organized two groups in San Francisco, which survived to celebrate the anniversary of the Paris Commune in March 1885—a celebration from which the "Red International" publicly disassociated itself.[21]

Nevertheless, the two overlapped much more than the rhetoric of their respective leaders implied. The speaker who scandalized the local papers with his "frothy, foolish" speech before the anarchists also served as a member of the executive committee of the Pacific Division

19 Ira B. Cross, *A History of the Labor Movement in California* (Berkeley, Los Angeles, London: University of California Press, 1935), 156–64.

20 Cross cites material from Haskell's estate in his *A History of the Labor Movement in California*, 161, 329n6. See also the directory of local affiliates in the San Francisco *Truth*, December 8, 1883. Cross indicates that Haskell was certainly included in the "propaganda of the deed" insurrectionism of the "Black International," 163–4.

21 The press described it as "a small gathering of ladies and gentlemen." "Mr. Thomas F. Heggerty" gave "a frothy, foolish speech" that included "a fierce tirade against the press." "A Communistic Gathering," *Daily Alta California*, March 20, 1885, p. 1, c. 2. The Red International had disassociated itself from the IWPA plans: "Celebrating the Commune," *Daily Alta California*, March 19, 1885, p. 1, c. 4.

of the "Red International." The IWPA, whose members had clashed with the Chicago police in Haymarket Square, also had sections in Denver and Omaha with affiliates in Huron, South Dakota, and Kansas.[22] Peter Percival Elder, the aging veteran of the free state movement in antebellum Kansas, had never hesitated from taking up unpopular causes and now lent his support to the anarchists. He also gave his name to the national convention that founded the Union Labor Party.

Republican editors and politicians in Kansas denounced these new insurgents as secret anarchists. The handful of IWPA members in the state were mostly students of political economy and philosophy, however, rather than adherents of Johann Most's propaganda. But though the majority of them were American, their concerns alienated those who prided themselves on their mistrust of all things foreign.[23]

These strange circumstances generated regular complaints that the continued existence of two organizations required splitting hairs. Joseph Ray Buchanan, editor of Denver's *Labor Enquirer*, became a key figure in the organization of a Rocky Mountain division of the Red International and worked to link the two internationals. When a Southern Democrat accused him of being a Yankee ignorant of conditions in the South, Buchanan replied, "How do a Virginia father, a Kentucky mother, and a Missouri birthplace strike you, Colonel?" Buchanan's grandfather had run one of the first papers in northwestern Missouri. Born in Hannibal, Missouri, Buchanan's father had learned the craft there, alongside Samuel L. Clemens, the future "Mark Twain." Buchanan himself worked in the trade under the editorship of Champ Clark, the future Speaker of the U.S. House of

---

22   See the directories in *The Alarm*, Oct. 31, 1885, and April 24, 1886, both on p. 4. Haggerty on division executive of Red International, described as "a mechanical genius, an inventor of rare ability, but first and foremost a Socialist." Cross, *A History of the Labor Movement*, 159, 165, and description from 325n9. "Labor Leads the Way," *Chicago Daily Inter Ocean*, February 23, 1887, p. 6.

23   Weston, *The Real American Cowboy*, 94, though he confuses this West Coast–based "Red International" with the IWA involving German Marxists.

Representatives. Joe went to Colorado in 1878 and married the following year.[24]

One J. Allen Evans began writing anarchist papers from the Wyoming Territory. While several men of the same name and initials left a mark on the historical records of the West, the Illinois-born John Allen Evans—46 years old in 1885—seems most likely. He had married a Missouri woman twenty years before and had at least six children. The oldest, Martha, would have been nineteen and Ida May, the second oldest, fifteen.

Evans later described himself as having been a longtime reader of the *Truth Seeker*, and for several months past a reader of *Liberty*. He writes:

> I have spent the last ten years of my life on the extreme frontier, and now for the first time in ten years am a resident of so-called civilized town. Hence I know something of the operations of a vigilance committee . . . The best people are Anarchists if they only knew it.[25]

Taking work where he could, Evans spent more of his winter wages to bring his wife and daughter from the east. Although his employers had agreed to employ his wife, they backed out of the arrangement once she arrived and forced her "to work like a slave for board." When the seasonal school closed, their daughter also lost her employment. A rancher who had "gobbled up 2,000 acres of beautiful and fertile land that should belong to the people" also held a seat on the

---

24　John James Scannell, ed., *Scannell's New Jersey First Citizens: Biographies and Portraits of the Notable Living Men and Women of New Jersey with Informing Glimpses into the State's History and Affairs*, vol. 2 (Paterson, NJ: J. J. Scannell, 1917–25), 69–70. See also John B. Ewing, "Joseph R. Buchanan, 'The Riproarer of the Rockies,'" *The Colorado Magazine* 11 (May 1934): 116–18.

25　J. Allen Evans, letter from Greeley, Colorado, February 22, 1885; Evans, "Judge Lynch's the Supreme Court," *Liberty*, April 11, 1885, p. 7, c. 1. "The worst elements themselves often form vigilance committees, and commit crime under the guise of administering justice; but, if there was no civil law, the best elements would always prevail against the criminal class." Evans insisted that vigilantism represented work sometimes "done by the citizens."

school board and offered to employ Evans's daughter to provide music lessons to his three children "for very poor board, or for nothing."[26]

Given that Evans's letters are postmarked from various states, he seems to have been doing migratory and seasonal labor. By February 1885, Evans was in Colorado, where he found some respite. He attempted to organize a section of the IWPA in Greeley but found little interest among his coworkers. By May, Evans had written to the Chicago anarchists in Eaton, Colorado, suggesting "Agitators Wanted."[27] Denver remained the great labor center.

That fall, Evans spoke to an audience in the front of D. & R. G. hotel, on Fifth West Street in Salt Lake City, along with Lewis E. Odinga. Then about eighteen years old, the French-born Odinga had only recently come to the United States and seems to have quickly gone to work in the printing trades in Colorado.[28] If one had to guess, he likely worked for the *Labor Enquirer* in Denver.

Evans and Odinga's speech was titled "Why the Workingmen Are Poor." The *Deseret News* found them "intelligent, able speakers" who "expressed their ideas on the subject under discussion in a concise and forcible manner, which showed that they had made the question one of deep thought and research from the standpoint they have chosen."

26 J. Allen Evans, letter from Trading, Wyoming Territory, January 14, 1885; "Wyoming Territory. Overstocked Labor Market. The Fate of the Cow Boys," *The Alarm*, February 7, 1885, p. 4, c. 3.

27 J. Allen Evans, letter from Greeley, Colorado, February 22, 1885; Evans, "Judge Lynch's the Supreme Court," *Liberty*, April 11, 1885, p. 7, c. 1; J. Allen Evans, letter from Greeley, Colorado, March 12, 1885, "Greeley, Colorado. Want and Destitution in a Land of Abundance.—A Beautiful Country, but a Wretched People," *The Alarm*, April 4, 1885, p. 3, cols. 3–4; J. Allen Evans, letter from Eaton, Colorado, May 25, 1885; Evans, "The Social Revolution. 'Go West Young Man,' Is Played out—Agitators Wanted—Swarms of Tramps—The Denver Enquirer—Anarchists and Internationals," *The Alarm*, June 13, 1885, p. 4, col. 5.

28 New York, State Census, 1915. Babylon, Suffolk County. Assembly District 2, p. 3, line 41; New York, State Census, 1925 New York, New York, Assembly Dist 14, House number 331, p. 6, line 42. Died June 10, 1926 in Manhattan Louis Odinga in the New York, New York, Death Index, 1862–1948 Certificate Number: 17032. Ancestry.com. New York.

The two likely spoke at other places as they made their way to the Pacific coast.[29]

In November, Evans wrote from San Francisco to the Chicago anarchist paper, the *Alarm*, about uniting the internationals and about the Chinese workers. By May 1886, though, he had returned to the wilds of Wyoming.[30]

The Single Tax and Antimonopolism

Elements of the Industrial Brotherhood—reborn as the Knights of Labor after 1878—and the Alliance movements opposed extralegal killings and the use of private vigilantes by employers, but found very few effective means of preventing them. Both involved the political authorities, who had little incentive to challenge well-heeled interests. The Greenback movement had tried to make a political issue about the new rule of capital, but it remained disorganized in the wake of the 1880 campaign, and efforts to reconstitute the party faced a familiar set of problems.

Two ideas emerged in these years to challenge not only the status quo but the way in which oppositional forces had hitherto challenged it. The West produced an idea that rapidly supplanted the old Republican aspirations to secure equality through access to homesteads. Certainly, conditions in the West had vindicated the forebodings of the old land reform movement about monopolies. Since the California Gold Rush, one of the veterans of that movement, James McClatchy, continued to press for action against the great

---

29   "Radicalism. The Doctrine as Expounded by Two Able Advocates. The Question That Is Looming to the Fore," *Deseret News*, October 21, 1885, p. 9, cols. 3–5. *The Ogden* [UT] *Standard-Examiner*, October 17, 1885, p. 13.

30   J. Allen Evans, letters from San Francisco, November 11, 18, 1885; Evans, "Pacific Coast. Comrade Evans Makes Tour of Propaganda Across the Continent. His Experience Among the Mormons and Elsewhere. Uniting the Black and Red Internationals—the Coolie Slaves. The Proletariat," *Alarm*, November 28, 1885, p. 1, cols. 5–6; Evans, letter from Fort Laramie, Wyoming, May 22, 1886; Evans, "Anarchy in Wyoming," *Liberty*, August 21, 1886, p. 1, cols. 2–3.

landowners, fostering a "Settlers' League," which became briefly familiar in Kansas before it transformed into the Alliance. One of McClatchy's protégés, a printer named Henry George, labored through the 1870s on an updated application of the old ideas.[31]

An impoverished and struggling young worker from the East, George and his wife had deep ethnic and demographic affinities for Irish immigrants and the Catholic Church. Along with McClatchy, George had come to see the Republicans as the party having reconstructed not the South but the West in its image. Granted subsidies to build the Transcontinental Railroad and other lines, the new industries demanded the ruthless suppression of any opposition by the political authorities. While both parties proved their willingness to comply with this system, the dominance of the Republican Party nationally and across the North, Midwest, and most of the West made it particularly favorable to big business. This, in turn, increasingly cast the Democrats as the "lesser evil" of the two.

Despite such predispositions, George understood that serious change would not turn on which political party held power. Both had held office long enough to demonstrate that they would not do much to assist the people. What was needed was an idea, he thought, a seemingly new plan that would transform the American economy to match its democratic rhetoric.

For George, the Homestead Act had failed to establish a middle class of small proprietors. If large-scale capitalism could not be subverted for the public good in that way, perhaps the long-term dissolution of land monopolies would achieve equality, if gradually. George introduced this idea in his book *Progress and Poverty*, proposing a clearly focused strategy of discouraging land ownership beyond the needs of a family, with a particularly heavy tax on holding land without improving it, which could prove successful, regardless of which politicians held office.

---

31 Edward T. O'Donnell, *Henry George and the Crisis of Inequality: Progress and Poverty in the Gilded Age* (New York: Columbia University Press, 2015). I discuss George's single tax in Mark A. Lause, "Progress Impoverished: The Origins of Henry George's Single Tax," *The Historian* 52 (May 1990): 394–410.

More than anything, though, *Progress and Poverty* promised radical social change without class conflict or even class confrontation. In 1880, George moved to New York but had little interest in joining any organizations, though he had been a member of the Typographical Union and did join the Knights of Labor in 1883.

Ideas and rhetoric have their place, but organization provides their attendant political impact and social significance. Supporters of George's proposals launched an American Free Soil Society, recalling the antebellum convergence of political and land reform movements against slavery. As early as 1883–4, California had ten groups and Colorado three; there were two in both Kansas and Texas and one each in the Dakotas, New Mexico, and Oregon.[32] George himself had little interest in the Society, however, and the organization never gained firm political footing.

However, as important new national force emerged in 1881, subsuming the massive Greenback movement by offering a seemingly more radical alternative, the National Antimonopoly League. Later accounts confuse Antimonopolism with Greenbackism, but none of the prominent Greenbackers helped to launch the Antimonopolists. On the surface, Antimonopolism seemed to express a radicalism deeper than currency reform, and some individual radicals unimpressed by Greenbackism joined the Antimonopolists in expectation of something more critical of capitalism.

In reality, though, Antimonopolism had developed in New York City and represented a different set of ideas than those dear to the Midwestern, Southern, or Western insurgents. The new movement was not so much opposed to monopoly in general as to the specific practices of the most prominent and obvious of the monopolies: the railroads. In the East, manufacturers rather than small farmers challenged the unregulated freight rates imposed by the railroads. In response, the railroads accused the New York City Chamber of Commerce, which wanted the state legislature to link freight rates to the distance the freight traveled, of being "communist."

---

32 *John Swinton's Paper*, October 14, 1883, p. 1; *Free Soiler* 1 (March–Nov. 1884): 6, 15, 23, 28, 38, 46, 70.

The National Anti-Monopoly League appeared in 1881. Even after it became the National Antimonopoly Party in 1883, the group had not decided whether to nominate candidates or endorse the slate fielded by another party. Clearly, then, simply advocating for or even launching a third party no longer entailed independence from the two-party system. Those businessmen interested in turning mass disaffection with the railroad into a serviceable Antimonopolism found a ready ally in William A. A. Carsey, who had earlier engineered the unlikely Greenback presidential nomination of Peter Cooper.

Carsey led a variously designated "labor party" that enjoyed an episodic existence on paper. A former resident of Kansas, he could speak for the West in New York and employ New York credentials in the Midwest. He had done both in 1876 to help run the entire Greenback project up a blind alley, and he may have had a hand in torpedoing the 1880 Greenback–Labor campaign.[33]

Both newspapers and government bodies regularly quoted Carsey and covered his activities, presenting him as a spokesman of labor. He claimed to be a member of the bricklayers' union, sometimes identified himself as a builder, and sometimes spoke on behalf of something called "the Laborers' Union" as well as his "labor party."[34]

When a skeptical member of one congressional committee questioned his credentials, Carsey had few qualms about replying. He described the association he claimed to represent as "composed of the leading trades unions in New York," including "the presidents of fifteen or twenty organizations."[35]

Carsey made clear, however, that his organization was not one "to foster or oppress a special class or special interests, but one that will foster and protect and build up our industries, develop our resources,

---

33 It was amusing, then, that Joseph Dorfman seized upon Carsey as a case study of the insurgency's conservatism at the time. Dorfman, *The Economic Mind in American Civiliation, 1606–1935*, vol. 3 (New York: Viking Press, 1946–59), 17.

34 U.S. Congress, *Report of the Tariff Commission, Appointed Under Act of Congress Approved May 15, 1882*, vol. 1 (Washington, DC: Government Printing Office, 1882), 341.

35 *Report of the Committee of the Senate upon the Relations between Labor and Capital* (Washington, DC: 48th Congress, 1885), 341–44.

perpetuate our institutions, and make us a wealthy, prosperous, self-supporting nation, with a happy, contented, enlightened, and industrious people," particularly enhancing the "prosperity of our great middle and professional classes."[36]

Most consistently, though, Carsey functioned as an agent of various Democratic Party figures. Most prominent at this point was David B. Hill, who became Grover Cleveland's lieutenant governor in 1882. Hill later ascended to the governor's mansion himself when Cleveland went on to the presidency.[37] Carsey provided a significant part of their "labor" support.

Carsey claimed an important connection to the largest workers' organization of the day, the Knights of Labor. He later described himself as "one of the founders" of the order in that he became a member of "the original assembly" among the goldbeaters and bricklayers of this city. He reiterated that the Knights originally saw their goals as political and insisted that the order had nothing to do with strikes. After the strikes of 1886, he complained that the Knights had become "a mob rather than an organization." The order's proper place was working to put Democrats in office.[38]

As an alternative, Carsey became associated with the "Knights of Industry," which claimed to be a labor organization resurrecting the original goals of the Knights of Labor. It hated strikes and sought to encourage peace between socioeconomic classes through negotiations and mutual respect. In 1881, it surfaced in the guise of "a secret society." It was usually described as being "confined to Missouri and Illinois" by people who lived nowhere near those states.[39] The press already used the term "*chevalier de l'industrie*," in describing confidence tricksters.

---

36   *Report of the Tariff Commission*, vol. 1, 341–2.

37   Charles W. Calhoun, *Minority Victory: Gilded Age Politics and the Front Porch Campaign of 1888* (Lawrence: University Press of Kansas, 2008), 56–7, 58, 59–60, 164–5, 167–8.

38   "Knights Badly Organized, Surplus of Labor the Cause of All Trouble. W. A. A. Carsey Describes the Knights as in a Chaotic Condition—Compulsory Arbitration," *New York Times*, February 13, 1887, p. 3.

39   "Wage-Workers' Demands," *The Sun*, April 5, 1881, p. 1, col. 3; Rowland Hill Harvey, *Samuel Gompers: Champion of the Toiling Masses* (Stanford, CA: Stanford University Press, 1935), 40–1.

When a Republican paper in Kansas seized upon a statement by the Knights of Industry as proof that "workingmen" actually agreed with them, a newspaper run by the Farmers' Alliance contacted a supporter in New York City to confirm it. The latter replied that the Knights of Industry consisted of Carsey, John Kehoe, and "a fellow named Gilhooly," likely referring to A. H. Gallahue. Echoing what the *Times* had written earlier about Greenback groups, the writer described the Knights of Industry as one of those paper labor organizations regularly floated by one or the other political party.[40]

In 1881, Carsey sought to connect with like-minded Greenbackers interested in using labor rhetoric to establish ties to the Democratic Party. At that point, the Knights of Industry joined another, equally mysterious secret society, called the "Amalgamated Labor Union." This organization started in 1878 and should not be confused with the New York City "Amalgamated Trades and Labor Union," though it may have been named to encourage just such confusion. No reference has been found to such an association, which may, like the Knights of Liberty, exist only as a paper organization. In any event, the Amalgamated Labor Union and the Knights of Industry cosponsored a national conference at Terre Haute on August 2.[41]

The conference was miniscule; it had likely been convened simply to authorize another secret society that would oppose strikes. Although only a handful of trade unionists attended, they proved to be enough to postpone such a proposal until a later conference. Although the only eastern city to participate was Pittsburgh, the unionists suggested reassembling there from November 15 to 18. Such was the strange conception and birth of the Federation of Organized Trades and Labor Unions—what became the American Federation of Labor several years later.

40   "That Campaign of Argument—One of the 'Capital's' Samples," *The Advocate and Topeka Tribune*, August 3, 1892, p. 5, cols. 2–3. For praise of the order by an unnamed employer in the building trades—almost surely Carsey—see "Wage-Workers Demands. An Advance Generally Agreed to in the Building Trades," *New York Sun*, April 5, 1881, p. 1, col. 3.

41   Harvey, *Samuel Gompers*, 40–1; William Trant, *Trade Unions: Their Origins and Objects, Influence and Efficacy . . . with an Appendix Showing the History and Aims of the American Federation of Labor*, 18th ed. (Washington, DC: AFL, 1916), 39.

Carsey cashed in on this new organization in the service of various causes. Although on the payroll of Western Union at the time, he testified as a labor leader in opposition to the idea that the government should own the telegraph system through its postal functions. Instead, he urged the Senate Committee on Interstate Commerce to avoid all but a "moderate and discreet regulation" that would not "injure the business." His work inspired one scholar to recall the comment of William Henry Vanderbilt: "When I want to buy up any politician, I always find the Anti-Monopolists the most purchasable. They don't come so high."[42] More accurately, people like Vanderbilt could simply mass produce such officials.

Most importantly, though, Carsey became a vocal proponent of the protective tariff. In August 1882, he testified before a congressional commission on the subject. He claimed to be

a representative of that large class of workingmen who, after a long and bitter experience of the folly or inability of the non-political striking labor union system to obtain the rights or better the condition of the worker, have directed our efforts and energies to the education of the working classes in the use of the ballot as a cure for the evils of our labor system, its power to remove the cause, as well as cure the effect, and to the discussion of all questions, political, social, and economic, that affect their interests (such as the tariff, the question of all questions to American labor), prior to their peaceful, intelligent, and just settlement by that great power and privilege we possess over the workingmen of all other civilized or uncivilized countries—the ballot.[43]

Workers understood, he explained, that higher wages meant that "we must have a tariff of at least 100 per cent, to allow us to compete

42 David Hochfelder, *The Telegraph in America, 1832–1920* (Baltimore: Johns Hopkins University Press, 2012), 47; Vanderbilt quoted in Clarence P. Dresser, "Vanderbilt in the West," *New York Times*, October 9, 1882. "Although not one of the major figures" in the movements, "he had earned enough respect" to testify before Congress and attended the Farmers Alliance convention at Ocala in 1890.

43 *Report of the Tariff Commission*, vol. 1, 341.

with foreign manufacturers, or cease to manufacture goods for a competitive market, or else reduce the American to the wage and (its result) the condition of Europeans, or import the pauper laborer to take the place of the American laborer." Carsey assured the government that the workers wanted the development of the merchant marine, a tariff to keep out foreign goods, and the cessation of immigration that provided cheap labor as "as an injury to both employer and workman, and an injury and danger to our government and our institutions."[44]

Employers regularly turned to Carsey to provide a "labor voice" for whatever they wanted. In 1883, he shared the stage with a range of local luminaries at a mass meeting at the Cooper Institute to demonstrate popular support for high tariffs.[45]

Carsey's concern that cheap goods would undervalue American manufactures extended to other questions. He considered the introduction of cheap labor to undercut high wages as much as cheap goods did. By this time, despite the heavily Irish origins of the working-class Democratic organization in New York City, the shift to increased immigration from eastern and southern Europe had already inspired Carsey's concerns about the threat of "the hordes at Castle Garden."[46]

Based upon his credentials as the leader of a "National Labor Party," Carsey and his colleagues gained enough influence in the Antimonopoly League to claim 5,000 members in the city and 20,000 in the state. The League claimed that it had secured the establishment of the state's Labor Bureau and the Railroad Commission, despite being "denounced by labor organizations, which had, however, been quick to reap the advantages of its labors." At one point, League members complained that the Knights of Labor favored a strike in one case simply because they had not been bribed with beer.[47] Carsey's organization favored arbitration of all such conflicts.

44   Ibid., 342–3.
45   New York Association for the Protection of American Industry, *Proceedings of the Mass Meeting Held at Cooper Institute, New York*, February 1, 1883.
46   "[Untitled]," *Indianapolis News*, September 4, 1882, p. 2.
47   "Knights Badly Organized," *New York Times*.

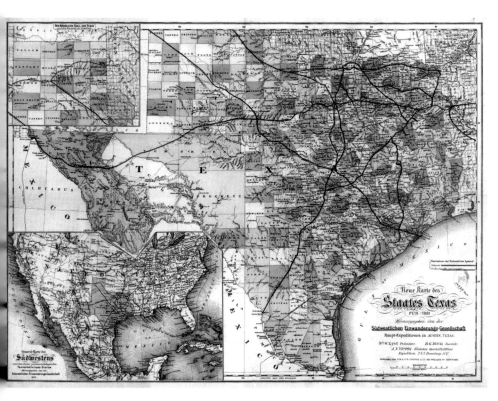

1 Texas in 1881. Library of Congress Geography and Map Division, Washington, D.C. Call Number/Physical Location G4030 1881.G3 TIL/Control Number 2003627050.

2 A Cowboy's Life—The Cowboy. Photographed ca. 1888 by J. C. H. Grabill, Sturgis, Dakota Ter. Reproduction Number: LC-DIG-ppmsc-02638. LC-USZ62-13227 (black and white film copy negative). Courtesy of the Library of Congress Prints and Photographs Division.

3 Cowboy on the LS Ranch. "A Texas Cow Boy" photograph by Erwin E. Smith, Bonham, Texas, ca. 1908. Reproduction Number: LC-DIG-ppmsca-08795 (digital file from original photo).

4 Texas Cowboys. A group of cowhands with their charges lingering in the background. Photographed by William Henry Jackson, 1901. Reproduction Number: LC-D4-13755_3a48282u.

5 LS Range Boss and Mexican Cowboy Pulling Cow from a Gully. Photographed by Erwin E. Smith, 1908. Reproduction Number: LC-DIG-ppmsca-07339.

6 Branding on the XIT Ranch. Photographed by W. D. Harper, 1904. Digital ID: cph 3b14504. Reproduction Number: LC-USZ62-67025 (black and white film copy negative).

7 Cowboys Eating Alongside Their Chuck Wagon. Photographed ca. 1880–1910. Reproduction Number: LC-USZ62-16318 (black and white film copy negative).

8 A Nicely Polished Sunday-Go-To-Meeting Look. Clean-shirted, nicely vested, well-scrubbed cowboys posing for a group photograph ca. 1904. Reproduction Number: LC-USZ62-48141 (black and white film copy negative) 3a48282.

9 Cattle in the 1886 Blizzard. Drawn by Charles Graham from a sketch by H. Worrall, from *Harper's Weekly*, February 27, 1886, p. 132. Reproduction Number: LC-USZ62-100252 (black and white).

10 Dan Bogan. One of the "troublemakers" in Wyoming, as well as the Texas Panhandle, he was particularly disliked by the big ranchers and their hirelings and was remembered as a rustler and gunslinger.

11 Nate Champion and Coworkers. Probably photographed in the 1880s, Champion, the late[r] cowboy martyr of the Johnson County War in Wyoming is on the left. A working cowboy long a[n] enemy of the big cattle men, Champion was the close friend and ally of strike leader Jack Flagg.

12 Nate Champion.

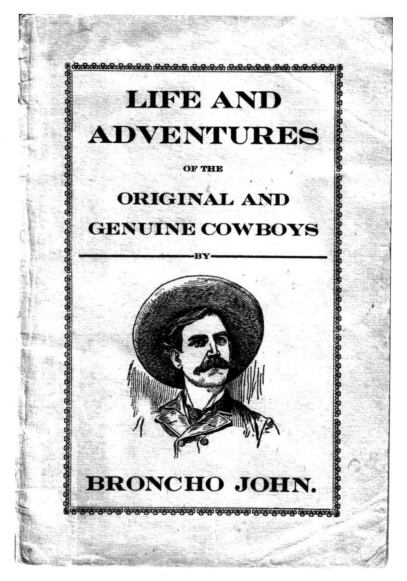

13 Cover of Broncho John's *Life and Adventures.*
The peripatetic working cowboy drew unabashedly radical
conclusions about class and labor in America.

"The Last Meeting of the First Farmers Alliance at their First House."

14 Farmers Alliance, Lampasas County, Texas. The original group founded in Pleasant Valley in the 1870s held their final meeting there in 1891. Wisconsin Historical Society. Image ID: 3397.

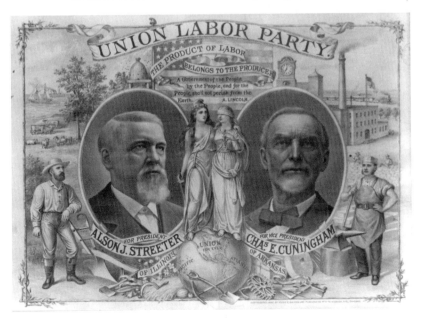

15 Union Labor Party Poster 1888. Poster produced by Kurz & Allison, Chicago. Reproduction Number: LC-DIG-pga-01952. LC-USZ62-7826.

16 Freight Depot at Coffeyville, Kansas. Photographed in 1931, the freight depot of the Atchison, Topeka & Santa Fe Railway Company was built in 1870 and target of the "anarchist" bomb used to discredit the labor movement and the Union Labor Party in 1888. Kansas State Historical Society. Item Number: 215899.

17 Samuel N. Wood.
From Margaret L. Wood's *Memorial of Samuel N. Wood.*

18 Cultural Appropriation—Three "Cowboys" at Dodge City ca. 1884–86.
Kansas Historical Society identifies the subject as three local businessmen
playing dress-up, wearing leather chaps and brandishing Colt
Army revolvers. KSHS Identifier: DaRT ID: 212446.

19 Dodge City Cow-Boy Band with Their Instruments ca. 1885. Studio Genelli, Hulbert Bros., St. Louis, Mo. Library of Congress Prints and Photographs Division. Reproduction Number: LC-USZ62-130931 (black and white film copy negative).

20 Tom Mix Doing Stunts. 1914. Poster on the making of early western movies, where
Tom Mix "told the story, and what he really did." Color lithograph by Goes Litho. Co.,
Chicago. Library of Congress Prints and Photographs Division. LC-DIG-ppmsc-03513.

Little surprise, then, that Carsey found himself a natural ally of those businessmen interested in turning mass disaffection with the railroad into a serviceable kind of Antimonopolism. This new party got the jump on the Greenbackers by holding a nominating convention in May 1884, nominating Benjamin F. Butler, the controversial reform-talking Democrat from Massachusetts, for president and Absolom M. West, a Mississippi railroad man, for vice president.[48] Among their presidential electors in Texas was Charles H. Jenkins, Jesse's brother and Tom Harris's lawyer.

What exactly Antimonopolism did or hoped to do in national politics remains unclear. Some angry Greenbackers charged that the Republicans funded the campaign, but New York City's Tammany Hall provided its Democratic anchor. Surely, though, Butler would not siphon off any votes from Democrats in the South, where he remained perhaps the least popular former Union general of the war. However, he could dent the Republican numbers in particularly strategic points in the North and help elect Cleveland.

This left the Greenback–Laborites either to divide the insurgents or endorse the Antimonopolist ticket, which most of them did, including D. G. Campbell in Kansas. Likely the most forthcoming source on the origins of the Farmers' Alliance, Campbell had then been in the legislature as a Democrat. By 1878, though, he chaired the Greenback Labor convention at Fort Scott for the Second Congressional District and remained active in the party in 1882. Two years later, with the Greenbackers swept easily to where the Democrats needed them to be nationally, he served as a presidential elector for the Butler–West ticket.[49]

Once more, the promise of merging the grievances of the West and the East dissolved into thin air. After the state convention at Utica in August 1884, Carsey presided over its "Executive Committee," which heard and approved the report on the convention "without discussion." Under Carsey, the group

---

48 Mark W. Summers, *Rum, Romanism, and Rebellion: The Making of a President, 1884* (Chapel Hill and London: University of North Carolina Press, 2000).

49 Wilder, *Annals of Kansas*, 659, 692, 707, 794, 829, 981, 985, 1007, 1077.

intervened in meetings sponsored by his former Greenback rivals. He assembled the Antimonopolist county convention of "about 50 persons" in the basement of Clarendon Hall on September 29. It explicitly declared its objective as simply "to gain legislation in the interests of labor." High on its list of principles "was the right to play baseball in Central Park on Sundays and holidays." Soon after, the local civil service board declared Carsey eligible for appointment as inspector of sewers and masonry.[50]

With the Antimonopolist organizations collapsing, Carsey graduated from being president of a nonexistent labor party to presiding over a nonexistent municipal Antimonopolist organization. Later, Butler chuckled that his campaign had placed Grover Cleveland in the White House, but that may not have been the goal for which committees were sent to both the Republican and Democratic state conventions "to ask that Anti-Monopoly principles be upheld in the party platforms." These self-described Antimonopolists also voted to promote railroad projects on the grounds that "the rich people who were interested in railroads had one in operation in front of their palatial residences."[51]

After the 1885 elections, Carsey, along with Keogh, another old Greenback faction leader, assembled "about a dozen retainers" in Knickerbocker Cottage on Sixth Avenue as "the Anti-Monopoly League of New York." Carsey presided. Keogh, who had gone to the Public Works Commissioner over "the wholesale discharge of city laborers," reported. Mayor Grace would not meet with them. Carsey discussed "alleged abuses in the Dock and Health Departments" and appointed a committee "to draft protectionist resolutions." This evidently led to a meeting with the city authorities over street-cleaning issues.[52]

---

50 "A Hot Meeting in Prospect," *New York Times*, August 18, 1884, p. 8; "Candidates of the Labor Party," *New York Times*, September 30, 1884, p. 5; *Minutes and Documents of the Board of Commissioners of the Department of Public Parks for the Year Ending April 30th 1885* (New York: Martin B. Brown, 1885), 648.

51 "Favoring a Fifth-Avenue Railroad," *New York Times*, September 13, 1885, p. 7.

52 "Their Law for the Mayor," *New York Times*, November 13, 1885, p. 8; "Appropriations for the Next Year," *New York Times*, December 24, 1885, p. 3.

By January 1886, what now called itself, without real competition, "the Anti-Monopoly League" passed resolutions "thanking the Governor for his advocacy of labor measures in his message to the legislature." Meanwhile, Governor Hill had proposed Keogh for Harbor Master and Carsey for Chief of the Bureau of Labor Statistics. The primary concern of the organization seems to have been contesting the renomination of a candidate for railroad commissioner.[53]

New York City had produced Democratic officeholders who had built careers flitting around the edges of the land reformers and the Greenbackers. The names of Gideon Tucker, Sanford Church, Nelson J. Waterbury, and Theodore E. Tomplinson all turn up in press accounts of politicians courting radicals and labor reformers.[54] In Carsey, though, the Democrats produced a new kind of figure. Superficially a labor leader and a radical organizer, he worked consistently against independent action by labor and radical organizations and to provide the party with what the ignorant or forgetful might see superficially as support among labor or radicals. The year 1884 marked the third successive presidential election in which Carsey demonstrated the value of such a novel combination of tactics, particularly to the detriment of the western insurgency.

For several years in the mid-1880s, the authorities faced expanding labor organizations, strikes reaching an unprecedented scale, and a persistent, dynamic radicalism forcing its way into new channels. Given the systemic blacklisting of strike leaders in the absence of a stable union, this meant that successive strikes generated a broad current of somewhat experienced organizers. At the same time, as Jenkins's saloon demonstrated, cowboys connected to the Greenback idea of seeking a redress of grievances through the ballot. As the strikes

53 "Anti-Monopoly Men," *New York Times*, January 12, 1886, p. 3.

54 For Carsey turning up with Waterbury, see "Joining the County Democrats," *New York Times*, February 19, 1886, p. 3.

reached a crescendo, though, the Antimonopolist "movement" and—
at least in the South—the Butler campaign thwarted the cowboys'
potential electoral expression.

In that 1884 national election, the masters of Oldham County sent
the state government their vote tally of 159 Democratic ballots without a single one cast for the Republicans or Antimonopolists. This
proved too much, even for the Democratic "redeemers." As a result,
Oldham became one of four counties in the state whose returns "were
received in irregular shape and were not counted in the official count;
omitted on mere technical ground."[55] Through one means or another,
the strikers found themselves disenfranchised.

Meanwhile, 1886 would see the lines of conflict drawn more clearly
than ever, particularly in the West, and clashes sharper than ever before.

---

55 *Tribune Almanac and Political Register for 1885* (New York: Tribune
Association, c. 1885), 82, note on 83. See also Peter H. Argersinger, "New
Perspectives on Election Fraud in the Gilded Age," *Political Science Quarterly* 100
(Winter 1985–6): 669–87.

FIVE

Destinies of the Industrial Brotherhood

A High-Water Mark of Western Worker Militancy, 1886

In 1886, as cowboy strikes swept the West, Eleanor Marx Aveling passed through Cincinnati in search of insights into the United States. The local socialists took her, her husband, and another European visitor to see a group of cowboys on tour there. The comrades lingered behind after the costumed performance and introduced themselves to one of the performers. "To our great astonishment," she recalled, the cowboy "plunged at once into a denunciation of capitalists in general and of the ranch-owners in particular." "Broncho John" Sullivan assured them that many of the cowboys had "awakened to the necessity of having a league of their own"—and that a Cowboy Union or affiliates of the Knights of Labor seemed likely.[1] After several years of strikes—followed by violent employer repression—organization seemed necessary, and the Knights, as shades of the old Industrial Brotherhood, seemed a natural choice.

The cowboy strikes of 1886 would be the last for many years and likely came about in part due to employers' responses to heightened competition, itself a result of increasingly unpredictable weather on

---

1 Bibbins and Marx Aveling, *The Working-Class Movement in America*, 158–9. See also Leslie Derfler, "The American Cowboy: Note on a Marxist Perspective," *Journal of the West* 38 (July 1999): 72–6.

an overstocked range. This was the high water mark of labor movements in the West as workers responded to a wave of employer repression, most dramatically evident in the Southwestern railroad strike. Repression by government authorities predisposed the repressed to seek political solutions.

The Strikes in the Southwest, 1886

The subjugation of the American heartland took place so quickly that the new arrivals hardly knew about the variations they would experience in rainfall or the intensity of the seasons. The weather had interrupted the antebellum fighting over Kansas with a series of droughts coupled with heat waves, while a postwar plague of locusts in Nebraska sent once confident whites scurrying for their Bibles. Decades later, the memory of the terrible freeze of 1880–1 remained vivid enough for Laura Ingalls Wilder to compose *The Long Winter* (1940).

As cowboy work stoppages escalated, nature began launching its own series of general strikes. By the winter of 1885–6, the relentless drive for profit had overstocked the range and further expanded the drift fences. A series of blizzards swept the southern plains in late December 1885. The herdsmen could not get food, water, or shelter to many of the cattle caught in the open, or protect them from wolves or coyotes. Packed into groups sometimes hundreds of yards deep, cattle seeking an escape from the temperatures found fences barring their way south. There they were smothered or froze to death.[2] The marketplace that had exterminated the buffalo ultimately did the same with its own living commodities; along with concerns over the

2   Henry D. and Frances T. McCallum, *The Wire That Fenced the West* (Norman: University of Oklahoma Press, 1965); David L. Wheeler, "The Blizzard of 1886 and Its Effect on the Range Cattle Industry in the Southern Plains," *Southwestern Historical Quarterly* 94 (January 1991); David L. Wheeler, "The Texas Panhandle Drift Fences," *Panhandle-Plains Historical Review* 55 (1982). See also "Cattle in a Blizzard on the Plaines," drawing by Charles Graham from a sketch by Henry Worrall, *Harper's Weekly*, February 27, 1886.

ticks that spread "Texas fever," widespread cattle death may have hastened the displacement of the longhorn by "short-faced" breeds.

The cattlemen tended to be less philosophical and more preoccupied with adjusting their bottom line to make up for losses. This meant an increasing reliance on the regulators—hired guns—to coerce the cowboys. After Pat Garrett left for New Mexico in 1885, the great bosses such as those on the LS Ranch fell back on henchmen of their own such as Ed King. He was aided by Frank Valley and Fred Chilton, a couple of gunmen who had gained a reputation in Dodge City some years before.[3]

Nearby, on the XIT Ranch, Mathew Bones Hooks, the black man barred from doing regular work as a cowboy, worked odd jobs and kept his eyes open. Probably because he worked closer to the ranch's home base, he later remembered that the gunmen had a password to participate in their murderous work. Hooks later recalled knowing of only twelve to fifteen men hanged by the group.[4] He seemed to mean the group associated specifically with the XIT, which would mean the regulators from other ranches left more bodies.

The grim losses of the winter demoralized the hired guns, who found themselves assigned the work of ordinary cowboys. King, Valley, and Chilton camped about four miles from Tascosa by the shallows of the Canadian River at Jerry Springs, where they supposedly worked at "bog riding." This meant running down strays who sought relief from the flies by going into the bottomland, where they tended to get stuck in the mud. King and his coworkers found the work tedious and began slipping off to town, where King took up with Sally Emory, who worked at Jesse Jenkins's saloon and had been the girlfriend of bartender Len Woodruff. She spent several days with King while his two pistol-packing amigos harrassed Woodruff, knocking him about and calling him "Pretty Lem." However annoying, what unnerved Woodruff was the realization that, at some point, the bored killers might murder him.

3 Sullivan, *The LS Brand*, 119–20.
4 Massey, *Black Cowboys of Texas*, 232.

After midnight on March 21, 1886, King, Valley, Chilton, and John Lang headed into town.[5] Valley and Chilton joined a card game at the Equity saloon while King headed to Jenkins's saloon to see Emory, Lang trailing behind him. There, Woodruff emerged from the shadows with his Winchester. "What does this mean, boy?" snarled King and grabbed the barrel.

Accounts of the night claim that someone else fired first, shooting King in the face. When King staggered off and fell into the street, Woodruff supposedly put the barrel of the Winchester against King's neck and pulled the trigger. Meanwhile, Lang and Emory scampered off down Spring Street into the dark.

Lang ran directly into the cowboy known as John B. Gough, or "The Catfish Kid," and the two quickly drew on each other. When Catfish fired and missed, Lang broke into a run, hoping to find other LS men. As Lang fled, though, he turned periodically and shot into the dark with his six-gun to discourage possible pursuers. He finally reached the Equity, where Chilton and Valley had apparently remained oblivious to the gunfire down the street. After they learned that King had been shot, though, the three men headed back toward Jenkins's saloon with Lang brandishing a fully loaded revolver he had borrowed from the bartender.

The LS gang got to Jenkins's saloon and found the front door locked. They hurried around the back into the alleyway and exchanged fire with some cowboys in the dark. In the flashes, they recognized Woodruff ducking into an adobe shack. Valley charged through the doorway where he took at least seven bullets, falling dead on the spot. However, two shots hit Woodruff in the stomach and through the groin, while another hit a cowboy named Charley Emory in the leg.

Lang and Chilton had taken cover in the alley, but found themselves in a cross fire. At this point, Jesse Sheets, a local restaurant owner, popped out of his back door to see what was happening and Chilton shot him in the face. Someone heard Chilton shout, "I got that son of a bitch Louis Bousman!" (Later, when it became clear that

---

5 "A Bloody Affair," *Fort Worth Daily Gazette*, March 26, 1886, p. 4.

it had been Sheets, Lang claimed that the restaurateur had been coming toward them blasting away with a Winchester.) Chilton's shooting had given away his location, and rifle fire dropped him. He passed his weapon to Lang, now the sole surviving regulator.

With all of his colleagues dead or dying, Lang took off up Spring Street to the Equity. Soon, he had assembled more LS guns in the street, but Sheriff Jim East and his deputy, the former LIT cowboy Charlie Pierce, had turned up to investigate what had happened. Once the group had returned to Jenkins's place, Pierce saw a figure breaking cover from behind a woodpile. Supposedly yelling for him to stop, he opened fire and the shadow fell. He ran over and found Catfish staring off blankly. Thinking him severely wounded, if not dead, Pierce rejoined Sheriff East on his way back to Main Street. At that point, Catfish quietly rolled over, unhurt, and headed into the dark.

Owners of the LS Ranch and other big spreads demanded action. The bosses suspected that Jenkins and Harris had been behind the shoot-out, though both had been out of town. East rounded up the remaining identifiable participants and got them to trial. These included Woodruff, Charley Emory, Bousman, and Gough, as well as Lang. Because of hostility over "the big fight" whipped up in Tascosa, the authorities moved the trial to Clarendon, which ended in a hung jury. A retrial at Mobeetie acquitted the accused.[6]

The dramatic gunfight at Jenkins's saloon preoccupied the newspapers, but there are indications that, with the gun thugs of the LS effectively out of the picture, the wage wranglers called a strike for the spring roundup a few weeks later. An account from New Mexico in May 1886 printed an account that a strike had taken place "last spring west of here in the Panhandle range, which deferred spring work considerably."[7] Ominously, though, there are no indications of its success, though it is clear that the longer a work stoppage lasted, the more difficult it would be for it to achieve victory.

The source for the strike in the Panhandle also reported that another broke out in adjacent New Mexico:

6 Sullivan, *The LS Brand*, 120.
7 "[Untitled]," *Cheyenne Transporter*, May 12, 1886, p. 1.

Did you ever hear of cowboys striking? Not to "chuck" at a neighboring camp, but for higher wages. Recently the cowboys out in New Mexico organized a meeting and demand[ed] higher salaries, else they would unsaddle their ponies and quit work.

This later came to be described as the effort of eighty cowboys to form the Northern New Mexico Small Cattlemen and Cowboy's Union. They did not want to work piecemeal for the five months of roundups and drives but have "living wages the year around" based on experience.[8]

In the spring of 1886, the *Fort Collins Express* in Colorado reported a strike for a raise of $5 a month,

refused by the employers, consequently there has been a general walk-out. Especially as not a man is left on the range . . . The occupation of a cowboy is one gained only by long experience upon the range. It is not the acquisition of a day. The stock owners will probably accede to the demands, as now is the time competent hands are most needed.

The most thorough historian of Tascosa, Frederick Nolan, interpreted this as indicating that a strike had broken out in Colorado.[9]

That same spring, a wave of strikes hit Wyoming. Literary scholar Jack Weston referred to "these and other attempts at cowboy unionizing," but it remains unclear if the idea of a permanent organization ever appeared in the area. Indeed, the employers seem to have instigated the action by trying to reduce wages. When at least four

8 Ibid; Richard W. Slatta, *The Cowboy Encyclopedia* (New York and London: W.W. Norton & Co., 1994), 361. The Wyoming paper unsympathetically added, "The cattlemen and the herder know what certain labor commands and without inquiring the cowboy can tell within a dollar what he will receive if told to go to work."

9 Clifford P. Westermeier, *Trailing the Cowboy* (Caldwell, ID: Caxton, 1955), 130, cited in Nolan, *Tascosa*, 296n15; *Field and Farm*, May 29, 1886, p. 5; John Clay, *My Life on the Range* (Chicago: n.p., 1924), 123, 125.

spring roundups started in central and northern Wyoming, "all work was stopped and word sent to the different managers that no work would go on until they agreed to pay the former wages." Once more, the cowboys had timed the strike very well, forcing employers "to comply with the demands of the strikers and restore their wages."[10]

In all likelihood, the northern range, which did not experience the crushing Panhandle winter, probably found employers less united, however determined they may have been to break the strike. A Montana newspaper reported on the tenth instant strike for $40 a month all around. "Not a wheel moved until the foremen submitted to the terms made by a committee from among the cowboys, to the effect that no man should work on roundup 23 for less than $40 a month."[11]

As in the aftermath of other strikes, employers conceded to the strikers' demands and then proceeded to take their revenge on the strike leaders. Joseph Carey, then president of the Wyoming Stock Growers' Association and later governor and U.S. senator, hoped to get back at the organizers of the strike. He had them arrested but, to his great frustration, none of the other cowboys would give testimony as to their activities. Unable to take legal action, the Association blacklisted the most prominent strikers.[12] Tensions and, perhaps, other work stoppages followed in the summer.

Workers responded in Wyoming much as they had done in Texas. Key strike leader Oscar Hite Flagg—Jack Flagg to his neighbors—had managed to set aside a modest herd of his own, which became the core of a common herd that included the cattle of other black-listed strikers. Flagg had been as much of a Southerner as Harris had

---

10 Quoted in Weston, *The Real American Cowboy*, 97–8.

11 Asa Shinn Mercer, *The Banditti of the Plains* (Denver: n.p., 1894), 101, 105, quoted in Weston, *The Real American Cowboy*, 98.

12 Weston, *The Real American Cowboy*, 98, 99; John W. Davis, *Wyoming Range War: The Infamous Invasion of Johnson County* (Norman and London: University of Oklahoma Press, 2010), 59, 209n21, which cites John R. Burroughs, *Guardian of the Grasslands: The First Hundred Years of the Wyoming Stock Growers Association* (Cheyenne, WY: Pioneer Print & Stationary Co., 1971), 112.

been. His father, George H. Flagg, had joined what became the Second Virginia in April 1861, got elected to a second lieutenant a year later, and took command of the unit in early 1864. Nevertheless, his rheumatism landed him in a Richmond hospital as the capital fell. Jack remained close enough to his family to return home regularly.[13] In the aftermath of the 1886 strike, Flagg led the most victimized strikers into the same kind of cooperative effort Tom Harris had initiated in Texas.

One of Flagg's closest associates in these activities was Nathan D. Champion. A Texas-born loner a few years older than Flagg, he had come north with the cattle business in 1881 and had decided to stay. At the time of the strike, he was working as a cowboy and surely participated, perhaps even helping to lead the work stoppage.

Any hope of survival for the strikers, if not success, would require organization. In the Southwest, the Northern New Mexico Small Cattlemen and Cowboys' Union failed. Cowboys also considered joining the successor to the old Industrial Brotherhood. "The cowboys have evidently been reading the newspapers," wrote the *Cheyenne Transporter*, "hence they follow the steps of the Knights of Labor. We have not learned if they accomplished their purpose." Even as the *Transporter* speculated on this, cowboys participated in a mixed assembly at Lander in Fremont County, Wyoming.[14]

Sullivan focused on the problem directly. The employers, he pointed out, have "one of the strongest and most systematic and, at the same time, despotic unions that was ever formed to awe and dictate to labour." Cowboys like Sullivan hoped for the success nationally of Henry George and his views, the potential of the new workers parties, and the prospect that a revitalized Knights of Labor could

13 Oscar H. Flagg, *A Review of the Cattle Business in Johnson County, Wyoming, since 1892 [i.e. 1882] and the Causes That Led to the Recent Invasion* (New York: Arno Press, 1969). See also "The Passing of 'Jack' Flagg," *Cheyenne Daily Leader.*

14 [Untitled], *Cheyenne Transporter*, May 12, 1886, p. 1; Jonathan Garlock, *Guide to the Local Assemblies of the Knights of Labor* (Westport, CT: Greenwood Press, 1982), 550; these assemblies are reported to have lasted until 1889. On New Mexico, see Slatta, *The Cowboy Encyclopedia*, 361.

spread across the West.[15] The Knights came to play a central role in the events of 1886.

The Wider Labor Movement: Railroaders to Musicians

The industry so intimately associated with the beef bonanza experienced its own labor strife in 1886. Moreover, the impact of action by rail labor proved to be far more significant than anything the cowboys might do to spread trade unionism, the idea of a strike, and fear of the dire consequences of their failure.[16] In many respects, if the railroads had first given rise to the cattle trade, the rapid and extreme impact of the beef bonanza made the railroads all the more important and rapidly transformative. Still, as with the cowboys, the industry created a workforce of largely single transient men around a less transient, though also disproportionately single, core of workers. The Chinese filled many of these jobs and were kept isolated in a distinctive working-class subculture, sometimes operating under conditions comparable to slavery.

At the time, Jay Gould owned nearly 12 percent of the nation's railroad tracks, including the Union Pacific, Missouri Pacific, and Missouri, Kansas & Texas Railroads. Taking on Gould gave the Knights of Labor unprecedented attention and popularity. However, the announcement by the Wabash, St. Louis & Pacific that it would implement a series of pay cuts of 10 to 20 percent and reimpose a ten-hour workday in the shops made it unlikely that a conflict could be averted.

On March 7, 400 workers in Sedalia walked off the job. John S. Marmaduke, who had destroyed those railroads as a Confederate general, sought to serve them as Missouri's newly elected governor, but he balked at sending the militia to break the strike. The

---

15 Bibbins and Marx Aveling, *The Working-Class Movement in America*, 158–9.

16 On the movement of railroad workers, see Theresa A. Case, *The Great Southwest Railroad Strike and Free Labor* (College Station: Texas A&M, 2010), 88–96, 108–9, 123–6, 142.

authorities intervened at every other level to do so and, eventually, the company accepted compromises on every point but an agreement not to cut the wages of its workers, which it rejected as "dictatorial." In August, more strikes broke out when the railroads closed their shops to lock out union members, reopening them with a newly hired or rehired workforce. A native Missourian, Joseph R. Buchanan of the *Labor Enquirer* in Denver came back to help organize the strike.

Within days, the strike spread across the region. The management fired a member of the Knights in Marshall, Texas, for allegedly attending a union meeting on company time. Discontent over wages, hours, and working conditions inspired the local Knights to walk out in sympathy. Across the Missouri Pacific and Union Pacific, their coworkers hoped to show their strength as well.

The pressure to call a mass strike became too great for Martin Irons, the tragic and enigmatic figure at the center of the movement. A native Scot, he had landed as a boy in New York in 1844. He later moved on to New Orleans, then to various locations in Kentucky, where he married in 1852. By 1859, he had reached Missouri, where he lived in St. Louis and, later Richmond. By 1880, he became involved with the Knights of Labor and quickly joined the regional leadership of the newly booming organization in the Southwest.[17]

Consistent with the aims of the old Industrial Brotherhood, African Americans joined the Knights of Labor in significant numbers, particularly in Arkansas and Texas. Local Knights understood that they needed black organizers and leaders to recruit African American members, who had been stung often enough by white leaders. Years later, Patrick Cassity recalled his experience in the 1886 strike as characterized by a remarkable level of interracial cooperation in the rail yards of Palestine, Texas.[18] Predictably, though, such experiences tended not to be universal and rarely lasted long.

17 On Irons, see ibid., 151, 152–3, 154.
18 Ibid., 129–30, 136–7, 176–7.

On March 19, Terence V. Powderly, the Grand Master Workman of the Knights, met in Kansas City with other Knights, railroad officials, and the governors of Kansas and Missouri to see if they could negotiate a settlement. After two days, the effort fizzled, and the Great Southwest Railroad strike rolled on to move over 200,000 workers in Arkansas, Illinois, Kansas, Missouri, and Texas. That made for twice the numbers estimated nationally for the earlier 1877 rail strike. Nor were the workers ready to accept intimidation.

Still, Gould was determined to make no concessions and began bringing in strikebreakers. Then, too, the Brotherhood of Engineers refused to honor the strike, and its members kept working. This time, Gould charged the strikers with "union violence" against strikebreakers and the seizure and destruction of railroad property. The governors of Missouri and Texas dutifully mobilized state forces and placed them at the service of the railroad, though those from Kansas refused. Under state protection, Pinkerton agents— often convicted criminals—went about beating and intimidating strikers. Gould reportedly sneered, "I can hire one half of the working class to kill the other half," and procured injunctions to prevent strikers from interferring with trains run by strikebreakers.

The railroad got the authorities to start enforcing these injunctions around Fort Worth. On April 3, the bosses ran a train south of Fort Worth to where the Missouri Pacific intersected the line of the Fort Worth & New Orleans, known locally as Buttermilk Junction. City Marshall Timothy "Longhaired Jim" Courtright brought a team of deputies to secure the line. The train driver saw that the switch had been thrown as the train approached the intersection, and the deputies jumped down to encounter half a dozen armed strikers or supporters. These included a switchman named Tom Nace, the one-armed peanut vendor Frank Pierce, who demonstrated real skill with a Winchester, and John R. Hardin, a carpenter described "as an out and out Communist." In twelve to fifteen minutes, the two sides fired about a hundred shots. The strikers shot three of the deputies, including Richard Townsend, who did not survive. After the incident, the authorities charged seven of the strikers of murder, though, in the end, three were acquitted, three avoided capture, and only one was convicted.[19]

Perhaps the most prominent of the strikers was Nathan Morris Lovin. One local account claimed that he had gotten away because he "had never been anything more than a bushwhacker and hired gun," and the authorities "could forgive him sooner for that than for being a socialist or union organizer, neither of which he never was." In fact, Lovin was the Mississippi-born Master Workman of a local assembly of the Knights and a veteran of the Eighteenth Mississippi Infantry in the Army of Northern Virginia through much of the Civil War. After returning home, he had helped defend Mobile with Captain Henry Gillum's Mounted Rifles. After moving to Collin, Texas, he participated in the strikers' negotiation, but—not surprisingly, given his background—he encouraged self-defense measures by the strikers. The authorities believed him to have been the prime mover at Buttermilk Junction and charged him as "an accessory before the fact to the murder of Richard Townsend."[20]

Not satisfied with arresting Lovin on the charge of murdering Townsend, law enforcement rearrested him on April 10 for incitement to riot. Released on habeas corpus, Lovin had returned to the strike, determined to secure a settlement. In mid-June, he turned up in St. Louis, attempting to save the jobs of the strikers at Fort Worth. He "claimed that the men had committed no depredations, had acted peaceably during the riots and now asked that they be reinstated in their former positions."[21] With the press clearly on the side of the

19 Hometown by Handlebar, "Buttermilk and Blood (Part 1): 'I'll Kill the First Man Who Touches This Engine,'" available at hometownbyhandlebar.com, and "Buttermilk and Blood (Part 2): 'For God's Sake, Don't Shoot,'" available at hometownbyhandlebar.com.

20 Case, *The Great Southwest Railroad Strike*, 160; Richard F. Selcer and Kevin S. Foster, *Written in Blood: The History of Fort Worth's Fallen Lawmen*, vol. 1 (Denton: University of North Texas Press, 2010), 101, 104–5, 111; see also Ruth Alice Allen, *The Great Southwest Strike* (Austin: The University Press, 1942), 38, 82.

21 "Grand Jury at Work," *Austin Weekly Statesman*, April 15, 1886, p. 2, col. 5; "'No Vacancies,' That Is the Answer N. M. Lovin Receives at St. Louis," *Fort Worth Daily Gazette*, June 15, 1886, p. 4, col. 2.

management, the strike movement shrank into the summer and finally collapsed in September.

What happened on the Gould railroads paralleled developments elsewhere in the country. That spring, for example, saw eight-hour strikes in Chicago that resulted in the May 1886 Haymarket Riot. The police moved to break up an otherwise peaceful rally, after which a bomb exploded. Who killed how many remains contested, but eight leaders of the local IWPA found themselves in the dock for criminal conspiracy to create the conditions that led to the death of the police officer killed by the initial blast. In the end, the strikes collapsed and the courts sentenced seven of the eight to the gallows, though eventually only four hanged, including Albert R. Parsons, a Texas-born Confederate veteran.

While uninterested in promoting anarchism, the broad workers movement in Chicago tended to rally to anarchists' defense. Very briefly, they also coalesced around the idea of challenging the capitalist parties at the polls. A wave of new local labor parties took to the field in response to a surge of direct government prosecutions aimed not only at the Southwest railroad strike and the strike wave in Chicago, but also at musicians in New York City.

This last issue galvanized the labor movement in that city. Furious over their perceived mistreatment by the courts and the government, the movement chose to run Henry George for mayor. The author of *Progress and Poverty* had moved to the city only a few years before, but remained skeptical as to the value of small independent campaigns, demanding that the labor organizations secure 50,000 signatures of voter support. When these signatures were supplied, George accepted the nomination on a United Labor Party ticket.

William A. Carsey made a predictable reappearance in the movement on behalf of the Democrats. At the time he held a patronage job as an inspector in the Department of Public Works and, like many in such jobs, threw his time and energies into helping to defeat George. The Democratic candidate Abram S. Hewitt mimicked the George campaign by issuing "blanks calling for signatures to a pledge to vote for him for Mayor" and "quietly catering to the George people by having his 'workers' give it out that he really believes in nearly all that George teaches." Carsey and his men also positioned themselves "to try and split up the labor vote in the interest of the Democratic Mayoralty candidate." In particular, they issued "purely imaginary reports of the decline of the George movement."[22]

The Democrats in New York employed various dirty tricks against the George movement, as the United Labor Party called itself. The Democratic organization remained far more concerned about losing the election than about the precedent such a defeat might mark. On the other hand, however impressive the numbers of the George movement seemed to be, it represented from the beginning a defensive response to the prosecution of trade unionists—a protest vote aimed at demonstrating the labor movements' ability to push one or both of the major parties into a less overtly hostile stance.[23]

Often touted as a great example of a third party movement, these new efforts in the 1880s by George and the earlier antimonopolists never seemed to share the old insurgent hope of becoming a major party, as the Republicans had in the 1850s. Rather, the reformers opened the door to a kind of religious "witnessing," shaping the modern idea of the protest vote as merely a means of "moral suasion" to influence one of the existing major parties.

The defeat of the strike movements and the failure of the electoral efforts also coincided with the final break between the Federation of Organized Trades and Labor Unions and the Knights. The craftsmen went on to found the American Federation of Labor, securing the hegemony of the "business unionism" or "pure and simple" unionism that abandoned the old vision of an all-inclusive labor reform association.[24]

---

22 "The Democrats Anxious," *New York Times*, October 27, 1886, p. 2; "Injuring Hewitt's Cause," *New York Times*, October 31, 1886, p. 9; "Found His Place Filled," *New York Times*, November 5, 1886, p. 2.

23 O'Donnell, *Henry George and the Crisis of Inequality.*

24 See Victoria C. Hattam, *Labor Visions and State Power: The Origins of Business Unionism in the United States* (Princeton: Princeton University Press, 1993).

Escapes and Safety Valves

Sullivan, one of the articulate, militant cowboys discontented with the new order on the range, went east, passing through several Wild West shows and freely sharing his views both with *John Swinton's Paper* and with Karl Marx's daughter when she visited Cincinnati.[25]

Sullivan faced the crisis unfolding in the cattle industry with skills beyond those of the ordinary cowpuncher. Wagon trains, freight services, and stagecoach lines all needed scouts, as did the U.S. Cavalry. Sullivan found work as an army scout through 1881 and 1882 and won considerable fame for his talents with a rope and a six-shooter. In the sparsely populated region, an active traveler may well have met all the people Sullivan claimed to have encountered—Kit Carson, "Wild Bill" Hickok, "Buffalo Bill" Cody, and "Texas Jack" Vermillion of Wyatt Earp's vendetta riders after Tombstone. He also mentioned Major Frank North of the Pawnee Scouts and Generals George R. Crook and George Armstrong Custer. In New Mexico, Sullivan encountered Frederick Remington who supposedly used Sullivan in a painting on which the statue of "The Cowboy" in Philadelphia's Fairmont Park was modeled.[26]

"Buffalo Bill" tried to recruit Sullivan for his touring show. When Cody planned his more elaborate "Wild West Show," Sullivan accepted the offer to become part of the first troupe. There was such a demand for the show that one of Cody's partners, William F. Carver—"Doc" Carver—started a new company in 1884, recruiting Sullivan as his right-hand man.[27] The end of the summer, though,

25 *Waterloo Courier*, April 1, 1891, p. 2; *Sioux County Herald*, April 8, 1891, p. 6; *Malvern* [IA] *Leader*, April 9, 1891, p. 2; *The Jackson Hustler*, April 17, 1891; *Topeka State Journal*, April 25, 1891, p. 6; *Hutchinson News*, May 1, 1891, p. 1; "A Cowboy Strike: The Strange Pranks of a Lot of Unruly Ranchmen," *Lawrence* [TN] *Democrat*, May 1, 1891, p. 1; "A Strike on the Ranch," *Bill Barlow's Budget* [Douglas, WY], May 6, 1891, p. 7; [Untitled], *Middletown* [NY] *Daily Press*, June 27, 1892, p. 1.

26 Sullivan, *Life and Adventures of Broncho John*.

27 "'Broncho John' Sullivan's Memories," *Vidette-Messenger*, September 27, 1951, p. 2.

brought legal difficulties for Carver that imploded the entire company.[28]

Carver's Wild West Show collapsed and stranded Sullivan, forty Indians, a dozen horses, two antelope, a deer, and a bear in Valparaiso, followed by Carver with another dozen cowboys, a "16-piece Negro band," and other sundry, newly unemployed entertainers. Then the creditors' lawyers descended on the group. Broncho John and others immediately appealed to the local residents, who organized a relief committee that kept the Indians together. He also raised money to get them to Chicago, from which point the Bureau of Indian Affairs agreed to get them home. Before departing, though, they gave a performance in gratitude to the people of Valparaiso.[29]

Out of this came Broncho John's old Wild West show, which generally toured in the Midwest, but its movements can be easily traced through newspapers from the period. The New York *Sun* interviewed Sullivan almost immediately after the show began touring—an interview likely arranged by the old radical John Swinton, long associated with the paper.[30] A few years earlier, Swinton had been the guest of honor at a banquet thrown by leaders in the news industry, one of whom apparently offered a toast to the independent press. Swinton reportedly scoffed:

There is no such thing, at this date of the world's history, in America, as an independent press. You know it and I know it. There is not one of you who dares to write your honest opinions, and if you did, you know beforehand that it would never appear in print. I am paid weekly for keeping my honest opinion out of the paper I am connected with. Others of you are paid similar salaries for similar things, and any of you who would be so foolish as to write honest opinions would be out on the streets looking for another job . . .

28 W. Thorf Raymond, *Spirit Gun of the West: The Story of Doc. W. F. Carver* (Glendale, CA: Arthur H. Clark Co., 1957).

29 "'Broncho John' Sullivan's Memories," *Vidette-Messenger*. "40 Destitute Indians Stranded in Valparaiso," *Vidette Messenger*, June 14, 1962, pp. 1, 7.

30 "A Talk with Broncho John," *The Sun*, August 29, 1886, p. 6, cols. 3–4.

We are the tools and vassals of rich men behind the scenes. We are the jumping jacks, they pull the strings and we dance. Our talents, our possibilities and our lives are all the property of other men.[31]

At the time of the banquet, the *Sun*, Swinton's own venture into independent journalism, had already begun to collapse; shortly thereafter, Swinton walked away from his *John Swinton's Paper* to try and revive it.

Around this time, Swinton also encountered Eleanor—also called Jenny or Tussy—Marx Aveling at a dime museum in Cincinnati. Her father had spent his life formulating a coherent social and economic critique of capitalism based on what he saw and studied in the Old World. Marx had always wanted a closer look at capitalism in the United States, whose politicians claimed to be taking an exceptional approach to nation-building, but never got the chance.

Eleanor, a striking woman, had become an important figure in her own right. Interested in the Irish cause by the age of twelve, she began accompanying her father to labor and socialist conferences at the age of sixteen. After losing her parents and a sister, she took on an even more public role in the movement. In 1884, she joined the dry-as-dust Social Democratic Federation and helped William Morris and others launch a new Socialist League, which looked to mass work as well as the distribution of socialist ideas. She also helped launch the Women's Trade Union League and lay the foundations for what would erupt a few years later in the Great Dock Strike. Her longtime interest in literary, artistic, and theatrical work explains not only her association with Morris but also her interest in Wild West theatrics in the United States. She would certainly have considered what Broncho John told her and her companions as a great vindication of her father's perspectives on class and capitalism.

31 "Sold for a Fact," *Carson City NV Morning Appeal*, September 13, 1892, p. 2; "Editors as Slaves," *Switchman's Journal*, 7 (January 1893): 688; "Socialists Make Good Copy," *Colliers*, 34 (November 29, 1904): 9. The statement is often repeated by right-wingers and sometimes refuted as a phony quote, so these early uses are particularly important.

Broncho John's troupe in Cincinnati may well have included refugees of the cowboy strikes over the previous years. The shows featured a touring group of cowboys; Sullivan would give "stereotyped speeches about them" while his subjects lounged about "in their picturesque garb, and looking terribly bored."[32] In finding the press remarkably disinterested in the truth about the domination of the West by big capitalists to the detriment of the small holders and cowboys, Sullivan was hardly alone.

By this point, Sullivan had largely made the complete transition to show business. In 1887, in Chicago, he married Mae Abbot Wallace, whose stage name was Sylvia Bidwell. He did not always maintain his own show. In 1889, he and "a group of Apaches and cowboys" working for Captain Jack Crawford's Wild West Show responded heroically to a fire that broke out in the theater, supposedly rescuing "the valuable coach of Revolutonary War hero Lafayette."[33]

Nevertheless, Sullivan carried his pro-labor message wherever he could to whomever might listen. While in Minnesota during a streetcar strike, he found himself horrified that the management put their strikebreakers into cowboy outfits. He told a local reporter that cowboys were "honest, hard working men." Watching the strikebreakers, he declared that "there wasn't a genuine cowboy in the crowd," because cowboys "don't go around taking another man's job from him."[34] Yet, Sullivan's own well-being, if not survival, had required getting out of the cowboy life.

The gunslinging strike leader Dan Bogan—alias Bill Gatlin—had far fewer options than Broncho John. After the Panhandle became too hot for him, he headed to Wyoming, where he took up yet another name: Bill McCoy. He found good, regular work on the Lake Vorhees

32 Bibbins and Marx Aveling, *The Working-Class Movement in America*, 156–7. See also Derfler, "The American Cowboy."

33 Darlis A. Miller, *Captain Jack Crawford: Buckskin Poet, Scout, and Showman* (Albuquerque: University of New Mexico Press, 1993), 136. See also Paul R. Nolan, *John Wallace Crawford* (Boston: Twayne Publishers, 1981).

34 Quoted in Elizabeth Faue, *Writing the Wrongs: Eva Valesh and the Rise of Labor Journalism* (Ithaca, NY: Cornell University Press, 2004), 59.

(LZ) Ranch, near Lusk. However, Texans populated much of the industry across the northern ranges and his identity was revealed almost inevitably. Bill Calkin, the editor of the local newspaper, described McCoy as a wanted man in Texas, who had used at least two other names in the past.[35]

Bogan headed to town with another cowboy, Sterling Balou, and cornered Calkin in the Cleveland Brothers Saloon. One of the Cleveland brothers produced a sawed-off shotgun and the two cowboys stood down. Shortly after, Constable Charles S. Gunn entered with his own pistol. A former Texas Ranger, Gunn had already killed two men while on the job. Bogan and Balou wisely retreated and left town.

On January 14, 1887, Bogan turned up in town again. The details remain unclear, though one account reported that Bogan was making a ruckus in a dance hall and Gunn arrived to get him to back down once again. It is difficult to imagine that anyone who needed to keep a low profile as much as Bogan did would have gone looking for trouble. In any event, a serious altercation took place. The next morning, Bogan waited at Jim Waters Saloon for Gunn to come in for his morning visit. When Gunn arrived, Bogan asked him, "Charlie, are you heeled?" Gunn replied that he was always armed, and Bogan apparently left the bar peaceably.

A few days later, Bogan returned to town once more to find Gunn looking for him and threatening him with arrest. To this, Bogan replied that he would do as he pleased. When Gunn responded, Bogan swung his unholstered gun from behind his back and shot him in the stomach. As Gunn fell, he drew his pistol and Bogan killed him, shooting him in the head. He then tried to make his escape but found Deputy Marshal John Owens in the street. Owens, too, was later reported to be a Texas-born ex-guerrilla who had ridden with William C. Quantrill. This was untrue: after brief service in a short-lived secessionist militia called the Missouri State Guard, Owen had spent most of the Civil War in

---

35 For this account of Bogan's activities in Wyoming, see DeArment, *Deadly Dozen*, 159–60, 161.

the West, working for the Union Army. While serving as a scout out of Fort Laramie, he had won a station and roadhouse on the road to Cheyenne in an all-night poker game. On this day, though, he certainly had had a good night's sleep. He reportedly fired one shot in the air and then put a bullet in Bogan's shoulder, knocking him from the saddle.[36]

Like Tascosa, Lusk had no jail, so the deputy marshal put Bogan in the back room of a saloon. The next day, Bogan escaped into a roaring blizzard. Realizing that a wounded man could not get far, Owen bided his time. Two weeks later, he got word from Bogan, who had an infected wound and a raging fever, offering to surrender. Owen met him sixteen miles from town and promised in exchange for Bogan's surrender that he would protect him from any attempt to lynch him. After a night shackled in the back of the Sweeney Saloon, Owen left with Bogan for Cheyenne and got him into a proper jail on February 4.

After a long trial, Bogan was sentenced to death for the murder of Gunn on September 7, 1887. Tom Hall—accused by detective Charlie Siringo of being Tom Nicholls, another killer from the Panhandle—paid a professional safecracker to commit a minor crime in Cheyenne in order to land himself in jail with Bogan. Hall had packed saw blades in his shoes, which he and Bogan used to remove the bars on October 4. Releasing two incarcerated horse thieves as well, they climbed through a ventilator onto the roof.[37]

Within hours, the authorities organized one of the largest manhunts in Wyoming history. They separated into groups of fifty men each to run down the fugitives, and put a $1,000 reward on Bogan's head, dead or alive.

---

36 Ibid., 162; Donald R. Hale, *Branded as Rebels*, vol. 2 (Independence, MO: Blue & Grey Book Shoppe, 2003), 240–1. See also Elizabeth T. Griffith, *House of Blazes: The Story of Johnny Owens* (Newcastle, WY: News Letter Journal, 1990), as well as Robert K. DeArment, *Knights of the Green Cloth: The Saga of the Frontier Gamblers* (Norman: University of Oklahoma Press, 1990).

37 "He Gets Another Lease. A Change of Judges in the McCoy Case Obligatory," Cheyenne *Daily Sun*, July 22, 1887, p. 3; "McCoy in Texas," *Lusk Herald*, July 29, 1887, p. 1.

Charles Siringo, the Pinkerton agent, made the most determined effort to run down Bogan. He followed a trail through Utah into the New Mexico Territory and then reached out to his old Panhandle friend Lem Woodruff, who had heard from one of Bogan's Wyoming friends that Bogan had written him from New Orleans, declaring that he was heading for Argentina. Later reports alleged that Bogan had been killed in Mexico by a gunfight or bucking horse. Others claimed that he had reached Argentina, where he built a ranch or died while riding with bandits. Still others reported that Bogan returned to the States under another alias, starting a small ranch and a family and raising his children to be what Siringo called respectable Roosevelt Republicans.[38] Of course, plenty of lawmen and regulators could have taken Bogan out of the picture, and the West had plenty of spaces where his corpse could have simply disappeared.

Another of the forgotten founders of the Western labor movement, N. M. Lovin escaped conviction for the shoot-out near Fort Worth associated with the Gould railroad strike. By early 1888, he had turned up in the Indian Territory, working for the Missouri Pacific as a car spotter, helping to deter thieves who preyed upon the company's freight cars. A Fort Worth paper reported that "the presumption is that while engaged in this good work he was assassinated by a gang of thieves, but full particulars are not yet known."[39] The only proof of this, however, is hearsay.

The railroad's armed enforcers seemed to have had less interest in running down those who killed their workers than workers who had gone on strike. It cannot be ruled out that his elimination might have been revenge for the killing of company men during the strike.

---

38 Charlie Siringo, *A Lone Star Cowboy: Being Fifty Years Experience in the Saddle as Cowboy, Detective and New Mexico Ranger, on Every Cow Trail in the Wooly Old West. Also the Doings of Some "Bad" Cowboys, such as "Billy the Kid," "Wess Harding and "Kid Curry"* (Santa Fe: Author, 1919), 165.

39 "Reported Killed. N. M. Lovin, Formerly of This City, Said to Have Been Murdered," *Fort Worth Daily Gazette*, January 26, 1888, p. 8, col. 5; *Fort Worth Weekly Gazette*, January 27, 1888, p. 8, col. 5.

The key leader of the 1883 strike, Tom Harris, had struggled heroically to hold together the little cooperative ranch of the blacklisted. In November 1886, Harris married Clara Paulus in La Grange, Fayette County. Her father served that community as its doctor and had brought the family over from Denmark.

That winter, which crushed so many ranching operations, fell heavily on the cooperative effort. J. E. McAllister, likely under pressure from the LS management that employed him, pulled out, as did Bill Ruth. Finally, Jenkins asked for the return of the money he had loaned to the enterprise. He and Harris quarreled to the point that they actually drew revolvers on each other and had to be talked down by Ruth. They settled, but Jenkins came out of it seventeen head of cattle short of his original investment.

Harris and his new bride left the area in the spring of 1887 to occupy a little patch of land on Chicken Creek in New Mexico, a gift from his friend Dave Lard that was some five miles west of Canadian City. Harris spent several years doing odd jobs, missing the trail, and lamenting the failure of the cooperative. Finally, claimed Lard, a sexually transmitted disease that Harris had contracted years before—and had thought was cured—flared up once more. It all became too much. On December 12, 1890, he scrawled a simple note, reading, "I'm tired of this" and "Put me away," after which he drank a bottle of morphine.[40] Like the orphaned sons of a defeated South, he remained a waif of the postwar economic order.[41]

So it was that, as Sullivan explained to Marx-Aveling, the staccato strikes that had served the cowboys in the past seemed to become less and less effective. Asking for a raise individually, he said, "means immediate discharge from the service," adding that the owners' association would then circulate the discharged worker's name, blacklisting him.[42] Despite the cowboys' efforts, the employers worked ruthlessly to establish and hold a $30 monthly wage, which meant that a

40 Nolan, *Tascosa*, 151.

41 For this and the following paragraph, see Nolan, *Tascosa*, 150–1, 123–4, 232; McCarty, *Maverick Town*, 124, 137. Jesse Jenkins died in 1947. Nolan, *Tascosa*, 232.

42 Bibbens and Marx Aveling, *The Working-Class Movement in America*, 162.

cowboy could make only $120 to $150 for his seasonal work over four or five months.

People still sought some way to live better by getting around the capitalist marketplace. Dr. Alfred Kimsey Owen proposed merging the ideas of Henry George with the interests of investors in the railroads of Texas. The plan involved raising capital to build a railroad across Mexico to Topolobampo Bay on the Gulf of California. Fueled by entrepreneurial greed, the projected utopia seemed to promise certain success. Among the interested Texans seems to have been Charles H. Jenkins, who was said to be involved in a socialist scheme in Mexico.[43]

From 1886 to 1894, some 1,200 Americans ventured south of the border to a colony on Topolobampo Bay. Kansas contributed far more proportionately than any other state, some Kansans coming from the old cow town of Baxter Springs and others from Winfield. Many of the settlers came from California and Colorado, though Texas contributed a surprising amount, as did Missouri. Representatives of all of the western states and territories showed up, including half a dozen who moseyed down from Laramie.[44] They represented the increasingly desperate hopes of people determined to live well without having to directly confront the capitalist social order.

Such revivals of communitarian strategies throughout the century had the usual mixed results, but these never included the destruction of capitalism. The series of successful cowboy strikes secured some mild and temporary relief, but soon faced the collapse of the beef bonanza, the end of the cattle drives, the implosion of the cowboy's job itself, and the ruthless violence of the regulators.

43   Nolan, *Tascosa*, 221.
44   Ray Reynolds, *Cat's Paw Utopia* (El Cajon, CA: Author, 1972): on California, 150–1; on Colorado, 151–2; on Kansas, 153–5; on Texas, 158; on Missouri, 156.

SIX

The Destiny of the Farmers' Alliance

*The Implosion of the Cattle Trade, the Union Labor
Party, and the National Election Fiasco of 1888*

Theodore Roosevelt's muscular Christianity never had a greater reason
to twitch in nervous self-doubt. He had invested a fortune in his
ranching before returning to New York City in the late summer of
1886 to receive the Republican nomination for mayor. The November
election saw his stunning defeat, coming in a distant third behind
Henry George, the United Labor candidate. Withdrawing briefly
from public life in the East as well as entrepreneurial pursuits in the
West, he married while visiting London, and the couple spent the
winter honeymooning in Europe.

Roosevelt and many of his peers remained so lacking in self-aware-
ness that they had great difficulty understanding the crises of confidence in their rule. Since the Civil War, their stated belief system
rooted the economic, social, and political order in nature. Now,
nature itself seemed to go into revolt, particularly in the West, even as
the courts and political system began modifying the structure of
power. At the same time, while Greenbackism may have been crushed,
what had been the Industrial Brotherhood—recast as the Knights of
Labor—acted in conjunction with the Farmers' Alliance to spark a
wave of new third-party efforts across the country. One of these, the
new Union Labor Party, promised a broad national campaign in 1888

that threatened to confront the ruling classes with the will of the producing masses.

Laws of Nature and of Society

Nature took its revenge on the market. In the summer of 1886, the victims of the rough winter in Texas moved cattle by the tens of thousands from their own overstocked fields to the northern ranges. When winter returned, it did not spare the Panhandle. The bodies of cattle trapped by the drift fence piled high once more. Later, an LX man reportedly supervised the skinning of 250 corpses a mile for thirty-five miles. Locals called it the "Big Die-Up" rather than roundup, and reported losses ran to three-quarters for fortunate ranchers. Mathew Hooks said you could put cows three feet apart and walk to Colorado on them. Mortality was said to be as high as 75 percent near Mobeetie. Many firms changed hands.[1]

However, the northern range got the full brunt of the season's fury, with temperatures falling as far as forty below zero and remaining arctic for long stretches. Late frosts, drought, and grasshoppers left little green on which the cattle might feed. Fires broke out, destroying much of what remained. Survival, many believed, would require a mild winter. Then, in late November, the first severe snowstorm hit. Subzero weather set in a month later, lasting for a month and leaving what cut grass remained under a thick crust of frozen snow capped by ice. In mid-January 1887 it warmed just enough to rain. Then, the temperatures dropped once more below zero, freezing the ground solidly and adding more heavy snowfall into mid-February.[2]

The devastation postponed hopes for a spring roundup, so the full impact remained uncertain until the summer. Roosevelt and

---

1 Massey, *Black Cowboys of Texas*, 232; H. Allen Anderson, "Big Die-Up," Handbook of Texas Online, Texas State Historical Association, available at tshaonline.org/handbook/online.

2 Ray H. Mattison, "The Hard Winter and the Range Cattle Business," *The Montana Magazine of History* 1 (October 1951): 5–21.

the other ranchers decided not to hold a roundup until they could find more of their missing cattle, sending scouts onto the Standing Rock Indian Reservation and elsewhere. However, most of the carcasses had already been stripped and the bones grown over with grass. By late summer, the general estimate of their losses ran to about 75 percent. Despite years of sending wolfers into the countryside, the overstocking of the cattle proved a bonanza for the beasts of prey.

The boom on the northern ranges came to an end. The De Mores packing plant in Medora closed for good. When a fire destroyed the local paper, *The Bad Lands Cow Boy*, its owners also decided not to rebuild the operation. The chateau of the De Mores stood empty, as did the town's new brick hotel and the church. Many residents of Medora and Little Missouri across the river moved to Dickinson.

As for the great ranchers, some of the larger local concerns limped on, but those fielded by eastern or European money tended to go under. As capital wandered off in search of greener pastures, Roosevelt told the *Mandan Pioneer* that

> the days of excessive profits are over. There are too many in the business. In certain sections of the West the losses this year are enormous, owing to the drought and overstocking. Each steer needs from fifteen to twenty-five acres, but they are crowded on very much thicker, and the cattlemen this season have paid the penalty.[3]

Roosevelt lost over half of his $80,000 investment in ranching. As soon as he could sell, he did, ending his career as a rancher and returning to a life in eastern politics.

A nature delivered its verdict, lawyers struggled to secure the future of American capitalism in the courts of California. There, the

---

3 Chester L. Brooks and Ray H. Mattison, *Theodore Roosevelt and the Dakota Badlands* (Washington, DC: National Park Service, 1958). Available at nps.gov/parkhistory.

expansion of the railroads that made the cattle drives increasingly marginal also transformed life in the settled districts of the country, making their impact felt most clearly in the far West. The Southern Pacific quickly gained control of the dominant Republican party in California. In the aftermath of bipartisan repression of the 1877 strike movement, the railroad also managed to placate the Democrats enough to bring them into partnership. In response, an independent political force brought white "workingmen" into the field, though under the leadership of shopkeepers, professionals, and small businessmen, such as the Irish drayman Dennis Kearney. Their "Workingmen's Party" moved quickly into prominence but carried the terrible burden of the white supremacist assumptions of the Democrats, focusing their attention less on African Americans than native peoples and, especially, the Chinese.

Early in 1878, the new party won elections in Alameda and Santa Clara counties, taking the mayoralities of Oakland and Sacramento and claiming 15,000 members in San Francisco. It had branches in 40 of the 52 counties and, in June, elected a third of California's constitutional convention. Still, much of it just as quickly collapsed into the Democratic Party, with its similarly overt white supremacism.[4]

As this power struggle raged, large companies decided to challenge payment of their taxes, creating a serious financial crisis. The Spring Valley Water Company and the San Francisco Gas Company owed the state nearly a million dollars by late 1883, but the state eventually settled for a fraction of the amount. The railroad decided that it would follow their example and refused to pay "unjust" taxes for years, complicating the problems of the state, which could not get interest on the amount either. The State Supreme Court eventually forced a settlement, though the railroad lawyers held out in Santa Clara, Colusa, San Benito, Monterey, and Los Angeles. The press described

---

4 R. Hall Williams, *The Democratic Party and California Politics, 1880–1896* (Stanford: Stanford University Press, 1973), 16; Carl Brent Swisher, "Motivation and Political Technique" in *The California Constitutional Convention, 1878–1879* (New York: Da Capo, 1969), 78.

the protests of those individuals and smaller businesses as mere disorders.

Judge Stephen J. Field—a longtime member of the U.S. Supreme Court— described the demand of local government for their taxes as an "agrarian and communistic" assault on the property rights of the railroads. Some years before, Field had dissented when the Supreme Court sustained the right of government to regulate business in *Munn v. Illinois* (1877). In the course of this agitation, some Democratic leaders such as George Hearst and Delphin M. Delmas in San Francisco decided that they would be well advised to get control of the iron horse while they still could. They suggested a strong railroad commission and the taxing of stocks, bonds, and franchises.[5] Yet, they saw no viable means of attack until the railroad provided them with one.

San Mateo County provided an opportunity to address the issue when it found the Southern Pacific Railroad unwilling to pay its taxes. In September 1882, the case reached district court, airing the arguments that would be repeated in *County of Santa Clara v. Southern Pacific Railroad Company* the following year. The case wound up in the state's Supreme Court, which ordered the company to remit what it owed the county. However, the Southern Pacific had not exhausted its possibilities.

The railroad had two strong arguments to get around the state authorities. First, they argued that the Federal Pacific Railroad Act of 1866 that granted public land to the corporation exempted it from state and local jurisdictions. It also based an appeal on the 1875 Jurisdiction and Removal Act, passed to protect former slaves in the South. Although not designed to get corporations out of paying taxes to local and state authorities; nevertheless, the railroad argued before sympathetic federal judges that it had been discriminated against. The issue crawled through the appeals process, starting with the U.S. Circuit Court in San Francisco in July 1883.[6] The railroad strategy stalled until its nonpayment of taxes forced a

5 Williams, *The Democratic Party and California Politics*, 20–1, 23.
6 Ibid., 34–6.

financial crisis, after which it would offer a compromise of partial payment.

By the spring of 1884, the cases against every railroad except the North Pacific Coast had reached the federal courts. Democratic authorities agreed to accept it, but Delmas still objected. One judge quipped that this was "the first time in history of a case where a taxpayer has been two long years trying to be enabled to get tax money in the State Treasury." Meanwhile, the Santa Clara case went into further appeal.[7]

Delmas made a strong argument for compelling the railroad to pay taxes. The State, he argued, created the railroad and

has delegated to it, this favored creature of its own creation, rights denied by it to the citizen, and the immense inequality between this creature and a man is so great as to be alarming . . . [The state] granted this creature the right to construct its road across streams; it has not granted such privilege to individual citizens. The State has granted it a right of way through cities and counties and towns, lands for depots; it has not to any human being. The State has given this creature the right to collect and take tolls, which right has not been given to any individual citizen. The State has given it vast sums of money, in the shape of subsidies from State, cities and counties, which has not been given to individuals. To these defendants the State has given the right to protect its life beyond the life of man . . . In the people inheres the right to regulate the creatures of its creation, so that they shall receive fair rewards for their labors and no more, and shall bear their just burdens in the support of the institutions of the country and in the maintenance of law and order . . . It may come

7 "The Railroad Taxes," *Sacramento Daily Union*, November 12, 1883, p. 2; "The Tax Case" [from *Oakland Times*], *Sacramento Daily Union*, November 13, 1883, p. 2; "Railroad Tax Cases," *Sacramento Daily Union*, March 1, 1884, p. 4; "Delmas' Flop. How He Gave the Railroad Tax Suits Dead Away—What the Officials Think of It" [from *Evening Post*, August 10], *Daily Alta California*, August 11, 1885, p. 4. See also "Marshall and Delmas. They Will Represent the State in the Railroad Tax Suits," *Daily Alta California*, November 12, 1883.

peacefully and quietly; it may come through tumult and revolution—but it will come.[8]

The issue loomed large in the Democratic conventions early in
the summer, as the party jockeyed to speak for the antimonopolist
sentiment in the state. The city convention in May sent Delmas to
the state convention where he headed the platform committee,
which denounced Field's ruling. When some delegates defended
the judge, Delmas spoke so eloquently against the court's siding
with the corporations that the resolution passed 453 to 19. His
views prevailed in the adoption of a platform generally characterized as a "New Departure" program for the Democrats. A
Democratic paper, the *Daily Alta California* argued that the
convention consisted "mainly of the representatives of the new
Constitution and Workingmen's parties" and that "the spirit of the
sand-lot" prevailed among the Democrats.[9] In the aftermath of the
1884 fall elections, the *Alta* groused bitterly about Delmas and
Heast's faction, blaming it for the loss of the legislature to the
Republicans:[10]

By August 1885, the *Alta* was complaining even more bitterly.
"The State and the counties thereof very badly needed the money
involved," it reported, "and, as the hearing and determination of the
appeal would take considerable time, a most satisfactory arrangement was offered by the railroads, and, after much discussion and
consideration, was accepted by the Attorney-General." Delmas was
described as a "small country lawyer" and "the second-class lawyer

8 "Shall the People Rule?" *Pacific Rural Press*, August 11, 1883, p. 108.

9 "The Convention" particularly "The Proceedings," *Daily Alta California*,
June 12, 1884, p. 1, and "The New Departure—the Platform," *Daily Alta California*,
June 16, 1884, p. 4. On the sandlot, see "The Convention and Its Work," *Daily Alta
California*, June 13, 1884, p. 4. For background to the convention, see "Democratic
Delegates," *Daily Alta California*, May 27, 1884, p. 4, and the "California
Democracy," *Daily Alta California*, June 11, 1884, p. 1.

10 "The Tax Cases. Justice Field's Orders in the Railroad Suits. Gen. Marshall's
Argument. The Court Orders That the Tender Be Made Good, and That the
Railroad Pay Over About $400,000," *Daily Alta California*, September 30, 1884,
p. 2; "Delmas' Flop," *Daily Alta California*.

from the third rate town of San Jose." "Never in the whole round of history," the paper wrote, "has so small a trouble created so big a row."[11]

The culmination of the case came on January 26–29, 1886. The result left corporations with the legal rights of people and human beings with what rights they could afford. On May 10, the U.S. Supreme Court issued its ruling on three cases: *Santa Clara County v. Southern Pacific Railroad Company* (by which the entire ruling has now come to be known), *California v. Southern Pacific Railroad Company*, and *California v. Central Pacific Railroad Company*.[12]

The particularly notorious reputation of the case came from its gloss, penned by court reporter Bancroft Davis, himself the former president of Newburgh and New York Railway. On May 26, Chief Justice Morrison Waite assured Davis in a letter that his gloss "expresses with sufficient accuracy what was said before the argument began. I leave it with you to determine whether anything need be said about it in the report inasmuch as we avoided meeting the constitutional question in the decision."[13]

The ruling cast a long shadow, but—as with the later *Citizens United v. FEC* (2010)—was less important than the climate that created it.

The Union Labor Party

By the early 1880s, the older Greenback insurgency had tapped into the deep discontent beyond the Midwest. Despite a general, national

11 "Delmas, the Demagogue. His Action in the Railroad Tax Litigation," *Daily Alta California*, August 17, 1885, p. 8.

12 *Santa Clara County v. Southern Pacific Railroad Company*, 118 U.S. 394 (1886). See also "The Great Case," *Sacramento Daily Union*; "The Railroad Tax Decision," *Sacramento Daily Union*, May 14, 1886, p. 2.

13 Jack Beatty, *Age of Betrayal: The Triumph of Money in America, 1865–1900* (New York: Vintage, 2007), 172–3. See also C. Peter McGrath, *Morrison R. Waite: The Triumph of Character* (New York: Macmillan, 1963), 117.

decline, Greenbackism survived and actually grew stronger in Kansas and Texas. In the aftermath of the 1884 Antimonopolist debacle, mass organizations—the Alliance in Kansas and Texas, the Agricultural Wheel and the Brotherhood of Freedom in Arkansas, and the Knights of Labor—provided the base for insurgencies powerful enough to anchor a national revival. For various, often localized reasons, a wave of local labor parties moved into the field.[14]

Toward the middle of the decade, a handful of insurgent leaders were determined to prevent their efforts from being derailed again. A small circle calling themselves the "Charitable Thirteen" decided to take a page from the Antimonopolists and launch a new party over a year before the usual nominating conventions.

They also formed a secret society: the Videttes. In military terms, "videttes" were mounted pickets posted far in advance to notify the rest of the army of an enemy movement. Notwithstanding the military origins of the word, this sense of protecting something—the integrity of a political project—was central to the Videttes' goals, though nothing in the secret rituals and pledges of the Videttes, later splashed across the local papers, hints at anything other than the usual hokum of the societies that grew as readily as corn across the heartland.[15]

The case of the Vincents demonstrates the deep abolitionist roots of this new effort. Years before, James Vincent had graduated from Oberlin and married Mary Seldon, the daughter of Henry Olcott Sheldon, who later became a prominent Greenbacker in northern Ohio. The couple had hoped to head for Kansas to join Free State efforts there, but only had enough money to reach

14 Although concerned with several case studies, Leon Fink's *Workingmen's Democracy: The Knights of Labor and American Politics* (Urbana: University of Illinois Press, 1983) includes what he acknowledges to be an incomplete list of generally unstudied political tickets on which the Knights of Labor were listed: "Knights of Labor Political Tickets, by State or Territory, 1885–88," 28–9.

15 See *Proceedings of the Joint Committee of the Legislature of the State of Kansas. Appointed at the Session of 1891, to Investigate the Explosion which occurred at Coffeyville, Kansas, October 18, 1888* (Topeka: C. C. Baker, 1891), 245, hereafter cited as *Legislative Investigation of Coffeyville.*

Tabor, Iowa. They settled in, establishing a station on the Underground Railroad and joining John Brown's efforts in the territory. Later, the entire family—including sons Henry, Leopold, and Cuthbert—helped establish and maintain a newspaper, *The American Non-Conformist*. In 1886, they moved the paper to Winfield, Kansas. There, it argued that sharecropping, sweatshops, and underpayment of workers should be as far beyond the pale of society as slavery was now considered.[16] For the Vincents, as for many, the openness of the West promised an opportunity for a new kind of society.

The new insurgent effort culminated in the formation of the Union Labor Party in February 1887. This new party—which later became the Populists—posed serious local challenges to both the Democratic Party in Arkansas and the Republican Party in Kansas. The former responded with a wave of illegal but unprosecuted and mostly uninvestigated violent attacks on black Arkansans and their white allies. Republican Kansas would find a similarly violent solution.[17]

The Union Labor Party included some familiar faces. Representing the Indian Territory, railroad striker Nathan M. Lovin served as a member of the Committee on Permanent Organization for the February 1887 founding convention. George V. Smith, a twenty-seven-year-old Missouri native residing in Wyoming represented that

16   Harold R. Piehler, "Henry Vincent: Kansas Populist and Radical Reform Journalist," *Kansas History* 2 (Spring 1979): 14. See also Vincent's PhD dissertation: "Henry Vincent: A Case Study in Political Deviancy," University of Kansas, 1975; Patrick N. Minges, *Slavery in the Cherokee Nation: The Keetoowah Society and the Defining of a People, 1855–1867* (London and New York: Routledge, 2003), 71–2, 73, 99. W. D. Vincent on the National Committee: "The Wind-Up. Close of the Union Labor Convention," *Cincinnati Enquirer*, February 25, 1887, p. 5.

17   Various students of agrarian unrest have discussed the incident in general terms, most notably Lawrence Goodwyn in *Democratic Promise: The Populist Movement in America* (New York: Oxford University Press, 1976), 188–9, 412; James C. Malin, *A Concern About Humanity: Notes on Reform, 1872–1912, at the National and Kansas Levels of Thought* (Lawrence, KS: Author, 1964), 162–4, 195.

state, probably one of a cluster of Missouri Greenbackers who found new homes on the northern range.[18]

Texas radicals played a proportionately large role in the organization. Born and raised in Kentucky, Samuel Evans taught school before going to Texas in 1853, gradually acquiring 300 acres in Tarrant County by the time of the war. He raised a company of cavalry without mustering with them, traveling to New Orleans and Montgomery. In early 1864, he married, raised another company, and went into the Twenty-First Texas. After the war, he traveled extensively to Kansas and back, winning election to the state legislature under the Reconstruction government in 1866 and going on to two terms in the state senate. With the overthrow of the Radicals, he had turned to Greenbackism. The Union Labor Party later appointed him one of five members of the committee instructed to discuss tension with the followers of Henry George.[19] Charles H. Jenkins—the elder brother of Jesse Jenkins—had a similar background.

The previous decade had badly battered the hope of displacing one of the two major parties. The frustrations had driven many in the Union Labor Party to the desperate hope that fielding the periodic protest ticket might suffice at pushing one or the the other major organization—most likely the Democrats—to embrace radical reform.

George clearly hoped to foster such an approach when he turned up in the same city as the founding convention of the Union Labor Party, though he insisted that his presence "is no way connected to

18 "Labor Leads the Way," *Chicago Daily Inter Ocean*, February 23, 1887, p. 6; Selcer and Foster, *Written in Blood*, vol. 1, 101, 104, 111. See also Symmes M. Jelley, *Voice of Labor* (Philadelphia, Chicago, Kansas City, San Francisco: H. J. Smith & Co., 1888), ii.

19 "The Wind-Up. Close of the Union Labor Convention," *Cincinnati Enquirer*, February 25, 1887, p. 5; "Where Will It End? Union and United Laborites Striving to Reach an Agreement," *Cincinnati Commercial Gazette*, May 16, 1888, p. 8; *History of Texas, Together with a Biographical History of Tarrant and Parker Counties* (Chicago: Lewis, 1895); Buckley B. Paddock, ed., *A Twentieth Century History and Biographical Record of North and West Texas* (Chicago: Lewis, 1906).

the convention." On Monday night, February 21, he spoke at Cincinnati's new Music Hall. Clustered about him on the platform were Leo Miller, the spiritualist-turned-anarchist from Chicago; Joel J. Hoyt, the old Greenbacker; Union Laborite Samuel Crocker, then living in Kansas; and a series of prominent local trade unionists.[20] The *Cincinnati Enquirer* reprinted George's entire speech, but what was really important was not what he said but where he was saying it.

Later, when George got back to New York with John McMackin, he explicitly declared:

> I had nothing whatever to do with the Labor Convention now being held in Cincinnati. I simply went there to deliver a lecture for the land and labor party, which is well organized in Cincinnati. We could have swamped the National Industrial Convention, but our people would have nothing to do with it.

McMackin had come along "just to see how matters were progressing, as he will soon make a trip as an organizer. When our work was finished we started home, and that is all there is about it." With regard to the Union Labor Party, McMackin added that a third party needed to avoid being plagued by "too many special hobbies, and that it would be hard work to get a platform." Such a party, argued McMackin, would likely consist of "a good sprinkling of cranks of all descriptions."[21]

In fact George had already decided that an occasional independent campaign for protest voting might be useful for raising issues and

20 "The Cincinnati Convention. No Room for Delegates Who Believe in the Land Theories of Henry George," *Chicago Daily Inter Ocean*, February 22, 1887, p. 5; "George. The Land Reformer on the Rostrum," *Cincinnati Enquirer*, February 22, 1887, p. 3; "Land and Labor. A Great Demonstration in Cincinnati," *The Standard* [New York], February 26, 1887, p. 1. See also "Mr. Henry George" under "Political. Prospects for a Large Attendence [sic] at the Polyglot Convention at Cincinnati," *Chicago Times*, February 22, 1887, p. 6; "United Labor Party," *Chicago Daily Inter Ocean*, February 26, 1887, p. 2.

21 "Henry George on the Cincinnati Convention," *Cincinnati Commercial Gazette*, February 24, 1887, p. 8.

demonstrating public interest in a particular concern, but serious politics required working within the two-party system. Moreover, the emergence of the Union Labor Party raised a real question about whether his own United Labor Party should fold itself into the broader national current. Instead, though, George decided to dismantle his organization in the interests of the Democrats. The purge started with the socialists but would continue until he had destroyed the party that had run him for mayor.

This then put George into a new kind of relationship with William A. A. Carsey, who had assisted Hewitt against him. The *New York Times* report on the testimony described Carsey as "the leader of one of the anti-monopoly bodies which makes themselves known during State and local elections, and who has managed occasionally to secure a minor office in return for services rendered."[22]

The executive committee of Carsey's Antimonopoly League met February 21 at the Queen City Hotel in Cincinnati. A James E. Curtiss of Kansas, listed as the secretary of the committee,

decided not to attend the Greenback Labor Conference for the reason that it is the purpose of the managers of that conference to arrange for the nomination of Presidential candidates, which is contrary to the policy adopted by the Anti-Monopoly League of supporting candidates and parties who will adopt anti-monopoly principles.

While there is no James E. Curtiss in the Kansas census, a "James W. Curtiss" later served as Buffalo's police commissioner and might well have presented credentials.[23]

Meanwhile, as Carsey worked for the Democrats to misdirect the Union Labor Party, Charles A. Henrie did much the same for the

22 "Knights Badly Organized," *New York Times*.

23 "Anti-Monopolists, Not to Attend," *Cincinnati Enquirer*, February 22, 1887, p. 8. See also James W. Curtiss, Acting Commissioner, Board of Police at Buffalo, *Manual of the Common Council, Containing a Sketch of Buffalo* (Buffalo: Wenborne-Sumner Co., 1897), 213, 242.

Republicans in the United Labor Party. This was the same fellow who later discussed resolving a Kansas labor dispute by deciding to

> get some dynamite and nitro-glycerine and put it in bottles, and put it under the macadam of the street from the depot up town, and the tramp of a good many people over the nitro-glycerine or dynamite concealed amid the rocks would probably cause an explosion.

Such, at least, was the version of Parsons's message that reached the authorities through Henrie.[24]

Henrie apparently implied that he had acquired his "socialistic and anarchistic" ideas working in Chicago. In reality, he came from an old American family, and his parents had married in Ohio. They lived downstate in Salem, Illinois—the birthplace of William Jennings Bryan—before moving to Kansas. Henrie married Margaret Mcintosh, born in Grafton, West Virginia, with her own ties to the adjacent corner of Ohio. Certainly, when he later found himself wanted for questioning in Kansas, Henrie turned up in Belmont County, Ohio. He also reportedly had a fondness for using aliases.[25] In Kansas, however, Henrie became the editor of the *Labor Chieftain* and operated the *Topeka Post*, an organ of the Knights of the Labor.

Once asked whether Henrie was a socialist, an old friend of his doubted it, though he had been "educated in that line," meaning that he understood "socialistic and anarchistic" rhetoric. Certainly, Henrie flitted around the edges of existing labor movements, however explicitly self-contradictory others thought them to be. He had been a member of the Typographical Union, edited a series of short-lived newspapers, and corresponded with Terrence Powderly, the Grand Workman of the Knights of Labor. He also participated

---

24 *Legislative Investigation of Coffeyville*, 179, 180, 181, 182, 183–9, 196, 197.

25 *David Benton and Nancy Pitts. Their Ancestors and Descendants, 1620–1920* (Rochester: DuBois Press, 1921), 93–4; *Legislative Investigation of Coffeyville*, 49, 137.

in the efforts of George's United Labor Party to establish a national presence, though he could have represented nothing more than a paper organization, comparable to Carsey's in New York. A neighbor later said that Henrie had received $150 to attend a national convention in 1888. Then, too, as we have seen, Henrie had become a prime mover among the handful of Kansans associated with the anarchist International Working People's Association, the so-called Black International.[26]

Henrie's critique of electoral action by the Union Labor Party might have made sense for an anarchist. However, his support for the United Labor Party seems to have been aimed primarily at keeping the insurgency divided.[27]

Approaching the 1888 Elections

The ferocious winters of the previous two years proved to be preludes to the disaster that befell the country at the start of 1888. From January 12 to 14, a terrible wave of storms swept the West from Montana down to Texas and east to the Great Lakes and beyond. The temperature fell as low as 53 degrees below zero. Because it came on so quickly, it caught many isolated rural schoolhouses still in session and came to be remembered as the "Schoolhouse Blizzard."

Then, over the weekend of March 10–11, several weather systems swept the United States. One rolled across Minnesota, Wisconsin, and Michigan before gaining strength over the Great

26   "United Labor. Dr. Edw. McGlynn Chairman of the Committee on Platform," *Cincinnati Commercial Gazette*, May 16, 1888, p. 8. See also "United Labor. A Desire to Join Forces With Other Organizations" under "In Convention. The Two Labor Parties at Work," *Cincinnati Enquirer*, May 16, 1888, p. 8; "In the Cause of Labor—The Two Cincinnati Conventions," *Chicago Herald*, May 16, 1888, p. 3; Henrie to Powderly, Dec. 23, 1887, cited in *Workingmen's Democracy*, 143; *Legislative Investigation of Coffeyville*, 178, 196, 198.

27   "United Labor. Dr. Edw. McGlynn," *Cincinnati Commercial Gazette*. See also "United Labor," *Cincinnati Enquirer*; "In the Cause of Labor," *Chicago Herald*.

Lakes. A second started in the Gulf of Mexico, driving ferocious winds and rain east across the lower South before entering the Atlantic, where it veered north just along the coast. This latter system dropped severe rain from the Virginia coast up to Philadelphia.

The heavy rains reached New York just as the other storm from the Lakes pulled temperatures rapidly down below freezing, coating everything with a thick layer of ice. Then the rain turned to snow, which dropped over four feet in places before it stopped on March 14. The unrelenting winds whipped the storm into a "Great White Hurricane" and left drifts up to forty feet. Nature had brought the northeastern United States to a standstill. With no reason to venture out, people stayed in bed or piled on layers of clothes to move about their inadequately heated homes, confronted with closed workplaces and no wages, though still needing food and rent.[28]

The weather put great strain on the expectations of the rich about their profit level while also pushing the workers and farmers to action. The nascent workers' movement in Denver, for example, generated a concrete new proposal around which it proposed to unite all insurgents. Sympathetic papers around the country reprinted Joseph R. Buchanan's nine-word platform from the *Labor Enquirer*: "Government ownership and operation of the railroads and telegraph."[29]

The Union Labor Party had been quick to organize itself, but others hoped to get a jump on the nominations, including the Equal Rights Party, which fought for women's suffrage. While the larger organizations sought to influence other political currents, the Equal Rights Party was continuing Victoria Woodhull's stillborn effort of 1872 to establish a viable third party around a single issue. Functioning by then under the leadership of Belva Ann Lockwood, a Washington lawyer with a national reputation, the group came to an agreement

---

28 Jose Marti, "New York Under the Snow."

29 Joseph Ray Buchanan, *The Story of a Labor Agitator* (New York: Outlook Co., 1903), 430.

with a handful of Greenbackers and other reformers who supported woman's suffrage, and promised to place a major emphasis on it in their electoral work.

The Equal Rights Party held its convention on Washington's birthday in 1888 at the national capital —a year after the Union Labor Party was founded. A reporter described the forty-five delegates at the first session as having pockets stuffed with tracts. One simply shrugged an admission that theirs would be a cranks' convention, "a sort of *omnium gatherum*, including all who are dissatisfied with the old parties." The reporter summarized the attendees' sense that "all the profits of labor instead of going to the corporations and capitalists should go to the government for the benefit of the whole people."[30] Yet, the platform they adopted centered on Greenbackism with little attention to either suffrage or socialism.

Almost immediately renaming itself the Industrial Reform Party (or sometimes just the Industrial Party in the press), the new organization brought several worthies to the convention. These included Robert S. Tharin, Southern, white, and a longtime opponent of the restoration of power to the planters, and O. P. McMains, the leader of the movement against the Maxwell Grants, fresh from the bloodshed in New Mexico. The ubiquitous Carsey also attended.

With a new name and the platform out of the way, the smaller group of attendees present on the second day decided simply to nominate a national ticket, though some delegates clearly thought the move premature and probably divisive. The pick for president was Albert Ellis Redstone, a New York native roughly fifty years of age. Although he had run for office as a Greenbacker, he became more well known as an inventor and engineer. He had an industrial operation going in Indianapolis during the Civil War, when he offered the War Department a pioneering design for a tank or "land monitor." He then married and moved his family to California, where he became active in the local Workingmen's Party, the Greenbackers, and the

---

30 "The Industrial Party. Their National Convention Meets Today," Washington *Evening Star*, February 22, 1888, p. 1, col. 6.

mysterious "Red International."[31] His vice presidential candidate, J. A. Colvin, was so obscure that even the census taker seems to have missed him—at least under that name.

In the end, though, Lockwood remained dissatisfied and decided again to run her own campaign. She initially picked Alfred Henry Love of the Universal Peace Union as her vice presidential candidate, but he had no interest in serving as second in line to any commander in chief. Lockwood replaced him with Charles Stuart Weld, the son of those stalwart old abolitionists Theodore Dwight Weld and Angelina Grimké.[32]

Then, in mid-May, the Union Labor Party returned to Cincinnati to nominate its national slate. The subhead of the article in the *Cincinnati Enquirer* declared, "Nearly a Thousand Delegates Now in the City." The *Commercial Gazette*, more accurately, described several hundred delegates arriving, including "prominent Laborites, both Union and United, from all parts of the country."[33] That is, the United Labor Party—the followers of Henry George, now without George—arrived to hold a convention alongside that of the Union Labor Party.

31   "Redstone and Colvin. The Industrial Reform Conference Nominate a Presidential Ticket," Washington *Evening Star*, February 23, 1888, p. 3, col. 7; "Another Reform Party. Candidates Selected and Executive Committee Chosen. The Delegates Dissatisfied. A Feeling That Action Has Been Premature," Washington *Critic*, February 23, 1888, p. 1, col. 7; Albert E. Redstone, "Land Monitor" [watercolor], August 18, 1862, National Archives and Records Administration, Records of the Office of the Chief of Ordnance; "Four Tickets Already in the Field," *New York Times*, May 20, 1888, p. 10. See also Jay O'Connell, *Co-Operative Dreams: A History of the Kaweah Colony* (Van Nuys: Raven River Press, 1999), 24–5, 60–1, 71, 82, 171.

32   Laura Kerr, *The Girl Who Ran for President* (New York: Thomas Nelson, 1947); Jill Norgren, *Belva Lockwood: The Woman Who Would Be President* (New York: New York University Press, 2007). See also "Four Tickets Already in the Field," *New York Times*.

33   "Labor and Politics. Gathering for the National Conventions," *Cincinnati Enquirer*, May 14, 1888, p. 8; "For Labor's Cause—The Two Conventions Here To-Day," *Cincinnati Enquirer*, May 15, 1888, p. 5; "Union Labor. Everything in Readiness for To-Day's National Convention," *Cincinnati Commercial Gazette*, May 15, 1888, p. 4. See also "Men of Two Labor Parties," *Chicago Herald*, May 15, 1888, p. 3.

Union Labor's May 1888 nominating convention in the Odeon seems to have drawn far fewer attendees than the founding convention. The convention noted the deaths of four of its founders since February 1887.[34] They did not mention the killing of the strike leader, N. M. Lovin, near Muscogee in January.

Alongside the Union Labor Party convention, the United Labor Party assembled in the Grand Opera House—sometimes called the Grant Opera House—in hopes of determining its policies in the coming election. Over the previous year, George had managed to exclude the socialists, who went on to form their own short-lived Progressive Labor Party and distinguish themselves from what became the Union Labor Party upstate. By 1888, George had openly declared his support for the Democrats based on his support for "free trade," though the Democrats did not actually have this position. George, explained one newspaper, "does not believe that the time is ripe for a labor candidate for the Presidency," while his childhood friend and old ally, Father Edward McGlynn, did. McGlynn stuck to the party and tried to help it position itself to foster the George idea. On Monday night, May 14, McGlynn spoke to "about seven hundred people, including ladies in the audience."[35]

Union Labor delegates talked freely about finding some common ground as a basis for unity between their party and the United Laborites. One predicted "a combination of the three parties," because, in fact, a handful of Greenbackers had also convened to condemn the formation of the Union Labor Party. These stalwarts did not share the view of many old comrades who saw "no opposition on the part of the

34 "Knocked Clean Out. Union Labor Will Have Nothing to Do with Georgeism," *Cincinnati Commercial Gazette*, May 17, 1888, p. 1.

35 The Coming Labor Convention," *Chicago Herald*, May 14, 1888, p. 3. See also Manuel S. Shanaberger, "Edward McGlynn: A Missionary Priest and His Social Gospel," *U.S. Catholic Historian* 13 (Summer 1995): 23–47; "Dr. Edward McGlynn. A Three-Hours' Talk at the Grand Opera House," *Cincinnati Commercial Gazette*, May 15, 1888, p. 4; "The United Labor Party" under "For Labor's Cause," *Cincinnati Enquirer*. See also "National Labor Conventions," *Chicago Daily Times*, May 15, 1888, p. 2.

Union Labor party to the Greenback party, and vice versa." Most prominent among these reportedly stalwart Greenbackers skeptical of the Union Labor Party was Samuel F. Cary, a local figure described in the press as "an old-time Greenbacker." In fact, while Cary had lent his name as a vice presidential candidate of the Greenbackers in 1876, he "still claim[ed] to be a Democrat." Cary's presence clearly aimed to keep the Union Labor effort divided.[36]

In point of fact, though, representatives of other insurgent parties also mingled among them. In addition to a handful of identifiable members of the Socialist Labor Party, the *Commercial Gazette* noted "a sprinkling" of Industrial Reformers, including their candidate for president, Albert E. Redstone, of California.[37]

The Odeon where Union Labor convened was "very handsomely decorated with the National colors and with the banners of a number of the ward Labor clubs of this city." Reportedly "about 120 delegates" attended, "including four ladies in the hall, and an audience of eight in the gallery." In the end, they actually credentialed 243 delegates, not counting the seated representative of the Women's Christian Temperance Union. Together, Illinois, Indiana, and Ohio had well over 41 percent of the convention. Other states included Alabama, Arkansas, California, Colorado, Connecticut, Iowa, Kansas, Kentucky, Maine, Michigan, Missouri, Nebraska, New York, Ohio, Pennsylvania, Texas, West Virginia, and Wisconsin.[38]

Arguments about the necessity for unity largely came to nought. The women at the Union Labor Party convention included Juliet Severence of Milwaukee and Mrs. Marion Todd and Mrs. Sarah Emery of Michigan. Severence, a spiritualist and socialist, discussed

36 "Union Labor. Everything in Readiness," *Cincinnati Commercial Gazette*; "The Greenbackers. A Meeting to Revive Old Associations" under "For Labor's Cause," *Cincinnati Enquirer*. "Fighting Greenbackers" under "Union Labor," *Cincinnati Commercial Gazette*; "Greenback Conference. Greatly Disturbed Over the Desertion of Chairman Gillette, of Iowa," *Cincinnati Commercial Gazette*, May 17, 1888, p. 6.
37 "Union Labor. Everything in Readiness," *Cincinnati Commercial Gazette*.
38 "Where Will It End?" *Cincinnati Commercial Gazette*.

women's suffrage with a reporter, saying that she had seen "no opposition except on the part of some of the delegates from the South."[39] That opposition justified Lockwood's Equal Rights Party in fielding its own ticket.

McGlynn presided when the conference committee met at the Gibson House, and the press reported the unity and high hopes expressed by participants. The two sides agreed on everything except the land tax measure, over which debate became "quite animated." Many Union Labor delegates expressed a willingness to adopt George's land tax, but the United Labor Party leader insisted that any independent political action should avoid everything but the "Single Tax." One Union Labor leader told a reporter that the United Labor Party would not actually nominate a ticket because it "dare not show their weakness. They can not poll 5,000 votes in the United States, and will either indorse our ticket and platform or support the old party nominees."[40]

The Union Labor Party had several prominent potential candidates, including James B. Weaver, Henry Smith, Gilbert Delamatyr, and others, all of whom held seats in Congress and hoped to keep them. In the end, though, the Midwestern delegations swept the convention for Alson Jenness Streeter. The press described him as "a portly man, with flowing white beard and hair, and withal a fine looking man." Fifty-five years old New York native residing at New Windsor, Illinois, Streeter had gone into business as a farmer and stock dealer, but had also spent two years in the legislature and was then ending a four-year term in the state senate.[41] He also owned hundreds of acres in the West, including Texas.

---

39   "Union Labor. Everything in Readiness," *Cincinnati Commercial Gazette*.

40   Ibid.; "The Conference Committee" under "Where Will It End?" *Cincinnati Commercial Gazette*; "The Conference. An All-Night Session Probable—The Other Committees" under "In Convention," *Cincinnati Enquirer*; "The Conference Committee" under "Where Will It End?" *Cincinnati Commercial Gazette*.

41   "Knocked Clean Out," *Cincinnati Commercial Gazette*, p. 6; Alfred W. Newcombe's *Alson Jenness Streeter—An Agrarian Liberal* (Springfield: The Journal of the Illinois State Historical Society, 1945–46). "Mr. Streeter Is Grateful. The Union Labor Party's Candidate for President," *Brooklyn Daily Eagle*, May 21, 1888, p. 4.

For vice president, Union Labor selected a sixty-five-year-old farmer from the Little Rock area named Charles E. Cunningham. He had actually lived the life of a Western entrepreneur more than that of a Southern agriculturalist. A Maryland-born Missourian, Cunningham had crossed the Mississippi River early in life and participated in the California Gold Rush. Returning to Missouri before the war, he had been a Whig and headed south after the war as something of a "carpetbagger." An early Greenbacker in Arkansas, Cunningham's nomination, in part, reflected the national movement's solidarity with a state insurgency that remained crippled from its inception.[42]

The United Labor Party did not begin its convention at the scheduled time of noon on May 15, but delayed another two and a half hours for "a score of delegates" to assemble before beginning. In the end, representatives of fourteen states met in a hall that "was cold and dark, only two electric lights furnishing the illuminating power." It limped into the second day, and adopted both women's suffrage and "the defense of all people, no matter what sex or color." However, since it already had one plank for its platform, the focus seemed to settle on how best to deal with the Union Labor Party meeting across the way.[43]

United Labor responded to the Streeter ticket by spending its last session on Thursday making its own nomination, as urged by "E. A. Henry" of Kansas. The name is missing from the census, and likely

42 On Cunningham, see *Biographical and Historical Memoir of Pulaski, Jefferson, Lonoke, Faulkner, Grant, Saline, Perry, Garland and Hot Spring Counties, Arkansas* (Chicago, Nashville, and St. Louis: The Goodspeed Publishing Co., 1889), 438–49; Lause, *The Civil War's Last Campaign: James B. Weaver, the National Greenback–Labor Party and the Politics of Race and Section* (Lanham, MD: University Press of America, 2000), 116–17.

43 "United Labor. Dr. Edw. McGlynn," *Cincinnati Commercial Gazette*, May 16, 1888, p. 8; "United Labor. Another Day of Debate, and Now Ready for Business," *Cincinnati Commercial Gazette*, May 17, 1888, p. 6. See also "United Labor. A Desire to Join Forces With Other Organizations" under "In Convention," *Cincinnati Enquirer*, May 16, 1888, p. 8; "In the Cause of Labor—The Two Cincinnati Conventions," *Chicago Herald*, May 16, 1888, p. 3; "The United Labor Party" under "For Labor's Cause," *Cincinnati Enquirer*.

represents a typographical mistake for "C. A." and a misspelling of "Henrie." He charged that the Union Labor candidates got their nominations "through trickery and fraud, and that the Democratic party had a hand in all their proceedings, as they had sent paid men here to prevent any union of the two parties."[44] To thwart the Democratic plan to keep the parties divided, the United Labor Party had to make a definitive break with the Union Labor Party.

Reporters heard rumors of John H. Blake or Victor A. Wilder of New York as the chosen candidate, but the talk increasingly centered on the thirty-six-year-old Robert H. Cowdrey, an Indiana-born druggist with a common school education. He went to Chicago's College of Pharmacy at nineteen and had remained there to run his own drugstore. He had been "a Republican up to the campaign of 1876." Three years before the convention, he gained a certain amount of public attention with his novel, *Foiled by a Lawyer: A Story of Chicago*. In it, the second wife of a prominent businessman, Stewart Graham, tries to marry off his daughter to Arthur Howard. In Cowdrey's book, however, the dastardly Mrs. Graham, a school principal, tried to thwart this plan by adopting a malleable school-marm and using her to get control of the real daughter's rightful inheritance. Cowdrey's skill as a presidential candidate did not exceed his imagination nor originality as a novelist.

Having "dressed himself in rather dapper style in anticipation of the nomination," Cowdrey held "a lighted cigar between his fingers while he made his speech of acceptance." Observers in the gallery "yelled with delight" when he mentioned "the responsibility thrust upon him," and again when he confessed that he didn't expect to be elected. A few of the more irreverent even answered with an "Amen!" "The United Labor party is a grand party, well able to take care of itself," he declared, adding that he would do what he could "to cement the bond of fraternity between all labor organizations."[45] The pledge

---

44 "United Laborites Indorse the George Theory and Wind Up Their Convention," *Cincinnati Commercial Gazette*, May 18, 1888, p. 8.

45 "M'Glynn's Man for President—Robert H. Cowdrey, of Chicago, to Head the United Labor Ticket," *Chicago Herald*, May 18, 1888, p. 5. "United Laborites Indorse the George Theory," *Cincinnati Commercial Gazette*.

directly contradicted what he was actually doing in dividing the insurgent vote.

A reporter from the *Commercial Gazette* described their nomination to vice presidential candidate of the editor of the *Anti-Monopolist*, W. H. T. Wakefield of Council Grove, Kansas. Gray-bearded and bespectacled, he had long been immersed in the development of the movement in Kansas. He had, in fact, become a member of the Videttes, founded to protect the Union Labor Party. Concerns that the Democrats might be manipulating the deliberations of the Party seems to have drawn him to the United Labor gatherings. However, he seems to have quickly reconsidered his choices, weighing the merits of resigning from the ticket. Later asked about his nomination, he responded that "I never considered myself a candidate."[46]

The nomination of Cowdrey represented a great concession to more than the Henry George Club of Chicago. Clarence S. Darrow arrived in the city that year and quickly involved himself with the Georgists. His father had been a Liberal Leaguer and small-town atheist. Darrow recounted:

At the Henry George Club I formed some congenial friendships and never missed one of their meetings; here I found a chance to talk so that I would not completely forget how to form sentences and feel at home on my feet.

Like George himself, though, Darrow campaigned for the Democrats and their incumbent president, Grover Cleveland.[47]

George's embrace of the seated administration did not kill or discredit his ideas, which continued to resonate particularly among urban reformers in the West as well as elsewhere. However, in 1888, the United Labor had transformed itself from a potential movement into

---

46 "United Laborites Indorse the George Theory," *Cincinnati Commercial Gazette. Legislative Investigation of Coffeyville*, 206, 511, 534–5; for Wakefield's testimony, see 204–6.

47 Clarence Darrow, *The Story of My Life* (New York: Da Capo Press, 1996[1932]), 43, 46–7. See also Andrew Edmund Kersten, *Clarence Darrow: American Iconoclast* (New York: Hill and Wang, 2011).

an abstract idea requiring little more from adherents than a profession of faith. Repackaged as a non-partisan "single tax," it found followers in almost every political party, and its chief adherent after George, Louis F. Post, later became the Assistant U.S. Secretary of Labor.

Certainly the believers, particularly among urban reformers, continued to gather to profess their faith. Adherents organized scattered groups from Minneapolis and St. Paul down to New Orleans. California Single Taxers organized in Los Angeles, Oakland, Sacramento, San Diego, and San Francisco, as well as the Contra Costa County Single Tax Committee in Black Diamond. A Colorado State Single Tax Association formed, with local groups in Canyon City, Mesa, Pueblo, and Denver. Kansans had a Single Tax Club in the cow town of Abilene and Grove Hill in Dickinson County, with associations in Omaha and a Henry George Single Tax Club in nearby Otoe County, Nebraska. Portland, Oregon, had a group, and a South Dakota statewide association had clubs in Gary, Madison, and Rapid City. A Texas Tax Reform Association adopted the measure, as did the El Paso Tariff Reform Club, with explicitly Single Tax groups in San Antonio and Houston.[48] However, none of these clubs felt impelled to channel their deep social criticisms of the American class structure into an independent political force.

In hindsight, the national campaign produced few real surprises. A conservative Democrat who favored the gold standard, Cleveland still alienated many industrialists with his support for lower tariffs. In the fall of 1888, the Republicans voted down his proposed Bayard–Chamberlain Treaty that resolved fishing disputes with Canada, recasting him as pro-British and blocking the support he needed among the Irish, especially in New York. Victory went to Republican Benjamin Harrison, the grandson of the U.S. victor in the battle of Tippecanoe and the father of Teddy Roosevelt's colleague in Montana's fraternity of gentlemen stranglers.[49]

48   New York *Standard*, July 3, 1890, p. 15, and Sept. 3, 1890, p. 15.
49   On this particular presidential campaign, see Charles W. Calhoun, *Minority Victory: Gilded Age Politics and the Front Porch Campaign of 1888* (Lawrence: University Press of Kansas, 2008).

Official returns gave the Streeter–Cunningham ticket of the Union Labor Party only 146,605.[50] As for the United Labor Party, the prediction that, without Henry George, it would not be able to get 5,000 votes in a national election proved correct; most members likely followed George into the Democratic Party. A few votes went to the slate of presidential electors from the Socialist Labor Party, pledged to vote "no president" in the electoral college. No returns appeared for Redstone, Lockwood, or others, and it is reasonable to assume that they did not poll enough to pose a problem.

༄

Between 1886 and 1888, cowboys on the desolate cattle ranges of the West felt the future for which they had worked slipping through their fingers. Hardly alone in this sense, they had struggled, like other workers and small proprietors, to survive the rise of the large corporations. The courts had begun to define the rules of economic and civic life more tightly, making explicit their previously vague assertions of corporate personhood. Old Joshua K. Ingalls surveyed the collapse of the Greenback, Greenback–Labor, and Antimonopolist parties, the implosion of Henry George's United Labor Party, the farce of the Industrial Reform Party, the persistence of the Equal Rights Party and the refusal of the Union Labor Party and the Socialist Labor Party to cooperate with other insurgents. Recalling the sectarian madness that had thwarted efforts to unite antislavery voters in 1848, he now asked bluntly, "Are we to have a repetition of this consummate asinine stupidity in 1888?"[51] History answered.

Yet, persistent effort always allowed for the possibility of serious, radical change. And the heartland remained remarkably stubborn. In Texas, Streeter of the Union Labor Party, in fact, carried Rains County

50 In 1891, the Illinois legislature, for reasons of its own, put Streeter within five votes of getting a seat in the U.S. Senate. J. McCan Davis, "The Senator from Illinois—Some Famous Political Combats," *Transactions of the Illinois State Historical Society for the Year 1909* (Springfield: Illinois State Historical Library, 1910), 94.

51 Ingalls, "Land Reform in 1848 and 1888," *The Truth Seeker*, April 28, 1888, p. 258, and May 5, 1888, p. 278.

by a plurality of over 45 percent. Oldham County, the epicenter of those annual Panhandle strikes, returned 24 votes for Republican Benjamin Harrison, 247 for Democrat Grover Cleveland, and 170 for Streeter—39 percent of the total vote, a vastly larger share than the party won elsewhere in the area. If we assume that the bosses and their supporters would hardly have cast such ballots, something like half of the Southern white cowboy strikers voted for a party that explicitly practiced interracial cooperation against the restored Democratic power.[52]

Such was the shadow of the great cowboy strike.

---

52 *Tribune Almanac and Political Register for 1890* (New York: Tribune Association, c. 1890), 84, and *Tribune Almanac and Political Register for 1892* (New York: Tribune Association, c. 1892), 287.

SEVEN

From Coffeyville to Woodsdale

Kansas Variations on the Uses of Political Violence

On October 18, 1888, a teeth-rattling blast shocked the peaceful residents of quiet little Coffeyville, Kansas. Montgomery County Deputy Sheriff N. M. Clifford saw the smoke billowing over one neighborhood and hurried over. There he found about 150 people milling about in the yard of what had been the house of the local railroad clerk, Henry M. Upham. One of those neighbors had already found Upham wandering in a stunned daze among the scraps of kindling and plaster and took him in, though his wife and daughter were still missing. Dr. J. A. Wood, who also arrived early, began sorting through the crowd, recruiting those who knew the layout of the house to get into the ruins and locate Mrs. Upham and their daughter. They found both of them, though they had lost a lot of blood and had compound fractures in their twisted arms and legs. Clifford immediately began gathering evidence and mapping out a quick plan to find the parties responsible for the blast.

The Coffeyville explosion shattered the public peace just as voters prepared to cast their ballots in the 1888 election campaign. Local law enforcement found leads and began to pursue them. A private detective took up the investigation, and a formal investigation by a new state government documented what little we know of the event. More importantly, perhaps, the incident demonstrated a variation in the uses of political violence: wherein the dominant authority in the state leveled the accusation of violence to deal with insurgent threats. Finally, the fate of one of the very founders of the state demonstrated that good old-fashioned murder, committed in broad daylight, remained a perfectly viable option for those in charge of the government. In the end, developments in Kansas raise serious questions about the commonplace faith that insurgent movements faded because one or both of the two dominant parties assimilated their proposals and personnel.

Conspiracies and Bombs

Republicans in Kansas, like the Democrats in Texas, found themselves under serious attack. In Winfield, three papers, representing three parties, battled for readership and influence. The Republican *Winfield Courier* vied with *The Telegram* of the Democrats. Over in the Hackney Building, Henry Vincent and his allies labored on the *Non-Conformist*, arguing the merits of the Union Labor Party.

Located in Cowley County on the state's border with the Indian Territory, Winfield represented the southernmost outpost of the Kansas insurgency and the most immediate connection to the movement in Texas. After all, as Greenbackism ebbed and flowed nationally, it had actually grown stronger in both Texas and Kansas.

Republicans believed that the tolerance Kansas accorded to the Union Labor Party virtually invited the kind of violence their papers imagined to be taking place in the streets of Chicago. At the Union Labor state convention in Wichita, stories circulated of a secret organization within the party that controlled and dictated its policies.

Some of the Union Labor militants, such as transplanted Iowa Greenbacker James Culverwell, used rhetoric that might well confuse those inclined to superficial reading. Hardly a young hothead, Culverwell was an English-born forty-four-year-old family man, whose parents had emigrated to Canada. He had found his way to Davenport by 1860, married sixteen years later, and become a Greenbacker before taking his family to Kansas. In the wake of the Haymarket Trial, he urged his fellow Union Laborites and Videttes to organize what he called the "National Army of Rescue" to save the Chicago anarchists.[1] Such talk could easily conjure images of armed Kansas anarchists marching about the countryside gathering weapons, but Culverwell's "army of rescue" meant a successful third party.

Edwin P. Greer of the *Winfield Courier* caught wind of these rumors initially from George W. Poorman, the son of a Republican politician back in Ohio. Poorman had gone to work as a printer on the *Non-Conformist*, but quarrelled with the Vincents; his politics had always been closer to those of the *Courier*, a mere two blocks away. Greer encouraged him to dig up information on the conspiracy, and Poorman came back claiming to have infiltrated a group called the Videttes in South Haven, Kansas, giving Greer a copy of what he called its secret handbook. Using this for background, Greer set to work on an exposé, charging the Vincents with being leaders of the secret society, which he accused of taking blood oaths, using secret codes and signs, and generally being revolutionary and treasonable. Before it appeared, Poorman collected his payoff and left for Belmont County, Ohio.[2] Because infiltrating a group and acquiring its secrets would probably have required more than a few days, Poorman and Greer may have been working on this longer than they later implied.

On October 4, this full exposé of the Videttes appeared in the *Winfield Courier*, from which Republican papers across the state reprinted it under headings such as "Evidences of Anarchism in Kansas Are Increasing." Kansas, it appeared, faced a full-blown, homegrown revolutionary conspiracy.

1   James Culverwell, *A History of the National Army of Rescue* (Dentonia, Kansas: Author, 1888).

2   *Legislative Investigation of Coffeyville*, 49, 54.

About a week later, Greer met Charles A. Henrie in the Windsor Hotel. Henrie promised more information. On October 18, the *Courier* publised a second exposé.[3]

Around 11 a.m. on that day, a man stepped up to the counter of H. M. Upham at the Pacific Express Company office on Eighth and Walnut in Coffeyville. Although later said to have grown up in New England, the thirty-six-year-old Upham had come as a child with his missionary parents to the Cherokee nation but had lived in Kansas for years. His visitor presented a package for delivery to one "L. Louden" in Winfield.[4] The man seemed contented that the next train there would be at 4:30 the next morning, and paid his twenty-five cents to cover the package's delivery.

Upham later said that his customer identified himself as "P. Jason" and described him as "about five feet six or seven inches, dark eyes, dark hair, and dark complexion," weighing about 130 pounds. He guessed the man to have been his own age, but added that he might look younger without "a dark beard that was of about two or three weeks' growth," though Upham thought the beard might have been false. In addition, the man "had on a soft hat, narrow brim, and low-crowned; white shirt, and turned-down collar, and long neck-tie; rather nervous in his actions, and winked his eyes quickly."[5] The mysterious Mr. Jason assured careful treatment of his package by explaining that it contained bottles of medicine, which would also explain any rattling sounds.

Soon after, Upham locked up for a long lunch with his wife Emma and their adopted daughter. Since the little depot had no place to keep packages that needed more careful handling, he usually took them to his nearby home for safekeeping. He entered the house through the dark room which he, as an amateur photographer, had just equipped with the necessary chemicals. It seemed a perfectly reasonable place to stash the box.

---

3 Ibid., 69, 70, 74, 75, 97. Henrie continued to edit the *Topeka Post*, claiming that it was the state organ of the Knights of Labor. He discontinued it in September 188.

4 Upham was the son of Rev. William P. Upham, a missionary in the Cherokee Nation, according to the U.S. 1860 Census, 1875 Kansas State Census, and U.S. 1900 Census for Coffeyville.

5 *Legislative Investigation of Coffeyville*, 246.

After a bite, Upham knew that he did not need to hurry back to the depot, and decided to take advantage of the daylight by photographing his daughter, promising both her and Emma a quick lesson on how to develop the plate. Around 3:30 p.m., the three of them crowded into the darkroom. Needing water for the process, Upham went out into the backyard and started for the cistern.

At that point an explosion threw enough wood into the air to knock him to the ground. Neighbors ran to help, as well as to rubberneck. Fortunately, Dr. Wood and Deputy Sheriff Clifford arrived when they did. Clifford, a Confederate veteran from Texas and an experienced lawman, had seen enough blood to keep his wits about him. He called in the city marshal and had him close off the area. He then located Upham and took rapid action to find the mystery man who had delivered the package. Back at the station, Clifford sent his own decoy package in hopes of luring the person who expected to receive it, and telegraphed the sheriff in Winfield, alerting him to bring in L. Louden.

Deputy Clifford also quickly covered the town's few hotels, boardinghouses, and restaurants, asking for someone who answered the man's description and finding one clear lead. The landlord at the Southern Hotel told him that a man of that description had registered there with another man. Just before lunch, both had boarded an eastbound train for Valeda, a tiny settlement in Labette County. Clifford sent urgent telegrams up the line in hopes of alerting the authorities ahead of the culprits' arrival.

Later, I. M. Waldrop, the Valeda agent of the Missouri Pacific Railroad and Pacific Express Company and an acquaintance of Upham, had a strange encounter. He returned from supper to the depot, where he found two men in the waiting room. When he later got the alert about suspicious characters, he immediately thought to himself, "My God! Those men at the station!" The two of them got a ticket to Chetopa, and asked about connections from there.

At about 10 a.m. the next morning, Clifford showed up in Winfield, where the sheriff assured him that no "L. Louden" lived there. Clifford then hurried to the express office to alert the local agent about the decoy box, which the agent confirmed had arrived from Coffeyville. At the end of conversation, the deputy pushed a revolver across the counter toward him, with some advice: "If anyone claims that box, pull the gun on him and place him under arrest," he said. "Then send for an officer." Clifford then went outside and sat down to wait for someone to claim it. Nobody did.

The more time passed during which no one picked up the package, the less likely it seemed that anyone would. Then, too, as news of the Coffeyville bombing swept through Winfield, the chances grew even more slim. In the end, Clifford sighed and boarded a train for home.

Greer later recounted how he had heard about Coffeyville. He claimed that he ran into an acquaintance at the Farmers' Bank, who told him about the bomb. A conductor on a train from Coffeyville supposedly had brought the news to Winfield. Greer said that, after the news, he retreated to his office to brood over what it meant.

Greer's account is implausible in every particular. Clifford had telegraphed the story to the authorities in Winfield the previous day, so the word was already out. It is hardly imaginable that, after two major stories sounding the alarm about bomb-making Union Laborites in Kansas, Greer had to ponder the meaning of the explosion. Yet, if we are to believe the Republican editor, it was only after weighing the evidence that the *Courier* claimed that it had been vindicated in its warning about the violent nature of the threat posed by critics of monopoly.

S. W. Chase, then a self-described "red-hot Republican," had been at the First National Bank of Winfield that day and encountered a group of men gathered around the central table in the lobby. As Chase finished his business with the teller, he heard the group discussing whether to tell the Vincents to leave town on the next train, though "others were in favor of hanging them." According to him, the men assumed that the *Non-Conformist* group had been "the parties that caused the dynamite explosion."[6]

6 Ibid., 254.

Unobstructed by the lack of any proof, Greer and the Republicans reported that the Vincents had shipped the box to Winfield with the goal of blowing up the *Courier* building. As the Republican press bounced this story around the state over the next week or so, the governor called for the arrest and conviction of the guilty parties. Although Vincent's *Non-Conformist* had repeatedly urged the Republican officials to investigate the charges, they never did. Indeed, the officials curiously failed to pursue any of the leads generated by local law enforcement.

Still, the story conveniently dominated the public discussion on the eve of the 1888 election, contributing directly to the Republicans' success in placing Lyman U. Humphrey in the governor's mansion.

The Investigation

The Vincents emerged from the election determined to clear their name. Given the disinterest of the state authorities in the case, they hired the forty-year-old Ohio-born cattleman Israel D. Highleyman to investigate further. Highleyman had periodically conducted investigations as a detective "since 1874, I believe," with the Ohio Valley Detective Association and as a freelance investigator. He had also been "connected with the Missouri Pacific and M. K. & T. railroads," starting in the investigation of claims and then moving on to the tax department. Seven years before, he had moved to Chetopa where he raised livestock, dealt in lumber, and took what private investigative work came his way.[7]

Highleyman lived where the trail of the two suspects had run cold. Nevertheless, he started his inquiries in Coffeyville with Upham, who provided a detailed description of the moment when "we were standing on a dray or just on the platform of the depot at Coffeyville." Upham also told Highleyman of the man who had

---

7 Ibid., 49, 54, 247–8, 253. For the Ohio Valley Detective Association out of Bellaire, see *Annual Report of the Secretary of State, to the Governor of the State of Ohio for the Year 1886* (Columbus: State Printer, 1887), 140.

dropped off the package that "he could identify him among any number of men if he would see him." Or, if he had a good photograph, "he said he could recognize the party even if he had taken the false beard off."[8]

It quickly emerged that descriptions of the two suspects fit those of Charles Henrie and George W. Poorman. Henrie described Poorman to William H. T. Wakefield as an important Republican operative.[9] Poor Wakefield, who had originally meandered from the Union Labor Party over fear of Democratic influences, found himself at one point with United Labor people who had ties to the Republicans.

Both Poorman and Henrie may have had their own grievances against the Vincents. Poorman had quit his job at the Vincents' paper within hours of the *Courier's* first exposé, and members of the Republican county committee later admitted that they had paid to get him to Ohio after the bombing. The *Courier* acknowledged that Henrie had provided more allegations linking the Videttes to the anarchists, and his own wife said that he regularly met with Republican editors and officials and traveled around the state using aliases. He himself talked about learning how to make bombs, which, on one occasion, he publicly urged strikers to use—advice which they wisely shunned. Within days of these connections, two men showed up in Coffeyville with a bomb that effectively blasted the Union Labor Party to oblivion and pushed the Republicans to an even heftier margin of victory at the polls.

Moreover, an acquaintance of Henrie's over the previous four years reported that he had left Topeka a day or two before the Coffeyville incident and had not returned until after it. A neighbour heard Henrie heading into the house around 10 or 11 p.m.[10]

When Highleyman tried to find Henrie, he was unsuccessful. As of mid-November, he "instituted a search for him in Topeka by other

---

8 *Legislative Investigation of Coffeyville*, 246, 251.
9 Ibid., 534–5.
10 Exhibit 28, Edwin French, Linn County, before John C. Cannon, notary public, September 2, 1888. *Legislative Investigation of Coffeyville*, 178.

parties; who they are I do not know. I obtained the information, but how I do not know, that Mr. Henrie was not here at that time." "I learned that Mr. Henrie was not in Topeka," he explained elsewhere, "and his wife did not know where he was; that information, as I said before—I do not know from whom I got it, nor how I got it."[11] The disappearance of a newspaper editor from the state capital seemed suspicious enough.

Highleyman hoped to gain evidence against Poorman, forcing him to testify against Henrie. He contacted William M. Drugan, who he had known "nearly all my life," and who had police connections in Belmont County, Ohio, where Poorman was hiding. It turned out that, in that small community, Drugan also knew Poorman. Highleyman tried to send a camera and equipment to Bellaire, a process hampered by Drugan's inexperience with photography.[12]

Then, Drugan reported a remarkable development. A newcomer had turned up, "a man by the name of Henrie," who got his mail through the Poormans. Drugan reported that mail also came and went from Greer in Winfield. Rumors were already swirling in Kansas that the new Republican governor-elect Humphrey planned to appoint Henrie to a clerkship in the state's new labor department. Drugan also reported that Poorman had turned up in town and sent a policeman to question Poorman's father, who "came very near fainting." Convinced that the Poormans knew something, Drugan advised offering a $20,000 reward, a fifth payable upon Poorman's arrest and the balance on his conviction. Drugan had confidence that Poorman "will squeal when he is arrested."[13]

As inquiries seemed to make slow progress in Ohio, the investigation in Kansas fell apart. Convinced that he had enough to get the authorities started on an official investigation, Highleyman approached Samuel C. Elliott, the prosecutor for Montgomery County, in

---

11 Ibid., 247, 253.
12 Ibid., 245, 248, 249, 251, 252, 253.
13 Ibid., 249, 250, 251–2. Drugan to Highleyman, November 21, December 5, 1888, Exhibits 33 and 34 in *Legislative Investigation of Coffeyville*, 253.

Independence. Elliott responded "that he had looked that matter up carefully, and was satisfied himself that there had been no crime committed." When pressed, he agreed to consult the state's attorney general and get back to Highleyman. Even if the state approved, he said, he could do nothing without Upham making a complaint. Then, he coughed, rose suddenly, and said that he had an engagement.[14] Plainly the county attorney wanted to hear no more about the explosion. Besides, his term was running out.

On December 2, Highleyman again reached out to Upham, whose circumstances had changed considerably. Certainly, he and his family had been through a lot. There had been a question for a while as to whether his wife and daughter would survive. Dr. Wood did his utmost and even moved into the Upham house to look after them. It took some weeks and they remembered little of the blast, though just before the explosion, they had heard a hiss. The express company awarded Upham $700 and arranged to transfer him to a position back east, in Maine.[15]

When Highleyman heard from Drugan that Henrie was back in Ohio with Poorman, he tried urgently to secure Upham's cooperation, but found him much more muddled. The clerk replied:

> I can't make the complaint against this party; I don't know anything about him, haven't even seen his picture, and I have no evidence at hand that he is guilty of any offense against me. If he has committed an offense against the state or the laws of society, the county officers will take hold of it, and if he is bro't to me for identification as the party who bro't the box to my office I will do the best I can; but you know I have my doubts about being able to identify him when I only saw him a few moments and he then had a full beard, and this man you say has only a mustache. Altho' he may be the party, yet if I can't identify him positively, how is he to be convicted? I hope, most assuredly, he is the right one, but with the case as it stands I can't make any complaint.

14 Ibid., 249, 243.
15 Ibid., 246, 397, 601–2, 630–1.

In short Upham reversed himself, declaring that he had not seen the picture, would not see it, and would therefore "be unable to identify the parties that delivered that box."[16] As far as the detective could see, the payment, promotion, and removal of the star witness from the investigation capped the remarkable unwillingness of the authorities to investigate the affairs.

After this, Vincent and Highleyman together approached Oliver P. Ergenbright, the county attorney in Independence. By this point, though, the detective had become "disgusted with the case . . . and I did not have much to say." Vincent laid out the argument for using state powers to investigate the incident, but Ergenbright "was in a hurry" and asked Vincent to supply what evidence he had. In the end, of course, they had nothing that would not be hearsay without official action to secure testimony. Prosecutors continued to raise that innovatively modern legal yardstick for wrongdoing by the authorities, declaring that nothing could be done "unless the parties had intended to hurt somebody with the bomb, or destroy some property."[17]

Clearly, the officials of the state did not want to investigate—much less prosecute—the case, and even threatened Vincent with legal action should they perist in pushing the matter. Ergenbright later approached Highleyman near the station at Coffeyville. "I have got to do something in this dynamite matter," said Ergenbright. "I have either got to arrest the Vincents, charging them with libel, or have Henrie and Poorman arrested; I am between two fires." Highleyman pointed out that either course "would bring out the facts in the case." Ergenbright then probed to see if Highleyman had any new information. The detective said simply that the investigation had already convinced him that if Henrie and Poorman were arrested, "the trial would be nothing but a farce, and that I did not propose to have anything more to do with it."[18]

---

16 Ibid., 244, 246, 247, and Upham to Highleyman, December 3, 1888, as exhibit 32 in *Legislative Investigation of Coffeyville*, 248–9.

17 For this and the next two paragraphs, see Ibid., 243–4, 251.

18 Ibid., 244.

Meanwhile, in the wake of the election, the same officials who had charged their opponents with being secret anarchists appointed Henrie—nominally the most prominent anarchist in Kansas—to be the assistant director of the Bureau of Labor Statistics. One neighbor recalled Henrie's joking about bombs and dynamite, adding to his recollections that

> a suit of clothes was sent to the house for him in his absence, and at first he appeared not to know where the goods came from, but subsequently said to me: "I am not satisfied with a suit of clothes, but I will have the position promised me in the labor bureau or I will raise hell." It was common talk between his family and mine for some weeks, that he was to have a position in the labor bureau.[19]

Finally, on August 26, 1889, Highleyman confirmed to Elliot that they had concluded the investigation because "these parties could not be convicted unless this evidence of Poorman could be obtained." Highleyman himself had become "fully convinced after I had a conversation with Mr. Elliott that no conviction could be had."[20] There the matter rested for months.

The Later State Inquiry

Despite the discouragement and threats, the Vincents pressed the issue. In the *Non-Conformist* they continued to demand the facts behind the Coffeyville outrage, calling on the state legislature to investigate it, which it predictably declined to do. The Vincents also documented what Highleyman had discovered, taking him to make a formal statement in the office of John W. Breidenthal. A fellow resident of Chetopa, the Minnesota-born Breidenthal had been a pioneering advocate for the Greenback movement and, later, the Union Labor Party. In preparation for the next Alliance campaign, he paid a

19 Ibid., 178.
20 Ibid., 250.

stenographer to take testimony that would be used for a political tract.[21]

The insurgents burdened their message with a complex tale of conspiracy implicating people on high. In 1889, Vincent published *The Plot Unfolded! or a History of the Famous Coffeyville Dynamite Outrage*. One of the uncooperative Republican state officials entered the cabinet, and when President Benjamin Harrison appointed Edwin Greer postmaster for Winfield, the Vincents suggested that the conspiracy reached into the national government. Publicizing the Republican "outrage" became part of the campaigns of the Union Labor Party and persisted through the "Alliance Party"—the electoral expression of the Farmers' Alliance—and, finally, the Populist or People's Party.[22]

Despite the regular and systemic efforts to obscure the issues they sought to raise, the insurgents eventually prevailed at the polls. After 1890, they had the strength in the state government to ensure a formal investigation of the Coffeyville incident. During that legislative session, a joint committee was selected to get to the bottom of the explosion, once and for all.

On Friday, February 13, 1891, its members filed into Senate Committee Room No. 5 in Topeka and opened a hearing. Spectators flocked to the sessions, which were then moved to more spacious rooms. Day in and day out, the hearing went on. Everyone the

---

21 *Kansas: A Cyclopedia of State History, Embracing Events, Institutions, Industries, Counties, Cities, Towns, Prominent Persons, Etc . . . With a Supplementary Volume Devoted to Selected Personal History and Reminiscence* (Chicago: Standard Pub. Co., 1912), 3, 30–1; *Legislative Investigation of Coffeyville*, 253.

22 *The Plot Unfolded! or a History of the Famous Coffeyville Dynamite Outrage, October 18, 1888. The Boldest, as Well as the Most Murderous Political Stroke of the Late Campaign. A Series of Articles Containing Correspondence, Interviews and Statements Step by Step* (Winfield, KS: American Nonconformist, 1889). Vincent condemns cabinet-level intrigues and even implicates President Benjamin Harrison. R. Alton Lee, *Farmers vs. Wage Earners: Organized Labor in Kansas, 1860–1960* (Lincoln: University of Nebraska Press, 2005), 63–4, 66; *Populist Hand-Book for Kansas. A Compilation from Official Sources of Some Facts for Use in Succeeding Political Campaigns* (Indianapolis: Vincent Bros Publishing Co., 1891), 92–186.

committee could find who knew anything about the matter, nearly 100 witnesses, testified under oath.

Their testimony required some shifts of position. For some time, those who disparaged the Vincents' suspicions actually suggested that Upham himself had set off the bomb, intending to kill his wife for the property she owned. After the Uphams' payment, promotion, and move to Maine, however, the family remained silent, and the detectives found nothing to back up this assertion.

The legislative hearing finally centered its probe on two probable instigators of the explosion. At the time, the Republicans had charged that the National Order of Videttes had sent the bomb as part of a plan by the Vincents to blow up the *Courier* plant. They had never retracted this accusation. The Vincents believed that the bomb had been sent in the interests of the Republican State Central Committee and had been intended to be discovered before it went off.

On May 9, the gavel sounded in the hearing room and the investigation ended. Across the state, some citizens awaited the verdict of the committee, hoping that, at long last, the guilty would be punished. They would be disappointed.

The three Republican members of the committee (C. H. Kimball, J. G. Mohler, and C. N. Bishoff) vehemently denied that their party had been connected even remotely with the explosion. They further concluded that Henrie, the anarchist whom the Republicans had put into public office, was not the man seen in Valeda and that he had no connection with the explosion whatsoever. They bemoaned the fact that $12,000 had been spent on the hearing and had only one recommendation: that law enforcement agents, not the state legislature, handle such cases in the future. This drew laughs from the lawmen in the audience.

The report of the Alliance Party committee members (Ezra Cary, M. Senn, G. W. Crumley, and T. M. Templeton) came to very different conclusions. It vindicated the Vincents' position that the Republican officials had staged the event, even questioning as to whether it had involved a vastly larger conspiracy.

It continued, "There was a conspiracy on the part of someone to do certain things for the purpose of breaking the ranks of the Union Labor Party and adding strength to the Republican Party in the political campaign of 1888." Upham's removal from Coffeyville after the explosion, the Alliance Party members argued, "leaves the impression on our minds that there was an influence brought to bear on him, which in the first place would prevent him from testifying, when the Vincents made their efforts to prosecute the guilty parties."

They found Henrie's appointment to the state labor commission even more strange, as he claimed not to be a Republican, while many qualified Republicans had sought the job. Moreover, no labor organization had sought his appointment. From their perspective,

> it is impossible to think of any explanation of C. A. Henrie's appointment, except that he knew about the damnable plot of preparing and sending the box, and that for the purpose of keeping him silent, the position was given him.

Therefore, they argued, "the refusal of the legislature of 1889 to investigate the explosion seems to us a confirmation" of the Republican connection with the Coffeyville explosion. They called Henrie's appointment "a reward for the part performed by him, and to prevent him from revealing what he knows of the affair which would implicate other parties." They could not account for Henrie's activities at the time and strongly suspected that

> he had some connection with the preparation of, and delivered said box at Coffeyville, to be shipped by express to Winfield to be exploded . . . and under the excitement following the explosion, a raid would probably be made on the office of *The Non-Conformist*.

The outcome of the hearings turned on the lone Democrat on the committee (Senator Edward Carroll). He acknowledged that he found it difficult to believe that Henrie's appointment had been honest. However, he dismissed the entire conflict as a political quarrel and sided with the Republicans, arguing that no conclusions should be drawn nor any legal actions taken.[23] Deadlocked, the committee adjourned and the Coffeyville bomb became, officially, a closed matter.

Summer had descended, sweltering, over Kansas. The sodbusters and their mules had gone back to the fields. No one would ever be punished for the Coffeyville outrage except, of course, those innocent of the crime. Or, rather, those guilty only of challenging the hegemony of the dominant party.

As modern scholars lack the power of subpoena, the threat of perjury, and any living witnesses to question, historians can be as sure about Coffeyville as about anything based on similarly circumstantial evidence. The committee did publish an account of the hearing the size of a phonebook: *Joint Committee of the Legislature . . . to Investigate the Explosion Which Occurred at Coffeyville.* If nothing else, this publication documents the crime and the dereliction of duty by local and state officials in failing to conduct such an investigation.

The construction of the bomb and its mode of delivery involved multiple persons, confirming the existence of a conspiracy. The conspirators were surely neither the farmers organizing their Union Labor Party nor the students of political economy in the IWPA. Greer, Henrie, and others who were involved in an alleged anarchist conspiracy among the Populists and predicted violence gained the most in terms of their careers and finances.

There is no reason to believe that the detonation of those bottles of explosives at Upham's was anything other than an accident; their mere arrival in Winfield would have sufficiently confirmed media predictions of violence. It is also likely that the strength of the explosion owed much to the chemicals in Upham's darkroom. Wherever and however the blast took place, it had the desired impact, and the victorious Republicans thwarted Union Labor at the polls. Furthermore, there seems to be no better explanation as to why they

---

23 There was no connection between the anarchists and the Videttes. *Proceedings of the Joint Committee*, 192. See also *Populist Legislative Investigation: Testimony Taken Before the Joint Committee Appointed to Investigate Charges of Bribery and Corruption* (Hutchinson: The News Co., 1897).

would have given the alleged "anarchist" Henrie a government job. Finally, the bizarre decision not to investigate clearly made the Republican government of the state the biggest beneficiaries of the crime.

The absence of a serious criminal investigation and trial leaves all evidence as hearsay, but testimony given before a legislative investigation confirms the Vincents' charges, of not their speculations about a national scheme. William J. Branden said that Bion S. Hutchins, secretary of the Republican State Central Committee, "admitted that Henrie had helped him, and others, at Topeka in a plan 'to show up the Vincents, and the anarchists and dynamiters.'"[24]

Hutchins thought it "a good political scheme to have the people believe that the Vincents were anarchists and dynamiters, and thereby do away with the union labor movement." He further admitted that his targets had not been "dynamiters or anarchists," but "anything was fair in politics."

Finally, Secretary Hutchins asked if Branden thought there would be an investigation. When Branden noted that some people wanted one, Hutchins looked amused and "made the remark to me that he did not think there would be an investigation." When Branden suggested that there had not been any explosive prepared, Hutchins "laughed, and said he probably knew more about it than I did." There can be little serious doubt that he did, and there was no investigation until the Alliance briefly got control of the state government.

Coffeyville showed how violence could be emplosed in order to frame others for the crime. Moreover, this variation maximized popular support for the marginalization and silencing of critics in the sphere of civic discourse.

24 On this exchange, see *Legislative Investigation of Coffeyville*, 255, 256.

The Legacies of Misdirection

The presence of figures such as C. A. Henrie and W. A. A. Carsey hint at the roots of a sinister practice.

Henrie got ample rewards. The Republican government gave the post in the state Bureau of Labor to the only person in the state who tinkered with anarchist bomb-making and advocated the use of bombs as a matter of public record. By 1894, Henrie went on to assume the editorship of a Republican paper in Garfield County, Colorado, and the Victor Typographical Union in Goldfield elected him president in 1901. The following year, Henrie returned to Kansas, settling just outside of Kansas City, where the Republicans made him the assistant docket clerk of the state senate and his son-in-law a warden in the state penitentiary system.[25]

Still, history had a more revealing reward for Henrie, who wound up in an advertising job for the Jones Motor Car Company of Wichita. While in the West, he received an invitation to attend a family reunion at Plymouth Rock. He responded in praise of the "remarkable code of ideal citizenship" the colonists had founded and urged an understanding of "human nature," which will encourage "the strong" to be "more willing to assist the weak." When "we shall be less exclusive in our likes and dislikes; the Fatherhood of God and the brotherhood of man will be the more prevalent creed." Soon after, the born-again adman seems to have retired to Oklahoma with his family, appearing in Tulsa's directories before dying on September 9, 1927.

Around the time Henrie's cover began to unravel, so did that of the transplanted Kansan, Carsey. With the collapse of the national third party after 1888, Carsey rechristened his own paper labor group the "Union Labor Party," making himself the local spokesman of a once large party which he had actually opposed. Still, one newspaperman reported that its executive committee "composes almost the entire party here." Carsey's "party" sought only to question candidates of the

---

25 "Local Briefs," *Aspen Tribune*, February 6, 1901, p. 4; "[Untitled]," *Glenwood Post* at Glenwood Springs, May 17, 1902, p. 5.

major parties. Discontented with his old arrangements with Tammany, he denounced the organization for hiring "alien scabs" to construct the subway.[26]

In early 1890, Carsey had a much publicized brawl with Curtis Dunham, a newspaperman and minor literary figure. When Carsey showed up in Albany to present the views of the now nonexistent Union Labor Party before the state senate's Committee on Miscellaneous Corporations, one of the committee members described his group as "political tramps." Carsey not only threatened the state senator should he ever return to New York City, but spotted Dunham and knocked him down. When an assemblyman tried to protect the reporter, one of Carsey's sons jumped him from behind. This "veritable Donnybrook" continued as "Old Man Carsey" punched a former nominee for state railroad commissioner in the eye. When he later returned to Albany, the authorities arrested him for assault, even though the "Executive Committee of the Union Labor Party" voted to vindicate him.[27]

By then, Carsey had been enjoying a series of rewards. He seems to have begun commuting from New York City to Washington and playing a minor role in the efforts of upstate New Yorker and former president Grover Cleveland to return to the White House over the opposition of Tammany. Notwithstanding his feistiness in Albany, Carsey filed for a Civil War pension as an invalid. In time the Cleveland connection began paying off.[28]

As the new People's Party took form, Carsey tried to present himself as one of the movement elders whose work went back to the Greenback days. In May 1891, his extant Union Labor Party

26 "Labor Agitators Busy," *New York Times*, September 20, 1889, p. 5; "Labor Men Oppose Tammany," *New York Times*, October 25, 1889, p. 3; "City and Suburban News. New York," *New York Times*, April 8, 1890, p. 3.

27 "Assaulted a Reporter. A Fight in One of the Corridors of the State Capitol," *New York Times*, March 6, 1890, p. 1; "City and Suburban News. New York," *New York Times*, April 1, 1890, p. 3; "City and Suburban News. New York," *New York Times*, April 8, 1890, p. 3.

28 *Index to the Grover Cleveland Papers* (Washington, DC: Library of Congress, 1965), 63.

sent Carsey and a former Antimonopolist leader as representatives to the state convention to "elect delegates to the Cincinnati Convention of the Farmers' Alliance and other organizations" that launched the Populist Party. At first, the Populists seem not to have known what to make of Carsey, but he actively opposed their ticket in 1892, supporting Cleveland and the Democratic Party instead. By August 1893, the Populist Party of New York declared that Carsey would be barred from deliberations in the state organization.[29]

Indeed, Carsey's main concession to the Populists had been to rechristen the "Union Labor Party" as the "Industrial Alliance." At a Cooper Institute meeting, the new organization claimed to control 6,000 votes, though local press reminded readers that the group "consists of about sixteen men . . . who for years have never done any actual work. They have posed as professional labor agitators, and are nothing less than political strikers." Not only did unions not recognize the group, but it had a history of approaching employers during strikes, offering "to get up mass meetings of workingmen to support their position. At such times the members of the Industrial Alliance usually assume some name that resembles some well-known union."[30]

When the Republicans returned to power in Washington, Carsey returned to New York City. By the turn of the century, he worked in the Bureau for Collection of Arrears of Personal Taxes, and later as an inspector in the city's Bridge Department. He died June 1, 1914, in Brooklyn, and his widow, Adelle, filed for his veteran's benefits two weeks later. His obituary reported high honors and a position in the leadership of Tammany Hall, but these may have reflected what he claimed at home. It mentioned none of his serious contributions to the history of insurgent party movements.

Yet, Carsey's real achievements were serious enough. With nothing

29   "Local Labor Matters," *New York Times*, May 15, 1891, p. 2; "A Snare for New-York Farmers. An 'Encampment' to Be Run by the People's Party," *New York Times*, August 13, 1893, p. 2.

30   "Political Bandits, These People. Unsavory Reputation of the Industrial Alliance Which 'Supports' Mr. Myers," *New York Times*, October 22, 1893, p. 2.

more than a title in a nonexistent organization, he had buffaloed his way through the Gilded Age as a freelance agent of various Democratic factions and a "labor" voice for hire by companies willing to pay. From the days of the First International to the Populists, Carsey found that persistent fear of mass strikes and armed insurrections generated a market for what he was selling.

Figures such as Henrie and Carsey demonstrate the new managerial skills of the owning classes and ruling institutions to shape not only the course of the mass opposition they inspired, but also the nation's memory of the experience. However, no sooner than the Coffeyville hearings closed, another incident reminded Kansans that those who controlled their politics ultimately had no real qualms about the assassination of opponents in broad daylight and in front of multiple witnesses.

And Murder Remained an Option

The wave of political insurgencies in Kansas through the later 1870s brought the old radical Samuel N. Wood back into action. The old abolitionist and Civil War veteran reentered the Kansas legislature in 1876 and 1877, becoming the Speaker during the last session. He then became the editor of the *Kansas Greenbacker* in Emporia and the *Kansas State Journal* in Topeka.

Alongside such radicalism, Wood became deeply involved in the cattle business in Texas and also served as the director of the Atchison, Topeka & Santa Fe Railway. All of this drew him into the development of western Kansas, particularly Council Grove, where Wakefield edited his militant newspaper.

By the mid-1880s, Wood and I. C. Price of Meade, Kansas, began organizing the settlement of a new town to be called Woodsdale, while a rival group from McPherson headed by Cyrus E. and Orin J. Cook promoted Hugoton eight miles away. The Woodsdale group offered free town lots to anyone who would build on it, and one Sam Robinson took the offer and built a hotel there. In 1886, Hugoton won the county seat when the Republican state authorities sanctioned the creation of Stevens County. The victory lured Robinson from Woodsdale with the promise of being placed in charge of local law enforcement. However, the settlers at Woodsdale protested that the population at the county seat existed only on paper, to which the town fathers of Hugoton replied in August with a lawsuit against Wood for libel.[31] In fact, as late as the 1890 Census, Stevens County had a total population of only 1,418, little more than half of what had been claimed at its formation.

Determined to silence the questions, a posse from Hugoton seized Wood and Price, then on their way to Garden City in the spring of 1887. At the new county seat, something of a kangaroo court found them "guilty" of opposing the town's interest and sentenced them to join the posse for a buffalo hunt into the Indian Territory, though no herds had been there for several years. An old Indian scout, S. O. Aubrey, led a rescue party of two dozen Woodsdale men to save Wood and Price. Although they failed to return with the two men, they did seize some of the Hugoton kidnappers and carted them to Garden City, where they turned the matter over to the authorities, who then transferred the case to a Hugoton court, which unsurprisingly found the kidnappers "not guilty" in the fall.

The conflict intensified when the two towns lined up behind respective candidates for county sheriff. John M. Cross, the Woodsdale candidate, defeated Robinson, then the city marshal in Hugoton. Early in 1888, Robinson stepped out of his official role in the local government to help secure bonds to bring the railroad to Hugoton rather than Woodsdale, and a warrant was issued for his arrest. Local supporters of Robinson used firearms to drive off an attempt to serve him with the warrant. Afterward, they dug trenches and erected barricades at the approaches of the town in expectation of an attack from Woodsdale.

Both sides seemed to be trying to avoid an actual shooting war, but

---

31   Mason, "County Seat Controversies in Southwestern Kansas," 55; Ken Butler, "Kansas Blood Spilled in Oklahoma," Kansas State Library, available at ksgenweb.com/stevens/haymeadow.html. See also "Biographical Sketch of Samuel Newitt Wood," available at usacitiesonline.com/kshistoryswoodbio.htm.

nobody could sustain that balance.[32] Kansas authorities sent the militia into the area from June 19 to 24 just to make sure that no shootouts occurred. Undismayed, Wood and his supporters remained determined to get the matter before the courts. Still, in July, Woodsdale Marshal Charles Edward Short heard that Robinson had left Hugoton with a camping party headed for the Indian Territory. Reputedly a cousin and sometimes partner of the notorious gambler and shootist Luke Short, Ed Short had a violent career in his own right. He had supposedly killed a man back in Indiana, and the woman he married in September 1887 committed suicide the following February. Just the sort of fellow to get the blood stirring and the bullets flying.

Short convinced County Sheriff Cross to raise a posse to intercept and arrest Robinson. Cross headed south with Ted Eaton, Bob Hubbard, Roland Wilcox, and Herbert Tonney to rendezvous with Short and his group on Goff creek in No Man's Land (near present-day Guymon, Oklahoma). By then, though, a posse from Hugoton had set out to meet Short and his men, running them back to Woodsdale in a gunfight. Meanwhile, Robinson had returned from the Indian Territory to Hugoton, and—later claiming to have known nothing of the other Hugoton group—raised his own posse of fifteen men and headed back into the Indian Territory to find Short's group. In the meantime, Sheriff Cross and his four men had reached Wild Horse Lake (in present-day Texas County, Oklahoma), where they found A. B. Haas and a small crew gathering hay. Assuming that the excitement had ended, Cross and his men decided to spend the night of July 25 where they were and settled down to sleep.

Shortly after they turned in, Robinson, backed by his large posse, showed up and confronted the man who had defeated him in the election for sheriff. The Hugoton thugs quickly disarmed the sheriff

---

32 For a discussion of how this conflict unfolded, see Mason, "County Seat Controversies in Southwestern Kansas," 56–8, 58–61, 61–2, 62–4; Jack DeMattos and Chuck Parsons, *The Notorious Luke Short: Sporting Man of the Wild West* (Denton: University of North Texas Press, 2015), 298n12. Ed Short was later killed by the Dalton gang in the Indian Territory. He was involved in the county seat fight in Grant County in which he, Bat Masterson, Luke Short, George Earp—one of Wyatt's cousins—and others won seats for Ulysses.

and his four men. "Sheriff Cross," Robinson reportedly said as he raised his rifle, "you are my first man." He coldly pulled the trigger. Then, one by one, the people whom the state had placed in charge of the county dispatched Hubbard, Tonney, Eaton, and Wilcox. The gunmen tested their work by holding lit matches to the faces of their victims and shooting any that reacted. Robinson and his posse removed the Haas haying crew and left the five lifeless bodies as they had fallen.

Herbert Tonney, however, had feigned death, though he had been shot through the neck and was bleeding badly. After the Hugoton gunmen left the area, Tonney dragged himself over to check his companions and found them all dead. With great effort, he made his way to his horse, mounted, and rode away, fighting his pain and exhaustion, made worse by the mugginess of the night. After a few miles, he found some relief from the heat of the night by collapsing into a buffalo wallow. Somewhat refreshed and hopeful, Tonney remounted and headed north. At daylight the next morning, Herman Cann, a constable from Vorhees, found him wandering on the prairie, stubbornly hanging on to life. After Robinson's murderers had released Haas and his men, one of them had gone to the law to report the massacre; the constable was looking for survivors. Cann got Tonney to a doctor in LaFayette, and the wounded man filed charges against his assailants.

Forewarned, Robinson fled to Colorado. There, the following May—in 1889—he robbed the combined post office and store in Florissant and got caught. The court sentenced him to fourteen years in the Colorado State Penitentiary in Canon City.

Meanwhile, the state government back in Kansas struggled to keep a lid on the situation. The governor again sent in the militia and imposed temporary martial law until tempers cooled. Wood and others eager to secure some justice managed to bypass the authorities' predisposition to leave the entire matter in the hands of the Hugoton officials. After all, the killings had taken place on U.S. territory. By October 1889, Wood got the case before a federal court in Paris, Texas. In July 1890—with Robinson still behind bars in Colorado—Wood made the prosecution's case against the Cooks and four others for cold-blooded murder of four unarmed men. In eight hours, he presented enough evidence to convict the six, who were then sentenced to be hanged December 19.

Nevertheless, in the end, the authorities never held the perpetrators to account. The U.S. Supreme Court suspended the executions until it could consider the matter. From December 11 to 12, it considered the case of *United States v. C. E. Cook, Orin Cook, Capt. C.E. Frease, Johnnie Jackson, Ed Boudin, John Colbert, et al.* On January 26, 1891, the high court voided the convictions. It declared that neither the federal court in Paris nor any other court had jurisdiction over the site where the crimes had been committed. The ruling was extraordinary given that, at the time of the killings, the federal authorities had exercised jurisdiction over the Indian Territory for decades. Indeed, that a Gilded Age Republican high court could place something as basic as the prohibition of murder beyond the responsibility of government has delightfully anarchist implications.

Not only did the murderers walk off in freedom, but Wood faced a series of legal charges in Hugoton levied as revenge for having prosecuted the killers, including charges of bribery while in the legislature. On June 23, 1891—less than five months after the Supreme Court decision—Wood turned up to give testimony before the court in Hugoton. Judge Theodosius Botkin, despite a personal friendship with the governor and a fondness for drink, had a terrible record of both partisanship and failure to disguise it. Wood, for his part, was "rather easy-going but would fight and fight hard in self-defense." In 1891, the Populist-controlled legislature, in which Wood served as clerk of the House Judiciary Committee, impeached Botkin. While the House voted to convict the judge, the requirement of a two-thirds vote in the Senate kept Botkin employed. The judge, however, was not a forgiving man.

Wood, his wife, and a Mrs. Carpenter had pulled in front of the Methodist Church that the court used for its sessions. He quickly clambered down from the buggy and went inside, expecting to find judicial activities under way. James Brennan, the gunman hired by Judge Botkin as a "bodyguard" and a defense witness for the Hay Meadow killers, was waiting in the church. When Wood found the judge absent, he turned to leave. Brennan came up behind him and shot him several times in the back. As Wood collapsed, Brennan put the pistol in his face and delivered the coup de grâce. Unlike the Hay Meadow murders, this one targeted one of the founding pioneers of the state and took place in broad daylight before multiple witnesses, including the victim's wife, and on the very site where a court met.

Neither the courts, local law enforcement, nor the state authorities called Brennan to account before the holy bar of justice. The last attempt to do so came in 1911, when Kansas extradicted him from Oklahoma, only to release him when they got him back into the state.

In the new year, Judge Botkin reported that he had been warned that an attempt would be made on his life on the three-mile route from his home to the court in Springfield, Seward County. On January 5, 1892, Sheriff Samuel Dunn took a posse along the route around dawn. A volley of fire from a ravine killed the sheriff, but no shots were fired on others in the party. In short order, the state sent the militia, which turned the community into a modified military camp, with pickets posted to regulate access to the town. Botkin charged Wood's widow with an attempt to kill him. Who or why Dunn was killed remained the unanswered question. But evidence of a conspiracy among those with power to do whatever was necessary to keep it seemed to have produced its mirror image: a conspiracy aimed at preventing those with power from exercising it.

The dominant, most well-armed and ruthless powers in Kansas engaged in remarkably reckless and potentially lethal activities in order to validate libel against political opponents. They created fictional problems to obscure real ones that might have moved people to vote against the status quo. They worked to defraud political opponents. In Kansas, no more than in the Deep South, those who killed for the power structure never needed to lose sleep over whether they would be called to account for their actions. Without these actions, of course, American history would be very different.

These developments demonstrate that politicians did not debate whether to rely on political violence or conspiracy, but who could take advantage of these tactics and, as Coffeyville clarified, who defined them. Those who controlled how incidents of political violence were processed defined the very importance and meaning of those incidents. A brief look beyond Kansas demonstrates how processes like these were common across the American heartland.

EIGHT

The West Beyond Kansas

*Murders and Range Wars—Arkansas,
Texas, Arizona, and Wyoming*

On April 9, 1892, the Texan Nathan D. Champion wiped the
grime from his face and surveyed his situation. About the same age
as Tom Harris, the Panhandle strike leader, Champion had surely
been organizing in Wyoming before finding himself on a death list
compiled by the bosses. Champion had enough ammunition to
keep the hired guns at bay for hours, and scrawled in a small note-
book. He confessed to feeling "pretty lonesome just now. I wish
there was someone here with me so we could watch all sides at
once." At points, he had to meet efforts to rush the cabin with brisk
gunfire, killing at least four assailants and wounding others. Then,
the besiegers began peppering the cabin to keep Champion under
cover while they gathered kindling. "Well, they have just got
through shelling the house like hail," he wrote. "I heard them splitting wood. I guess they are going to fire the house tonight. I think
I will make a break when night comes, if alive." When it became
clear that assailants would not wait, Champion knew he would
have to make his break in daylight. "Shooting again. It's not night
yet. The house is all fired. Goodbye, boys, if I never see you again."
And out he went, six-guns blazing.

Beyond the division between civilization and savagery marked by

Main Street in the Kansas cow towns, populations in other states held similar discussions. In the case of Arkansas and Texas in the old Confederacy, the social order required the suppression of African American voices and interests that sounded—however garbled by the Republican structures—through the Reconstruction. Arizona, like Kansas, pit the civilizing Protestant mission of the Republicans against various others, including Texas cowboys and Mormons migrating down from Utah, some to be opposed and others assimilated in a political process that included overt violence. Then, too, the conflict in Wyoming brought parts of the state to conditions of civil war, in a process that demonstrated the vital importance of the local cowboy strikes and of violence in fueling a mass popular insurgency.

Direct Violence as a Persistent Option

The attempt to launch the Union Labor Party gained considerable support in Arkansas and Texas, as well as Kansas. Political violence in these states represented a particularly exaggerated version of what happened across the old Confederacy. With deep antebellum roots, the masters of the Old South employed an unprecedented scale of violence to cripple efforts at postwar Reconstruction. That violence long outlasted the formal collapse of Reconstruction, reversing its gains for the outsiders to power and wealth in the South.

Violence became an essential feature of social control. Lynching—almost always aimed at African Americans—provided the dominant party with an indispensible mechanism of repression, as well as a stopgap solution to any threat of electoral defeat. From 1886 through 1893, the annual reported number of lynchings across the South came to 138, 122, 142, 176, 127, 193, 205, and 200.[1] Just in 1885,

---

1 Ralph Ginzburg, *100 Years of Lynchings* (New York: Lancer Books, 1962), 94. From *Chicago Tribune*, December 31, 1914. See also Norton H. Moses, *Lynching and Vigilantism in the United States: An Annotated Bibliography* (Westport, CT: Greenwood Press, 1997).

Texas saw twenty-two mobs lynch forty-three people, including nineteen blacks and twenty-four whites, one of them a woman.

From the perspective of the restored Democratic Party, Republicans seemed to be as insurgent as any third party elsewhere.[2] Over much of the South, the Republicans—with mixed motives—sought to make common cause with the insurgents, who in turn took up issues that revisited the Republican arguments during Reconstruction.

The insurgents learned from bitter experience that the disenfranchisement of any minority did not leave the majority a particularly representative government. Black disenfranchisement did not adjust the electoral college and other arrangements that disproportionately represented the more deferential and docile Southern whites, and in the name of what they called democracy. Riding roughshod over the minority sufficed to control the total electoral process. Paramilitary bands inflicted armed violence on citizens for their political views, seized control of elections, and reported false returns.

The Democrats had waged attacks on the new party movements as soon as they appeared in the state. Greenbackers near Little Rock in 1880 brought their holstered revolvers to a racially mixed picnic and hung them from trees near where they socialized with friends and family. Streeter's vice presidential candidate eight years later, Charles E. Cunningham, had come out of that state's movement. So the national party remained well aware of the situation in Arkansas.

The Knights of Labor and the Farmers' Alliance recruited large numbers in the state, while indigenous associations such as the Agricultural Wheel and the Brotherhood of Freedom provided an even larger base. For these reasons, the new Union Labor Party quickly emerged as the strongest threat to the Democrats. In 1888, Charles M. Norwood polled nearly 46 percent for governor, and recent research has implied that he lost only due to violence against his campaign and fraud in the vote count.[3]

2 On the two-party balance, see Calhoun, *Minority Victory*, 152–3, 179–80.
3 Clifton Paisley, "The Political Wheelers and Arkansas' Election of 1888," *Arkansas Historical Quarterly* 25 (Spring 1966): 3–21; Matthew Hild, "Labor, Third-Party Politics, and New South Democracy in Arkansas, 1884–1896," *Arkansas Historical Quarterly* 63 (Spring 2004): 24–43; Jason McCollom, "The Agricultural

One of the candidates most dangerous to the restored Democratic order was John Middleton Clayton. The Pennsylvania-born Clayton had been a federal officer in the Civil War and joined his older brother, Powell Clayton, in Arkansas in 1867. Four years later, he served on the board of what became the University of Arkansas at Fayetteville and helped establish a college at Pine Bluff. He also entered politics as a Republican, eventually becoming the speaker of the state senate.

Throughout, Clayton remained a militant proponent of Radical Reconstruction and the rights of African Americans. During the Brooks–Baxter War over the disputed gubernatorial election, he raised troops in Jefferson County and marched them to Little Rock on behalf of Joseph Brooks. Brooks lost the position when the Grant administration sided with Baxter, a key event in the national collapse of Reconstruction. Clayton, however, won five successive terms as the county sheriff, starting in 1876.

As part of the Bourbon Redemption of the state, Democrat Clifton R. Breckinridge won the 1882 election to the U.S. House of Representatives. Breckinridge was the son of John C. Breckinridge, one of the major architects of Southern secession. The end of Reconstruction created something of a backlash of its own in Arkansas, where large numbers of blacks fleeing from repression in other states swelled the Republican constituency and, with discontented whites, made a force capable of turning out the Democrats.[4]

In 1888, Clayton ran against Breckinridge in the Second Congressional District of Arkansas. On paper, Clayton lost by 846 out of over 34,000 votes cast, but the election became one of the most overtly fraudulent in the country. During the campaign, prominent black opponents of the Democrats, including ministers, were "disappeared." In the midst of the 1888 voting, four masked men

Wheel, the Union Labor Party, and the 1889 Arkansas Legislature," *Arkansas Historical Quarterly* 68 (Summer 2009): 157–75.

4 Breckinridge eventually alienated his base in Arkansas by supporting Cleveland's "gold standard" politics. Ultimately, he went on to serve on the Dawes Commission, adding to his personal fortune through the acquisition of Indian lands, though a later Justice Department investigation acquitted him of having done so fraudulently.

entered one predominantly black precinct in Conway County and stole the ballot box at gunpoint.[5]

Losing under such circumstances, Clayton and his supporters decided to contest the election, seeking information in particular on the intimidation and fraud at Plumerville, where blacks accounted for two-thirds of the population. Local Democratic officials agreed to testify regarding the events leading to Breckinridge's victory in return for Clayton withdrawing his indictments. On the evening of January 29, 1889—a day after Clayton and his people declined to withdraw the charges—he sat down at a table in his rooming house near the window. Someone—generally believed to be a local deputy sheriff or other Democratic partisan—fired a shotgun from outside, nearly removing Clayton's head and blowing bits of brain around the room.[6]

There seemed to be a general agreement that this had been yet another political crime, but the official investigations—even aided by a $5,000 reward—did not result in the arrest, much less prosecution, of the killer. In 1890, the U.S. House of Representatives agreed that Clayton had won the election and vacated the seat, a decision that came after the unelected Breckinridge had already served almost the entire term and was fairly sure of winning later that year. After all, who would challenge the Democratic hold on the district after what had happened to Clayton?

The normalization of political violence in Texas bore fruit in 1888 and after, as well. Conflicts over the enclosures of vast tracts of land sparked episodic outbursts of violence, broadly described as the "Fence-Cutter Wars." These disputes raised unanswerable questions about the corruption and brutality of law enforcement, as when the Texas Rangers rode into Navarro County in 1888 as active enforcers for the big spreads and their barbed-wire boundaries.

These functions coincided with the ongoing clashes over the unresolved issues of Reconstruction. The Opposition sustained their

---

5 Richard M. Perloff, "The Press and Lynchings of African Americans," *Journal of Black Studies* 30 (January 2000): 315–30; Case, *The Great Southwest Railroad Strike*, 214.

6 Kenneth C. Barnes, *Who Killed John Clayton? Political Violence and the Emergence of the New South, 1861–1893* (Durham, NC: Duke University Press, 1998).

control over the local government in Fort Bend County just southwest of Houston, despite the growing pressure from the regular Democratic "Jaybirds." The Jaybirds, who vied with "Woodpeckers" for control of the Democratic Party, represented the traditional formerly proslavery and secessionist leadership of that party, while "Woodpeckers" consisted of various dissenting Democrats and many former Republicans, including African Americans. In the course of this, a large cotton planter named J. M. Shamblin supposedly came up with the idea of taking power by getting blacks to support the Jaybirds in the interests of "better government," after which he allegedly received threats. "Then, on August 1, 1888—as the story went—the pious planter sat reading the Bible in his home when a shotgun blast dispatched him.[7]

In response to Shamblin's murder, a white Democratic posse with hounds did its own reenactment of the antebellum slave patrols in the interests of "better government." They descended on the shack of a black field hand named William Caldwell, arresting and carting him off to jail. An allegedly Negro jury in Harris County sentenced Caldwell to death by hanging for Shamblin's death. His defenders carried the case as far as the U.S. Supreme Court in December 1890, but the court dismissed the appeal in less than a month.[8]

This did nothing to relieve tensions in Fort Bend County, and someone reportedly shot Democratic leader H. H. Frost with a shotgun in front of his house while he was out on a moonlit "stroll." In traditional fashion, armed and mounted white Democrats responded to Frost's murder by descending on a "negro shanty," where they grabbed two suspects. They might well have lynched them on the spot had not word arrived that Frost's wounds were not mortal.

Nevertheless, the white Republican organization at the state level

    7 Sonnichsen, *I'll Die Before I'll Run*, 186–226; C. L. Douglas, *Famous Texas Feuds*, 2nd ed. (Austin: State House Press, 1988), 161–72. The source for Shamblin's story is laughably biased and riddled with racist assumptions, including references to "the long-suffering majority," 162. See also Jesse A. Ziegler, *Wave of the Gulf* (Galveston: Naylor Co., 1938), 154.

    8 *Caldwell v. Texas*, 137 U.S. 692 (1891) in Justia. U.S. Supreme Court, available at supreme.justia.com.

disavowed rumored black violence aimed at the landowning, office-holding white victims, armed with much more than shotguns.[9] The cowardly white Republican surrender included an agreement not to field their own ticket in the election. This amounted to turning the county over to the Democrats and leaving the black voters there to the tender mercies of the brutes who had been riding roughshod over them.

Determined, the local Woodpeckers nominated their own ticket anyway. In Wharton, Kyle Terry, a Woodpecker, accidentally encountered a Jaybird named Gibson, who was running for county assessor. Hot words became hot lead, leaving Gibson bleeding out on the street. A week later, one of his relatives, Volney Gibson, "happened to be visiting" Galveston, where he met Terry on the steps of the county courthouse and shot him dead.

Tensions came to a head on August 16, 1889, in the streets of Richmond. The Woodpecker Sheriff J. T. Garvey arrested the Jaybird Albert George, said later to have provoked his own arrest. As they approached the courthouse, deputy sheriffs Tom Smith and H. S. Mason and former county judge J. W. Parker came out to meet Garvey and the prisoner. Soon, though, they saw Gibson, who had shot Terry in Galveston, approaching the courthouse with a Winchester.[10]

Not surprisingly, somebody reached for a pistol and the gunfire began. Former sheriff J. W. Blakely fell first. Two of Garvey's deputies arrived on the courthouse lawn just in time to see him riddled with bullets. Deputy sheriffs Smith and Mason also dropped to the ground, Mason shot in shoulder. The Texas Rangers who rushed out of the courthouse also came under fire, and Judge Parker collapsed by the entrance, wounded in the groin. Although still suffering from his own wounds, Frost showed up and got shot again, fatally this time.

The casualty lists seem more horrifying given that the entire exchange took place on the steps of a courthouse. The state's solution

9 On the continuing violence of the Reconstruction, see Douglas, *Famous Texas Feuds*, 165–6, 166–7, 167–8, 168–9.

10 See Douglas, *Famous Texas Feuds*, 169–71, 173. Also Richard M. Brown, *Strain of Violence: Historical Studies of American Violence and Vigilantism* (New York: Oxford University Press, 1975), 258–9.

involved sending more Texas Rangers, who provided protection for the most conservative Democrats. By October 1889, a Jaybird Democratic Association entered politics by warning its political opponents to leave the county.[11]

In describing a later death sentence for William Caldwell, a Fort Worth paper noted that the county had seen "pitched battle between the Jaybirds and Woodpeckers in the streets of Richmond [which] resulted in the death of the sheriff and several citizens on each site." It added that "nearly all the leaders of these political factions have since died sudden or violent deaths."[12]

In hindsight, these killings in Arkansas and Texas appear racially— or even personally—motivated. This may have been largely true for the individual killers, but a cold political calculus underlay the decision of the authorities to permit the killers to avoid responsibility.

Saints and Sinners in the Pleasant Valley War

Perhaps nothing better embodies the political dimensions of even superficially personal violence as clearly as the events that broke out in Arizona. There erupted a range war so remarkably violent that it came to be remembered as having been fought "to the last man." This happened, in large part, because of disagreements between groups seeking to rule the territory.

On October 25, 1881, one of the most notorious events in Western history took place at the edge of Tombstone, Arizona. There, Town Marshal Virgil Earp, with his brothers Wyatt and Morgan and Doc Holliday, attempted to disarm Billy and Ike Clanton, Tom and Frank McLaury, and Billy Claiborne. The men clustered in a narrow lot next to a photographic studio, some six doors west of the rear entrance to the OK Corral.

---

11 Mike Vance and John Nova Lomax, *Murder and Mayhem in Houston: Historic Bayou City Crime* (Mt. Pleasant, SC: Arcadia Publishing, 2014).

12 "The Death Sentence. William Caldwell to Hang in Houston July 31," *Fort Worth Gazette*, June 23, 1891, p. 2, col. 6.

The cowboys were later said to have engaged in all sorts of violent criminal activities, but the lawmen did not move against them for these acts. Rather, the McLaurys, Clantons, and others moved about the street armed, in open disregard for the respectable "order" that cowboys observed in most places. The cow towns in Kansas—which had shaped the experience and expectations of the Earps—saw large numbers of gamblers, drunks, and gunmen sweep through seasonally. Their municipal regulations required gunmen to check their weapons when they entered the town limits.

The victors, for obvious reasons, cast the gunfight at the OK Corral as the work of a civilizing ex-Unionist Republican force to subdue the savage Democratic cowboys from Texas, even with the Georgian Holliday wielding the shotgun for the Earps. In the end, it seemed to have been as much of a feud as anything. Two days after the fight, Ike Clanton filed murder charges, and in case the courts failed to deliver justice the cowboys spent the next few weeks setting up ambushes of the Earps.

With their backs to the wall, the Earps hired Thomas Fitch to defend them. Just over fifty years old, the New York City–born lawyer had moved to Chicago and then to Milwaukee. There he became the editor for Sherman Miller Booth's *Free Democrat*, a paper that opposed slavery and supported land reform and that helped set the political climate for the emergence of Republicanism in Wisconsin. Fitch continued on to San Francisco, became an active Republican, and, in 1863, went to Nevada to work for the *Virginia Daily Union*, where he became acquainted with Samuel Clemens. He returned to California a lawyer and won election to Congress, where he gained his most consistent support by opposing federal efforts to suspend Utah's territorial government over polygamy. Ten years before Tombstone, he became a prominent legal voice for the Mormons, who hoped to send him to the Senate before their bid for statehood crashed. Fitch returned to Prescott in 1877, was elected to the territorial legislature, and moved to Tombstone a few years later.

Fitch's defense in the OK Corral trial proved expert. His questioning teased out the contradictions in the key testimony against the Earps by Democratic politician and Cochise County Sheriff Johnny Behan. The judge ruled that Virgil might have been injudicious in bringing the others to help him disarm the McLaurys and the Clantons, but that his choice had been fortuitous, given what had happened. Fitch added that the Earps had chased off the unarmed Ike Clanton, giving the lie to the claim that they had planned to murder the lot of them.

The victory boosted not only Fitch's well-earned reputation but the standing of the Mormons in Arizona as well. Mormons terrified their "Gentile" neighbors with their preoccupation with preserving their own separateness. In 1857, Utah's territorial governor Brigham Young had presided over the Mountain Meadows Massacre, where Mormon militia dressed as Indians attacked a party of settlers from Missouri, negotiated their surrender, and then slaughtered 120 men, women, and children on their way to California. Not until 1875 did the government prosecute anyone for these mass murders. Then, too, the closer Utah got to statehood, the more polygamy came into question.[13]

During these years, groups of Mormons had begun to colonize parts of Arizona. By the mid-1880s, they had their own newspaper, the *Orion Era*, and a key role in railroad development. As elsewhere, the Mormons introduced a distinctive and coherent force that encouraged cooperation to the exclusion of non-Mormons, who responded with tremendous resentment, as they had decades earlier in Missouri and Illinois. Mormons, though, believed that their neighbors victimized them and that they were compelled to enter politics in self-defense.[14] However, growing numbers of the Saints had begun to develop a pragmatic willingness to live and work with the Gentiles.

Mormons faced real challenges in terms of understanding circumstances in Arizona. While they saw Native Americans as the Lost Tribes of Israel in the Bible, they did not know what to make of

13 On this chapter of Mormon history, see Will Bagley, *Blood of the Prophets: Brigham Young and the Massacre at Mountain Meadows* (Norman: University of Oklahoma Press, 2002), and Ronald W. Walker, Richard E. Turley, Jr., and Glen M. Leonard, *Massacre at Mountain Meadows* (New York: Oxford University Press, 2008).

14 Daniel J. Herman, *Hell on the Range: A Story of Honor, Conscience, and the American West* (New Haven: Yale University Press, 2010). See also Rita Ackerman, *OK Corral Postscript: The Death of Ike Clanton* (Honolulu: Talei Publishers, 2006).

Chicano people, who often competed with them in raising sheep. Some rationalized their dislike of the dark-skinned Mexicans by claiming that they were descendants not of Indians but Africans. More problematic, they clashed with the Gentile rivals in the Aztec Land and Cattle Company, called the "Hash Knife" outfit because of the shape of its brand. This eastern-owned operation had a million acres, 32,000 cows, and skilled Texas cowboys to look after them. For many of the Mormons, the cowboys represented yet another face of the Gentile barbarians.[15] They thought they faced a rather undifferentiated opposition of sheepherders, ranchers, and Jewish merchants, and they protested U.S. anti-bigamy laws by flying the American flag at half-mast on July 4, 1885.

The Mormon presence added a vital force in the shaping of the territory's politics. The Saints who felt beleaguered returned to Utah to encourage heavier colonization, bringing two hundred families to Apache County, and tipping the balance of political power there in 1886. By then, Mormons in the eastern and western parts of the territory had begun to fall out with each other. Some of them convened with allies in Winslow to form a "People's Party," while others tried to establish a coalition with the Mexican population and the cowboys through a new Equal Rights Party, which included Ike Clanton's brother-in-law.[16]

In the Mormon stronghold of Apache County, adherents of the

15   Robert Carlock, *The Hashknife: The Early Days of the Aztec Land and Cattle Company, Limited* (Tucson: Westernlore Press, 1994); Jim Bob Tinsley, *The Hash Knife Brand* (Gainesville: University Press of Florida, 1993); William G. Robbins, *Colony and Empire: The Capitalist Transformation of the American West* (Lawrence: University Press of Kansas, 1994). See also Brown's *Strains of Violence* and his *No Duty to Retreat: Violence and Values in American Society* (New York: Oxford University Press, 1991), as well as William D. Carrigan, *The Making of a Lynching Culture: Violence and Vigilantism in Central Texas, 1836–1916* (Urbana: University of Illinois Press, 2004).

16   Daniel J. Herman, *Arizona's Secret History: When Powerful Mormons Went Separate Ways*, Common-Place 12, no. 3 (April 2012), available at common-place-archives.org. Two political dynasties of national importance grew out of Mormon politics in territorial Arizona—the Romneys and the Udalls—and the climate shaped the career of the Goldwaters as well.

"Winslow Convention" put forward the name of Commodore Perry Owens for sheriff, a candidate who also had the support of the Apache County Stockgrowers' Association. A bounty hunter employed by the more militant Mormons, he was expected to eradicate the criminal cowboys, and rival Chicano sheepherders, as well as corrupt local officials, particularly targeting the Jews. (One of these would have been Michel Goldwasser, a Jewish refugee of 1848 who had anglicized his name to Goldwater.) Shortly after Owens's victory in November 1886, an ambush took the life of the local prosecutor who initiated legal action against the Mormons.

The family of James Tewksbury, one of the gunmen, had been stealing livestock with the Grahams, but had a falling out. They then resorted to recriminations about pilfering horses and cattle from Jim Stinson. Stinson made a deal with the Grahams that he would pay for his cattle back if the Grahams turned the state's evidence against the Tewksburys, though the authorities found insufficient evidence to pursue the case. Both sides tried to use racism against the other. Describing Tweksbury as part Indian, the Grahams hoped to drive the "damn blacks" from the area.

Tensions escalated in 1885, when the Tewksburys leased some sheep and hired a Basque shepherd to bring them to Pleasant Valley. An ally of the Grahams, Andy Cooper—also called Andy Blevins—robbed and murdered the shepherd. However, it was the election of that particularly proactive sheriff Commodore Owens that sent the violence spiraling into the decade-long Pleasant Valley War, also called the Tonto Basic War or the Tonto Basin Feud.

When Fred Wells refused to help the Grahams drive off the Tewksbury cattle, the Grahams sent two deputies to seize Wells's cattle. Wells had already taken his goods, chattels, and family off toward the mountains, however. Two of the deputies caught up with the women, Wells's son, and a nineteen-year-old friend, Frederick Russell Burham. A deputy killed the family's pet dog. Using a good rifle, Wells dropped the lawman from a distance. The Tewksbury people seized the remaining deputy and held him hostage until they reached the safety of the mountains. Released, he returned to Globe, where private gangs had already begun to organize themselves to avenge the heroic dog-killer with a badge.

Burnham, meanwhile, made his own effort to get to Globe. He later told a memorable tale of spending several months in hiding before he could get into town and ask Judge Aaron H. Hackney of the Arizona *Silver Belt* newspaper for help. Hackney sheltered and assisted him in establishing several aliases before he escaped the area and found refuge in the relative tranquility of Tombstone.

In February 1887, Tom Graham ambushed and killed a Navajo man herding Tewksbury sheep in the Mogollon Rim. Graham buried his victim where he fell. An account of the murder appeared in William Owen "Buckey" O'Neill's *Hoofs and Horns*. This report described the beheading of the Navajo man's corpse.[17]

Memorably depicted by Sam Elliott in the *Rough Riders* TV series (1997), the real O'Neill became one of Arizona's pioneering Populists. The Missouri-born son of an Irish officer in the Union Army who was severely wounded at Fredericksburg, he sought to challenge the legislative special privileges of the railroad as a new manifestation of the government's subservience to slavery.[18] For the present, though, O'Neil still hoped to mount an offensive against the railroads from within the state's Republican Party.

The expansion of the violence in Pleasant Valley tended increasingly to involve figures such as O'Neill. Most officers of the law, however, found themselves involved in it. The expanding circle of Graham activity eventually had them driving off the horses of Jim Roberts, who O'Neill picked as his deputy in late 1889. Before leaving office in late 1890, O'Neill led an expedition into the contested district.[19]

Meanwhile, the Grahams's side recruited one of Billy the Kid's old partners, Tom Pickett. Because the authorities never had a warrant

---

17 Earle R. Forrest, *Arizona's Dark and Bloody Ground: An Authentic Account of the Sanguinary Pleasant Valley Vendetta that Swept Through Arizona's Cattleland in the Latter Eighteen-Eighties—the Graham-Tewksbury Feud* (London: Andrew Melrose, 1953), 38.

18 Mark Bevis, "The Legacy of Arizona's Populist Movement," KNAU Arizona Public Radio, August 22, 2012, available at knau.org.

19 See Forrest, *Arizona's Dark and Bloody Ground*, 117, 118, 173, 27, 28, 142, 184, 188, 208. Attacks on the Tewksburys in August 1887 represented "the first white blood" of the feud, 46.

when they kidnapped Pickett back in New Mexico, they had released him in Las Vegas. Pickett married in 1885 or 1886, his wife later rumored to have been the widow of Billy the Kid, and he soon drifted into Arizona where he went to work for the Aztec Land and Cattle Company. Early in 1887, Pickett and his firepower were engaged on behalf of Tom Graham.

Another self-described participant, Tom Horn entered the fray after hiring himself out as muscle in the spring of 1887. His later claim to have been the "mediator" of the Pleasant Valley War is questionable. He also boasted about having served as a deputy under three of the territory's most famous lawmen: O'Neill, Owens, and Glenn Reynolds.

Born to a rural northeast Missouri family, Horn had grown up with an abusive father among violent neighbors. He escaped to the Southwest at sixteen, around 1876, and allegedly killed his first man in a fight over a prostitute. The U.S. Cavalry employed him as a scout during its campaigns against the Apache, and he boasted of helping to bring in Geronimo in 1886. He returned to try his hand at ranching and mining, became utterly bored by the honest work, and began working as a regulator from Texas to Wyoming, gunning down suspected rustlers without "one shred of remorse." He worked for a rancher who became one of the prime suspects in the disappearance of Matt Blevins, but scholars never found definitive proof of which side used him.

In September 1887, the Graham faction surrounded the Tewksbury cabin in the early morning hours and shot down John Tewksbury and William Jacobs as they dashed for their horses. One story had a drove of hogs starting to devour their bodies until John Tewksbury's wife heroically walked out of the cabin with a shovel. The Grahams held their fire while she carved out shallow graves for the two men, after which both sides resumed firing. Tewksbury's wife denied this, noting that it took four men most of the day to bury the bodies about a foot down because of the hardness of the ground. They wrapped the murdered men in a sheet and piled rocks over them to keep wild animals from eating the remains.

A few days later, Apache County Sherriff Commodore Perry Owens in Holbrook heard that Andy Blevins had been bragging in a local store that he had killed Tewksbury and Jacobs. Owens rode over to the Blevins house on his own to serve a warrant. He found the house full, with a dozen members of the Blevins family present; Andy simply refused to come out and be served. When John Blevins, his half-brother, allegedly stormed out the front door with his rifle blazing, Owens shot him and Andy. Mose Roberts jumped through a window in the side of the house. Owens heard him running and fired instinctively, killing him on the spot.

Another of Andy's brothers, the fifteen-year-old Sam Houston Blevins, then picked up his pistol and broke free from his mother's arms to rush outside and take on the sheriff. He allegedly shot first, but the sheriff dropped him dead. Owens emerged unscathed and lionized by some factions in the territory, though the county commissioners fired him on the grounds that he overreacted in killing Sam Blevins.

The shootings continued. One of Owens's deputies subsequently killed Ike Clanton, who had escaped Wyatt Earp's wrath in Tombstone. In 1888, another of Owens's deputies handed over three more cowboys—probably all innocent—to a lynch mob. A posse under Sheriff William J. Mulvernon venturing out from Prescott caught up with John Graham and Charles Blevins during a shoot-out at Perkins Store in Young, Arizona.

By 1892, the vendettas had taken between twenty and thirty-four lives, leaving only one of the Tewksburys and one of the Grahams. Then, Tom Graham got killed in Tempe. Edwin Tewksbury, the last of that faction involved in the feud, became the prime suspect and faced trial for murder. Tewksbury turned to Thomas Fitch, the man who had defended the Earps in Tombstone. This proved to be a much tougher case, but the lawyer managed to stretch a straightforward issue into a legal technicality and he got Tewksbury off. Then, a second trial deadlocked the jury. The last Tewksbury was able to live until April 1904, when he died in Globe.[20] Less than twenty years later,

20 Leland J. Hanchett, Jr., *Arizona's Graham-Tewksbury Feud* (Phoenix, AZ: Pine Rim Publishing, 1994); Herman, *Hell on the Range.* See also Tom Horn, *Life*

Zane Grey's *To the Last Man* (1921) transformed the conflict into a morality tale on the futility of family feuds.

Meanwhile, after 1890, Buckley left his position as sheriff and took a position on the bench. From there, he launched a major direct effort to tax the railroads. As his fellow Republicans backed away from him, he edged closer and closer to the Populists. O'Neill became the mayor of Prescott and ran twice as the territory's delegate to Congress.[21] What he advocated may have been widely supported but his views were largely blasted out of civic life before the last Tewsbury bit the dust.

The Johnson County War

Developments in Wyoming dramatically illustrated the connections between cowboy discontent, range wars, and political insurgency. The arrogance of the big cattlemen in Wyoming created a general culture of resistance in the area. Between 1884 and 1886, cowboys—often transplanted or transient Texans—waged many well-timed strikes, apparently successful enough to inspire one last effort in 1886 that seemed to have won its demands but, without organization, could not protect the strikers from later reprisals.

The repression after the 1886 strike left Jack Flagg, Ned Champion, and others in Wyoming in the same position as Tom Harris and the more identifiable leaders in the Panhandle. Denied employment, the Wyoming cowboys resorted to the same solution as their Texas peers. In the fall of 1886, Flagg happened to encounter W. E. Hathaway, who wanted to sell a dozen head of cattle and get out of the business.

of Tom Horn: Government Scout and Interpreter (Denver: Louthan Book Co., 1904); *Life of Tom Horn, Government Scout and Interpreter, Written By Himself: A Vindication*, ed. Doyce B. Nunis, Jr. (Chicago: the Lakeside Press, R.R. Donnelley and Sons Company, 1987), 317–18.

21   Dale L. Walker's biography, with a foreword by Barry Goldwater, has been reprinted several times under different titles: *Death Was the Black Horse: The Story of Rough Rider Buckey O'Neill* (Austin, TX: Madrona Press, 1975); *Buckey O'Neill: The Story of Rough Rider* (Tucson: University of Arizona Press, 1983); *Rough Rider: Buckey O'Neill of Arizona* (Lincoln: University of Nebraska Press, 1997); and Ralph Keithley, *Buckey O'Neill* (Caldwell, ID: Caxton, 1949).

Flagg not only bought the cattle but also purchased Hathaway's registered Hat brand.

The operation developed quickly. Al Allison, Billy Hill, Lew Webb, and Thomas Gardner joined Flagg, together forming a small herd with a few hundred heads of cattle. As in Texas, all of them had friends working for the large ranchers, including foremen and even some owners. Allison, for example, used an alias instead of his real name, which was Martin Allison Tisdale, the brother of the rancher John A. Tisdale. The base of this operation was likely Flagg's little place on the Red Fork of the Powder River.[22]

The principal town in this area was Buffalo. The writer Owen Wister visited Fort McKinney, two miles east of Buffalo, and recorded his impressions of the place as "something horrible beyond words. They [Wyoming towns] all are." In a letter home, he suggested imagining the "most sordid part of Atlantic City, you can remember." After a bit more time there, though, he did find Buffalo "a shade better in its appearance" than most towns in the region.[23] As at Tascosa, the townsfolk tended to be skeptical and resentful of the large ranchers and sympathetic to the cowboys and small operators.

On the other hand, after the horrific losses in the terrible winter of 1886–7, most of the large owners nurtured a deep resentment of the cowboys. Flagg, particularly, made enemies with his rather blunt writings for the *Buffalo Bulletin*. The organized stockgrowers responded by agreeing not to do business with the small proprietors who competed with them. Those blacklisted or blackballed in this way also found themselves described—and increasingly treated—as "rustlers." Their Hat brand provided a rubric under which the smaller owners could participate in the spring roundup of 1887, pulling their own wagons.[24]

---

22 Helena Huntington Smith, *The War on Powder River* (Lincoln: University of Nebraska Press, 1967), 111–12; John W. Davis, *Wyoming Range War: The Infamous Invasion of Johnson County* (Norman: University of Oklahoma Press, 2010), 59–62; "The Passing of 'Jack' Flagg," *Cheyenne Daily Leader*.

23 Fanny Kemble Wister, ed., *Owen Wister Out West: His Journals and Letters* (Chicago: University of Chicago Press, 1958), 115–16.

24 Smith, *The War on Powder River*, 112–13; Davis, *Wyoming Range War*, 117–19.

Like Harris in Texas, Flagg even married as part of this attempted transition to respectability. The recently divorced Mariah Imogene Spang, a small women—nicknamed "Fairy"—had some education before marrying a logger at fifteen and coming to Wyoming, where they settled in Buffalo. To add to the family income, she took in sewing, baked, and cooked on ranches for the cowboys. After her husband abandoned the family, she began taking in washing and ironing and engaging in midwifery to support herself and her five children.[25] Flagg had done well enough to take the train home regularly to his remaining family back in Virginia during the off-season, and he took Mariah home to marry her there.

The worse conditions got, the more the big ranches sought to squeeze out the smaller operations, such as that of the Hat brand. The large concerns hoped to recover a portion of their earlier losses by claiming any and all unbranded cattle as their own. Then, too, the regulators they brought in continually asked for more men, more guns, and greater leeway in using violence against the small ranchers.

Key among these was Frank Canton. In the movie *Heaven's Gate* (1980), Sam Waterston presents a particularly upscale version of someone who was as proficient a murderer as any Texan in northern cattle country. Actually named Joe Horner, he had killed a black soldier in Jack County near the Indian Territory, launching a career of mostly rustling and robbery. Arrested, tried, and incarcerated, Horner escaped in August 1879 and fled the state. After arriving in Wyoming, he took the name Canton and presented himself as a respectable businessman and a Democratic office seeker.[26]

Flagg had managed to frustrate those ambitions, helping to elect as sheriff William Galispie "Red" Angus. A child of the Kansas border conflict, Angus had gone to war as a drummer boy with the Thirteenth Kansas and reenlisted to fight the Cheyenne. He had followed

25 Jennie Lee Pope Gibby, "Pioneer Grandmothers," Ogden and Taylor Family History, available at ogdentaylor.info.

26 Davis, *Wyoming Range War*, 51–3; Robert K. DeArment, *Alias Frank Canton* (Norman: University of Oklahoma Press, 1966). For his own account, see Canton, *Frontier Trails: The Autobiography of Frank M. Canton*, ed. Edward E. Dale (Norman: University of Oklahoma Press, 1966).

opportunities into Texas where he worked as a cowboy, then came north to Wyoming. He shared few of Canton's pretenses, marrying a former sex worker, and became known as the "mayor of Laurel Avenue," Buffalo's little red light district.[27] Flagg and Angus represented the broad political opposition of Populists and Democrats confronting the predominantly (but not exclusively) Republican membership of the Wyoming Stockgrowers' Association.

Defeated at the polls, Canton drew closer to the big operators, who themselves had become as frustrated as their Montana predecessors with politics, courts, and the law. Their private regulators became increasingly brutal in their dealings with the people. On July 23, 1889, they seized Jim Averell and Ellen Watson, who had defied the will of the large ranchers on several points and, therefore, came to be called "rustlers." The couple had been together for three years and applied for a marriage license a few weeks before. The thugs strung them up on a short rope, leaving them to strangle slowly, a warning to any who might be tempted to cross the big owners.[28] After the double murder, they started describing Watson as "Cattle Kate," a prostitute who took cattle for her services.

The arrogant brutality of the regulators grew worse. On June 4, 1891, U.S. Deputy Marshal Thomas G. Smith and Deputy Sheriff Joe Elliott, using bogus warrants, cornered and strung up Thomas Waggoner, a German living with his common law wife and a child. On December 1, they either ambushed or happened upon John A. Tisdale out on the road trying to get home with groceries and Christmas gifts. They shot him in the back and, for good measure, also executed his two horses and shot his dog. An attempt to take them to court sent Canton briefly fleeing the state. In November 1891, regulators also killed Orley Everett "Ranger" Jones, a Nebraskan who had been coming to Wyoming to work seasonally for several years.[29]

27 Davis, *Wyoming Range War*, 12–13.

28 Bill O'Neal, *The Johnson County War* (Austin, TX: Eakin Press, 2004), 42–54, 57–8. See also George W. Hufsmith, *The Wyoming Lynching of Cattle Kate 1889* (Glendo, WY: High Plains Press, 1993).

29 O'Neal, *The Johnson County War*, 69–70, 78; Davis, *Wyoming Range War*, 94–6, 97, 103.

Most of these paid killers may have been gentlemen hunters, as their apologist Wister claimed, but the work certainly attracted professionals, such as Tom Horn. In 1890, after participating in Arizona's Pleasant Valley War, he had turned up in Colorado operating with C. W. Shores to run down suspects in the robbery of the Denver and Rio Grande Western Railroad. Unlike law enforcement and much like extralegal enforcers in Texas, Horn and Shores tracked suspects across jurisdictional and state lines easily, finally running them down in the reorganized Oklahoma Territory. This kidnapping caused no problems for the kidnappers because their last captive "was considered by everyone in Colorado as a very desperate character." The Pinkertons sent Horn into Wyoming under the alias of Tom Hale. When the Wyoming Stockgrowers' Association began recruiting gunmen with no qualms about murder, Horn was a natural recruit, as was Tom Smith, a veteran of the Jaybird–Woodpecker war in Texas.[30]

The employers began planning a final solution in February 1892. They put Major Frank Wolcott in charge of a strike force to remove their enemies for good, and sent Smith down to Paris, Texas, to recruit gunmen for the enterprise. They hoped to repeat the successes of Stuart's Stranglers in Montana, but Wyoming had a much more dense population organized into towns who shared with the small ranchers a deep distrust of the power structure. So they would have to act quickly.

The force of about fifty guns spent Tuesday, April 5 in preparations and left Cheyenne around 6 p.m. They had provided their own evidence to justify the death list they carried. To carry out their plans, they would have to murder the law enforcement officers in Johnson County and execute the county commissioners before they could respond. This would allow them to control the area, for however long it might take to deal with the troublemakers.

Late Friday afternoon, April 8, they learned that Champion, Nick Ray, and other "rustlers" remained on Champion's Kaycee Ranch. Those who had a particular fear of Champion, a tough-minded little

---

30   Gary Scharnhorst, *Owen Wister and the West* (Norman: University of Oklahoma, 2015). O'Neal, *The Johnson County War*, 92–3, 97–8. Horn is alleged to have participated in much of the killing during and after the Johnson County War.

fellow who knew his way around a six-gun, suggested that they should mop up that problem on their way to Buffalo, while others worried about losing the element of surprise. The FORMER group prevailed and they set off for a nasty four or five hours struggling against gale force winds and heavy snow before reaching a gulley a few miles from the Kaycee around 4 a.m. Saturday, where they made a fire and rested briefly.

Around dawn, they approached Champion's cabin and began deploying their forces to ensure the outcome they wanted.[31] Since nobody wanted to knock on the door, they shivered outside for two hours before the people inside began to stir. Around 8 a.m., an old cowboy named Ben Jones stepped out with a bucket to get water from the stream downhill past the barn. He and his partner, Billy Walker, had been trapping to get through the winter and had stopped to shelter with Champion and Ray. The regulators waited for Jones to get past the barn, out of sight of the cabin, and jumped him. After a bit, Walker popped out, apparently wondering what was taking Jones so long. He dawdled just outside the cabin for some time before heading off himself. Once past the barn, he, too, fell into the hands of Wolcott's gang.

Then Nick Ray stepped out and met a volley of fire. Ray fell, badly wounded, and tried to crawl back to the cabin door. In the course of this, a small figure appeared in the doorway to provide covering fire, calmly returning shots in every direction. Only at this point did he and Ray become aware that they faced a large paramilitary operation that had surrounded their home.

In Ray's case, the realization did not last long, because he died quickly, leaving Champion on his own. However, holed up in his own cabin, he had a winter's worth of ammunition and several good firearms. After the first few attempts to rush the door met Champion's desperate and determined resistance, Major Wolcott's men seemed to lapse into some confusion. Nobody wanted to get killed doing this work, after all. The stalemate lasted through the late morning and into the early afternoon.

31 For the developments at the Kaycee, see Davis, *Wyoming Range War*, 145–52.

Around 2 p.m., a horseman and buggy approached the Kaycee. They started to turn in to the ranch but, unexpectedly, continued on. Actually, Alonzo Taylor and Jack Flagg, the man in the wagon, had hoped to spend the night with their friend Champion, but they sensed the unexpected activity there. Then, one of the regulators shouted, "That's Jack Flagg! Shoot him!" The two men raced over the little bridge nearby and Flagg managed to retrieve a rifle he used to discourage close pursuit. Some of the fire from the gunmen did hit some of the horses, and Taylor cut the wounded horses loose as he and Flagg mounted two that had not been shot and galloped off. However modest, Flagg's shooting persuaded the gunmen to give up the chase after about half a mile. Flagg and Taylor realized that they could do nothing to help Champion but get immediate help.

Meanwhile, the more sentient participants remaining around the cabin realized that they had lost the advantage of surprise and would get nothing for it unless Champion was killed. They prepared a wagon to torch and push into the cabin. Their prey could then choose to either burn to death where he stood or risk a run through dozens of armed men. To the unwanted admiration of those closing in on the cabin, the door flew open and Champion stormed out, a Winchester rifle in his left hand and a large pistol in his right. Even those who riddled him with bullets expressed their appreciation for a man who had died "game."[32] Left to his druthers, of course, Champion would probably not have chosen to be so remembered.

The mercenary would-be "invaders" of Johnson County now realized that they might soon face hundreds of armed men. They discussed the merits of making a mad dash for Fort McKinney. However, the fort would be near enough to Buffalo, where they would have the option of continuing on their mission should the county remain unprepared.

In fact, Sheriff Angus was on the verge of finding out that an invasion was on. Terrence Smith, a neighbor of Champion and Ray, had heard the first of the gunfire and watched the beginning of the siege

32 Ibid., 153–4.

from a ridge several miles distant. He had quickly taken off to Buffalo to warn Angus and the town.

Flagg and Taylor, meanwhile, stopped at a cluster of ranches that evening and found others preparing to move. Flagg gathered a dozen volunteers and headed back to the Kaycee. Only after sighting the regulator force did the locals become fully aware of what they faced. Flagg headed out again on the evening of April 10 with forty-nine men, enough to match the invaders.[33]

Meanwhile, the killers realized that Flagg would alert the countryside and thought their best chance would be to send word to Governor Amos Barber for reinforcements. Then, they holed up to wait at the TA Ranch, a few miles east of the Big Horn mountains. They spent much of Sunday, April 10 trying to fortify the long barn there in expectation of an attack. Around 1 a.m. the next morning, Sheriff Angus and the posse returned to Buffalo and began preparations to move against the "invaders" at the TA Ranch.

Remarkably, Governor Barber looked at the efforts of otherwise peaceful and unarmed civilians to prevent a band of hired killers from murdering to be a threat to public order. He telegraphed President Benjamin Harrison—the father of one of the "stranglers" in Montana—informing him of an "insurrection in Johnson County" and the need to send the army.

By Tuesday, April 12, a serious little battle raged around the defensive positions at the TA Ranch. Colonel James Judson Van Horn took nearly a dozen officers and some ninety men from Fort McKinney with orders to end the fighting by taking the besieged men into custody. A reporter for the *Cheyenne Daily Leader* wrote that the army found 175 attackers, of whom 125 were small ranchers, 25 mechanics and workingmen who owned some land, and 25 gamblers, rustlers, and riff-raff from the town. They had already built their own war wagon to provide moving cover to get close enough to fire the barn. Major Wolcott surrendered forty-five defenders with fifty revolvers and 5,000 rounds. Given that this had been a well-planned operation, the army clearly let Wolcott's men keep some of their weapons.

33 Ibid., 164.

Though Colonel Van Horn tended to vindicate the conduct of the attackers, what had happened had been little short of remarkable. A private armed force had set off to kill citizens who had not been arrested, charged, tried, or convicted of any crime. Canton's valise included documents indicating that the projected scope of their cleansing operation had been far beyond Johnson County. What they had in mind was nothing short of a bloodbath.

The army took its nominal prisoners into very loose custody, ultimately subjecting them to parole on the streets of Cheyenne. Meanwhile, the authorities took the two witnesses to the killing of Ray and Champion—the two trappers—into custody and took them into hiding, first in Omaha and then in Rhode Island. By the time the government permitted the civil officials in Johnson County to indict the men, the writing was already on the wall. The state sloughed the cost of prosecution onto the local government and then began piling on the expenses.

The residents of Wyoming became so distraught with such behaviors that the authorities had real difficulties keeping control of the situation. A journalist who had always supported the big operators, Asa Shinn Mercer wrote and printed his *The Banditti of the Plains*, exposing the conduct of the masters of the state. In response, they burned his press, had copies removed from the mail as obscenity, and arrested, jailed, and drove him from the state.[34]

After the Johnson County War, Flagg could no longer live comfortably away from other people. He moved his family to Buffalo and went into the newspaper business with the *People's Voice*.[35] Early on in Wyoming, figures such as Flagg bridged the emergent Populist movement and the Democrats.

In 1892, the state's Populists reached an understanding with the Democrats that elected Henry Asa Coffeen as the state's representative to the U.S. Congress. The Midwestern schoolteacher and former Illinois Greenbacker had moved with his family to Big Horn in 1884. He ran a store and a sawmill and brought horses from

---

34 See Asa Shinn Mercer, *The Banditti of the Plains* (Denver: n.p., 1894).
35 "The Passing of 'Jack' Flagg," *Cheyenne Daily Leader.*

Kentucky to the territory. When it became clear that the Burlington railroad would bypass Big Horn for Sheridan, Coffeen moved there and became a prominent figure in the community's development. In 1888, he became mayor and attended Wyoming's Constitutional Convention the following year. Interestingly, as historians gathered to hear Frederick Jackson Turner speak about the West's past, Coffeen served as Wyoming's official delegate to Congress. Bankers and financiers remained particularly eager to coax investments into the new state.[36]

The Populist leader in the state through all of this was a veteran of struggles elsewhere, a native of eastern Ohio and former school-teacher, Lewis Cass Tidball. After playing a prominent role in the Industrial Brotherhood's Greenback organization in Jasper County, Missouri, he had come west, marrying in Montana and taking up residence in Sheridan, Wyoming, in 1884. In the wake of the Johnson County War, Tidball won election to the state legislature and, in 1893, became the Speaker of the Wyoming House. He later ran for governor twice as a Populist and went on to establish the state's Socialist Party.[37]

One of the family histories of the Flaggs wrote of the big operators that "history records their humiliating defeat."[38] Yet, this was all very short-lived. The Populists were crushed, as were the Socialists and other radicals who never attained sufficient strength to get their concerns addressed. Despite the impression given by scores of movies, the squatters, homesteads, and "little people" could not vanquish the corporate goliaths. Quite the contrary. The movie *Blazing Saddles* was never a documentary.

36 Leonard Schlup, "I Am Not a Cuckoo Democrat! The Congressional Career of Henry A. Coffeen," *Annals of Wyoming* 66 (Fall 1994): 30–47; Davis, *Wyoming Range War*, 243, 245.

37 Tidball showed up in the 1880 Census at Leadville, but, for his later career, see Ichabod S. Bartlett, *History of Wyoming*, vol. 2 (Chicago: S. J. Clark Publishing Co., 1918), 626; Lewis L. Gould, *Wyoming: A Political History, 1868–1896* (New Haven: Yale University Press, 1968), 184, 437; Virginia Cole Trenholm, ed., *Wyoming Blue Book*, vol. 2 (Cheyenne: Wyoming State Archives and Historical Dept., 1974), 258, 259, 266, 380, 549, 568. See also Weston, *The Real American Cowboy*, 128.

38 "The Passing of 'Jack' Flagg," *Cheyenne Daily Leader*.

Then, too, the brutality with which the authorities dealt with the people of Wyoming created a very traditional kind of social banditry. Less than twenty-five miles southeast of Kaycee Ranch was Hole in the Wall, a remote pass through the Big Horn Mountains. Based there and in a few other sites nearby, the "Wild Bunch" launched a series of daring train robberies from 1899 on. Finally, pursued by Charles Siringo, Butch Cassidy and the Sundance Kid escaped in 1901 by leaving the country.[39]

As with the buffalo skinners or wolfers, those employed by the dominant institutions to eradicate what they deemed to be vermin rarely came to good ends themselves. Back in Texas, Thomas G. Smith and another veteran of the homicidal squad sent to Johnson County returned to their duties in official law enforcement. On November 4, they tried to force a black passenger to move back to the "colored" section of a train. The passenger, Commodore Miller, turned out to be a wanted man in no mood to take harassment. When the gunsmoke cleared, where he would sit had become a dead issue, as had Miller and Thomas G. Smith.[40]

After his role in the Johnson County death squads, Tom Horn worked briefly for the Pinkerton Detective Agency until they found him too homicidal to be reliable. From 1895 onward, he was implicated in a series of apparently unauthorized killings, capped by the 1901 murder of fourteen-year-old Willie Nickell, to which he confessed a year later while drunk. His old employers contributed to his defense, but former detective Siringo thought they had been motivated by fear that Horn would rat them out for extralegal activities. In November 1903, Horn faced his execution on the "Julian Gallows," the fancy new water-powered hanging machine.

39 Butch Cassidy's Wild Bunch consisted of Butch Cassidy (a.k.a. Robert Leroy Parker), the Sundance Kid (a.k.a. Harry A. Longabaugh), Elzy Lay, Tall Texan, "News" Carver, Camilla "Deaf Charlie" Hanks, Laura Bullion, George "Flat Nose" Curry, Harvey "Kid Curry" Logan, Bob Meeks, Kid Curry's brother Lonny Curry, Bob Smith, Al Smith, Bob Taylor, Tom O'Day, "Laughing" Sam Carey, Black Jack Ketchum, and the Roberts Brothers, along with several lesser known outlaw gangs of the Old West. Jesse James was also reported to have visited the Hole in the Wall hideout.

40 O'Neal, *The Johnson County War*, 225–6.

In a very real way, justice for Horn's fourteen-year-old victim had little to do with his hanging. The demands of the cattle trade subsumed everything into the slaughter. Buffalo, wolves, longhorns, Indians, Mexicans, Africans, hired cowboys, hired guns—all became ultimately disposable.

∽

The cowboy strikes, the range wars, and the political insurgencies underscore the extent to which the history became "heritage." Entertainment helped distill the experience of the American West into a memory that often inverted reality.

American culture has worked hard to create a comforting image of the West as a place that made theirs a free country of equal citizens. To some extent, this image seems to have survived the dawning recognition of the wholesale ethnic cleansing of native peoples from the region and the founding principles of racial stratification that informed U.S. settlement there. That comforting image required parsing the general social question into a range of issues, best accomplished by parsing them into distinct and disassociated issues. Thus, the overwhelming and ultimately common problem of the dehumanizing assumptions about the various peoples of color are broken into discrete problems. And these are severed from the translation of an old manorial sense of patriarchy and property into corporate agriculture and husbandry. To make the West what it became required the power and authority ruthelessly imposed by the established authorities back east, who used coercion and violence to impose its interests on the entire society.

An acknowledgement of these as part of a grand mythology and its brief exploration seems essential.

Conclusion

Wizardry, Empire, and the Final Subjugation of the West

Frederick Jackson Turner had only turned thirty-two before ascending to speak at the American Historical Association on July 12, 1893, at the Columbian Exposition in Chicago. He explained to his audience that the much-lauded democratic values of their society grew from the frontier experience. This thesis stressed the process—the moving frontier line—and the impact it had on pioneers and their legacy for the wider society. Turner described an American democracy

> born of no theorist's dream; it was not carried in the *Susan Constant* to Virginia, nor in the *Mayflower* to Plymouth. It came out of the American forest, and it gained new strength each time it touched a new frontier.[1]

The process of settling new lands freed Americans from the dysfunctional customs and values of the Old World. The frontier needed no standing armies, established churches, aristocrats, or nobles. Those who headed west found no landed gentry to control most of the land and levy their rents and taxes upon the toiling masses.

---

1 Frederick Jackson Turner, *The Frontier in American History* (New York: Henry Holt and Company, 1921), 293.

In this light, these unexpected labor revolts along the cattle trail—and their accompanying violent repression—both reflected and contributed to detonating the massive, popular insurgencies of the West in the Gilded Age. Turner became the first of a new profession that took on the specialized challenge of addressing the process of western expansion and the frontier in a materialist way. Yet, Turner's analysis threatened to conjure the old specter of American Exceptionalism that systematically relegated social discontent and political radicalism to the irrelevant margins. Paradoxically, perhaps, the development of a modern technology of communication and culture production actually strengthened the power of this ideology, which served to warp some of the best efforts to look through it at our history.

Turner

The man identified with a theory of the American frontier was born at roughly the same time as the cowboys who had pioneered the development of the economy and society of the West. Turner's father, the Republican editor of the *Portage Democrat*, had labored in the antebellum Wisconsin coalition that included a noisy group of land reformers who urged measures to secure a democratic redistribution of land as essential to republican government. A recognition of the significance of the frontier had been commonplace through most of Turner's youth. While, at its core, the land reformers repudiated Indian removal, slavery, and Manifest Destiny, the framework of political respectability within which they tried to operate naturally shaped more conservative interpretations.

Andrew Jackson Turner and Mary Olivia Hanford Turner provided their son with a far more secure early life than that of a frontiersman.[2] The future historian had barely reached the age of two when his neighbors elected his father to the legislature. As civil war swallowed the fathers of the cowboys, Turner's began passing through a series of

---

2   Richard Hofstadter, *The Progressive Historians: Turner, Beard, Parrington* (New York: Knopf, 1968), l.

public offices, including the mayoralty of Portage and state railroad commissioner. The old newspaperman developed an interest in the history of Portage and central Wisconsin strong enough to take up a pen on the subject.

Frederick Jackson Turner followed his father's interests into the University of Wisconsin at nearby Madison. Around the time that the cowboys were forming early labor combinations, Turner joined Phi Kappa Psi. He obtained his degree in 1884 and followed his aspirations into graduate work at Johns Hopkins, as Harris and his colleagues emerged from their second effort at organizing a roundup.

As the cowboys learned and relearned how to read the trail north to Dodge City, Turner studied Emerson, Charles Darwin, and Herbert Spencer. On paper, the West provided opportunity and mobility, but harsh realities chilled such expectations. While Turner made his way through the blasts of winter to his classes at Hopkins, that series of vicious storms blasted their whiteness across the West, visiting market-driven mass exterminations on the overstocked grazing lands and impoverishing most of those who sought to make a living there.

Turner obtained his doctorate in 1890, as the old mass cattle drives had already become a thing of the past and a despairing Tom Harris took his own life. The historian wrote his dissertation on Indian trade in Wisconsin without indicating much concern for the fate of the last of the indigenous peoples still striving to live beyond the control of the government concentration camps.

A few years later, at the World's Fair, though, Turner's thesis electrified his peers, who saw it as a brilliant contribution to an interpretive understanding of the past. His essential insight that the Census of 1890 documented an end to the frontier seemed straightforward enough. Yet, one cannot help but wonder whether any of his listeners, as they shuffled off to ponder the meaning of it all, even spoke with any of the native peoples present at the Fair, or the conductor of one of the stagecoach tours of the fairgrounds, Broncho John Sullivan.

Almost nobody denied that Turner had a point, but over time historians have offered several telling criticisms of his position. Some have pointed out that multiple factors always shape the course of American civilization, some going beyond the issues of the frontier.

Urban historians have pointed out that towns and trade became primary engines of expansion, not lone settlers establishing farms. Others have complained that Turner ignored the role of women and gender issues in shaping society.[3]

The generalizations central to the grandeur of Turner's thesis carried many risks. His sense of the West—like that of his similarly educated contemporaries—had been distant enough to overlook the specifics of settling places as different as Yonkers and Nome. Issues related to the presence of women and indigenous people may have loomed larger in some times and places than others. Moreover, settlers carried plenty of preexisting assumptions and values when they arrived in the West, just as people carried cultural and ideological baggage with them when they crossed the Atlantic. For Turner, "democracy" represented something new and disconnected from classical democracy; what happened on the frontier may have influenced the style of American politics but had very little impact on the institutional structures of power.

More fundamentally, Turner offered a plausibly materialist explanation for American Exceptionalism. This suited his new profession, coming into its own in an age characterized by "scientific racism," coupled with muscular Christianity. The business of interpreting the past—like any other business—might involve a woman or person of color or workingman who lived long enough or even a reformer of whatever background. However, white men from financially secure families with direct associations to the mechanisms of power had responsibility for raising the interpretive structures and defining safe boundaries for the discussion.

Some of Turner's intellectual children certainly acknowledged violence—particularly racialized violence—as central to the development of the West. The process of western expansion carried the implicit elimination of the native peoples, which made ethnic cleansing an essential feature of white civilization's development.

---

3 Wilbur R. Jacobs, *On Turner's Trail: 100 Years of Writing Western History* (Lawrence: University of Kansas, 1994); Patricia N. Limerick, "Turnerians All: The Dream of a Helpful History in an Intelligible World," *American Historical Review* 100 (June 1995): 697–716.

Patricia N. Limberick's *The Legacy of Conquest* in 1987 suggested that the West of the past never quite came to an end, and that the conquest it inspired continues to inform the U.S. sense of itself.[4]

Race was central to that violence. Among the bits of baggage the migrants to the West carried with them, white supremacy not only justified the violent removal of the Indians but informed the construction of "civilization" in the West. As with other transported ideas, it came to be applied somewhat differently from time to time and place to place when dealing with native peoples, Hispanics, African Americans, and others.

However sanctioned by a racial hierarchy, the violence had serious implications for the techniques of controlling "savagery" with the forces of "civilization." It created what Richard Slotkin termed, in the concluding volume of his highly acclaimed trilogy on the cultural impact of the West, a "gunfighter nation."[5] Class violence against the cowboy strikers obviously formed part of a wider legacy of repressive violence against workers, farmers, and social critics.

The use of violence became inseparable from an inversion of the responsibility for its employment. Exaggeration or actual misinformation about violence aimed at whites by Indians, insurgent political movements against the armed minions of the state, or strikers against employers became an issue only because it justified violent repression. What the mythology celebrated as "law and order" or "civilization" required brutal feuds and range wars, which treated as "savage" any serious movement of workers or radical criticisms of capitalism.

The West and the Persistence of Its Discontents

Conditions in the West, along with the rest of the nation, radicalized Americans. Certainly, the hard times that had begun in 1873 moved

---

4 Patricia N. Limberick, *The Legacy of Conquest: The Unbroken Past of the American West* (New York: W. W. Norton & Co., 1987).

5 Richard Slotkin, *Gunfighter Nation: The Myth of the Frontier in Twentieth-Century America* (New York: Atheneum, 1992).

desperate wage earners of all sorts to resort to versions of the mass strike inaugurated by African Americans to secure emancipation. From 1877 discontents with the system faced the inflexible institutional opposition of their employers and the government, so workers tended to accept the institutional limits imposed on them—focusing their efforts on the fight against particular employers in specific industries—or they tried to mount effective electoral challenges against the employers' control of the government.

When both of these approaches failed, the more radical social critics, interested in systemic changes, fell back upon old techniques in the hopes that they might produce better results than in the past. Former adherents of the Industrial Brotherhood, such as G. B. De Bernardi, fostered a new "Labor Exchange" project. The name itself recalled the antebellum projects of Josiah Warren, but the goal became part and parcel of Edward Bellamy's nationalism and of socialist projects through the end of the century.[6]

The weight of American Exceptionalism and its civilizing mission often shaped efforts to promote a more egalitarian society. Racism permeated most of those efforts, which regularly documented the hostility of their participants toward Indians, Hispanics, African Americans, and, especially in the West, Asians, though this hostility was often challenged. A proposed Union Labor party position to "absolutely exclude the Chinese from the United States" sparked some debate, one delegate pointing out that "the platform of the party declared that all men were born free and equal, and that the Chinese had a right to come here." Even as Delphin M. Delmas battled against "corporate personhood" in the California courts, he participated in Democrat-sponsored rallies urging action to stop Chinese immigration.[7]

---

6 On De Bernardi, see H. Roger Grant, *Self-Help in the 1890s Depression* (Ames: Iowa State University Press, 1983), 41–4, 47, 53–4; Buck, *The Granger Movement*, 97, 195; *American Annual Cyclopedia*, 1874, 576–9; Nordin, *Rich Harvest*, 178–9. See, for example, "People's Meeting at Sarcoxie," Carthage *PP*, Oct. 8, 1874, p. 3. Other political meetings took place at most localities listed in the Grange directory.

7 "Knocked Clean Out. Union Labor Will Have Nothing to Do with Georgeism," *Cincinnati Commercial Gazette*, May 17, 1888, p. 1; "Anti-Chinese," *Sacramento Daily Union*, February 24, 1886, p. 3.

Broncho John Sullivan did not give the question enough thought to avoid unconsciously accepting its standards. He complained that speculators claimed ownership of the land originally settled by the ambitious and industrious settlers of the West. He recalled with nostalgia how the original settlers of the West consented when they "turned their entire property over to people they never saw before, but knew they were the genuine native whites."[8] Racism provided a vital bridge to permit reconciliation with the dominant powers.

The Topolobampo community of 1886–94 revealed the particular limits of communitarian impulses. The architects of this particular utopia sought to fund their colonization of that promising bay on the Gulf of California through a railroad venture, jointly sustained by the Mexican government and American investors. No less radical a figure than the radical Populist John William Breidenthal embraced the project, invested heavily in it, and became its secretary.[9] Functioning as agents of American imperialism may have been the last thing participants hoped to do, but the strategic decision to operate within the framework of corporate capitalism doomed the colony.

Within a few years of Turner's paper, the United States embarked on violent globalization of its frontier experience with the Spanish–American War of 1898, to which policy makers welcomed appropriate representatives of the entire society. Buffalo Bill took time out from his Wild West show to suggest organizing a company of scouts. One writer suggested that 3,000 Indians under leaders such as Sitting Bull would make short work of the Spanish.[10] The Spanish–American War came to demonstrate how Indians, white cowboys, and black "buffalo soldiers" could all contribute to the civilizing mission of the United States.

Most famously, Theodore Roosevelt raised volunteer cavalry regiments among the cowboys of the West. The governor of New Mexico hoped to fill the first regiment with volunteers of Spanish

---

8   Sullivan, *Life and Adventures of Broncho John.*

9   *Kansas: A Cyclopedia*, vol. 3, 30–1.

10   Clifford P. Westermeier, *Who Rush to Glory: The Cowboy Volunteers of 1898: Grigsby's Cowboys, Roosevelt's Rough Riders, Torrey's Rocky Mountain Riders* (Caldwell, ID: Caxton, 1958), 45–6.

descent, but the War Department selected Captain Leonard Wood as commander with Roosevelt as his lieutenant colonel. Despite objections from Republican loyalists, Wood and Roosevelt sought the assistance of the Populist mayor of Prescott, William "Bucky" O'Neill, who had made enemies with his efforts to tax the railroad. Nevertheless, he became one of the most prominent figures in Roosevelt's "Rough Riders." The image of the regiment remained forever that of cowboys, though college athletes, Ivy League adventurers, aspiring local office seekers, and others likely outnumbered the cowpokes.

Cowboys may have been even more sparse in the other two volunteer cavalry regiments, which did not see action in Cuba. The authorities had mandated that the Third U.S. Volunteer Cavalry be raised in the east, but wound up taking on a surplus of enthusiastic Westerners. These included Seth Bullock, who had worn a badge in Deadwood.[11]

Nevertheless, in addition to O'Neill, the war involved a number of people already discussed. Tascosa's Doctor Henry C. Hoyt—the friend of Billy the Kid—became a surgeon general in the Philippines. After working on supply in Tampa, Tom Horn went to Cuba to get the trains to the front, supposedly witnessing the Rough Riders in action before San Juan Hill, where O'Neill lost his life.

Despite his socialist proclivities, Sullivan left his Wild West shows behind to serve as a trainmaster in Tampa for troops on their way to Cuba, and then in Seattle for those heading to the Philippines. He returned to make Valparaiso his home, where part of his story and artifacts from his career in show business are cherished parts of local history. He kept the bear, which he had raised from a cub and treated as a pet, to the astonishment of many locals. One of the Indian women who had performed in the Wild West shows also reportedly remained with him, and they had several children. He himself lived to a remarkably old age, dying in 1951. War doubtlessly contributed to the town's acceptance of what it surely saw as part of an emerging ability in spite of his eccentricities.

11   Ibid., 27–8. Melvin Grigsby of Potosi, WI; enlisted on December 11, 1861, as a private and mustered into "C" Co. WI 2nd Cavalry, taken prisoner on March 8, 1864, Big Black, MS and mustered out on April 17, 1865.

So, too, the militant old veteran of the movement Joseph R. Buchanan had inadvertently mapped out what became part of an emerging Progressive agenda with his nine-word platform of 1888. Conversely, his sense of government as a force separate and independent from the tensions and conflicts of the society it governs drew him ever closer to the early-twentieth-century reform agenda. It was not surprising, perhaps, that even as Gene Debs reminisced about Buchanan's courage and consistency, his old friend wound up supporting Woodrow Wilson, whose policies would later place Debs back behind bars.[12]

Even critics of this extroverted version of American Exceptionalism sometimes missed the point. They criticized the arrogance of the United States while assuming universal applicability of its version of "democracy." They protested that the 1898 war established a chain of banana republics across Latin America tied to U.S. corporations. However, they have often failed to see through the assumptions that the system prevailing at home had been somehow more democratic, more republican, more egalitarian.

In reality, many of the essential features of those banana republics were homegrown. Through the first part of its history, U.S. wealth had been firmly rooted in a plantation system that grew, harvested, and sold a product for sale in a world market. The story of the cattle industry in the West demonstrates that many features of that system survived the Civil War. From some perspectives, then, the large scale of commercial agriculture actually makes the United States the first banana republic, albeit without bananas.

Meanwhile, as resistance continued at home, it assumed forms that mixed new elements with traditional concerns. Shortly after Turner's paper, the Panic of 1893 began creating new kinds of cowboys, transient workers who mounted the Iron Horse. Some of the old romance of the trail and travel survived, along with the fraternal sense of being seasonally overworked and underappreciated. Steam and steel even translated the language of tramping into that of bindle stiffs. In 1894, as their numbers continued to grow with the depression, Jacob S.

12 *Scannell's New Jersey First Citizens*, vol. 2, 72.

Coxey, an old Greenbacker from Canton, Ohio, offered a new strategy that the authorities could not coopt or derail so easily.

"Coxey's Army" mobilized tens of thousands of the unemployed and homeless to converge on Washington, DC. They hoped to camp out there until the government addressed their needs. When the divisions from the West Coast reached Reno, Nevada, a former cowboy named William D. "Big Bill" Haywood joined them. He had taken to the saddle to work for his in-laws and enjoyed the work, but conditions forced him into the mines, where he became ever more painfully aware of the injustices he faced on the job.[13] He dropped out when the chance of a job came up in Chicago, but the world had not heard the last of Haywood.

Haywood left as the legions of the unemployed reached Henry Vincent, who was in Chicago at the time. Vincent had gone there in the hopes of bringing Populism to the urban workers and building a party on a truly national scale. He joined Coxey's army, pen in hand, and created a book-length account of the movement. A disapproving Owen Wister happened to cross their paths at Columbus, Ohio, but went unnoticed.[14] In the end, their arrival in the capital had an impact, but their numbers were never more than a fraction of what they might have been.

These new kinds of mass actions based their approach on the sense that "the people" ultimately had only one real asset: their numbers. The actions were designed to mobilize those numbers in the most effective way, but doomed to be sidetracked into categories that minimized the impact of those numbers.

A little more than two decades after Coxey's Army, a very traditional form of protest resurfaced briefly in the heartland, where cowboys once drove the longhorns from Texas to the Kansas railheads. In the 1916 presidential election, the Democratic incumbent, Wilson, secured his reelection with the slogan "He Kept Us Out of War."

13　Peter Carlson, *Roughneck: The Life and Times of Big Bill Haywood* (New York: W.W. Norton & Co., 1983), 35–6, 43–4.

14　Harold R. Piehler, "Henry Vincent: Populist and Radical-Reform Journalist," *Kansas History* 2 (Spring 1979): 24–5; Gary Scharnhorst, *Owen Wister and the West* (Norman: University of Oklahoma, 2015), 70.

Socialists cast more than a quarter of the ballots in Seminole County, Oklahoma, however, and almost as many in neighboring Pontotoc County. There, too, a radical tenant farmers' organization called the "Working Class Union" not only opposed imperialist war, but had a deep-rooted hatred of conscription going back over half a century, when Indians in the territory and white residents of Arkansas formed secret pledges to resist the Confederate draft.[15]

Despite Wilson's sloganeering, he not only led the United States into war, but inaugurated conscription in July 1917. From August 2 to 3, the "Green Corn Rebellion" brought an estimated 800 to 1,000 Seminoles, Muscogee Creeks, African Americans, and Euro-Americans—most of them young tenant farmers—into the field, arms in hand. The papers quoted their Working Class Union as declaring:

> Now is the time to rebel against this war with Germany, boys. Boys, get together and don't go. Rich man's war. Poor man's fight. The war is over with Germany if you don't go and J.P. Morgan & Co. is lost. Their great speculation is the only cause of the war.

They hoped to march on Washington, DC, drawing countless numbers of other opponents of the war into action with them. After several armed encounters, the federal authorities came down hard on them, killing Clifford Clark, an African American tenant farmer, and a few others. The government arrested nearly 450 people, filing

---

15   Garin Burbank, *When Farmers Voted Red: The Gospel of Socialism in the Oklahoma Countryside, 1910–1924* (Westport, CT: Greenwood Press, 1976); David A. Chang, *The Color of the Land: Race, Nation, and the Policies of Land Ownership in Oklahoma, 1832–1929* (Chapel Hill: University of North Carolina Press, 2010); Davis D. Joyce, and Fred R. Harris, *Alternative Oklahoma: Contrarian Views of the Sooner State* (Norman: University of Oklahoma Press, 2007); Nigel Anthony Sellars, "'With Folded Arms? Or With Squirrel Guns?' The Green Corn Rebellion," *The Chronicles of Oklahoma* 77 (Summer 1999); "Green Corn Rebellion," *Encyclopedia of Oklahoma History and Culture*, available at okhistory.org; "Treasonous Tenant Farmers and Seditious Sharecroppers: The 1917 Green Corn Rebellion Trials," *Oklahoma City University Law Review* 27, no. 3 (Fall 2002), via the National Agricultural Law Center, 1097–114.

charges against 184 and sentencing 150 to jail or prison terms of sixty days to ten years.

For all its triumphalism, the civilizing mission of Roosevelt and Wilson remained as incomplete at home as abroad. This reality made the civic mythology of the West, in which the cowboy provided an icon essential for cultivating a domestic memory of the past, all the more important.

Smoke and Mirrors

The new professional history of Turner and his contemporaries emerged alongside—and not particularly distinct from—what has come to be called "heritage." The Wild West shows demonstrated early on how to market a fundamentally comforting sense of the past as the natural prelude to an improved present. However, the careers of Owen Wister and Lyman Frank Baum offer an important insight into both the message and the way it was conveyed.

Wister's *The Virginian* (1902) became the novel that made the Western genre in American letters. Wister's father had been a well-heeled doctor born in Philadelphia, and his mother was the daughter of Pierce Mease Butler and Fanny Kemble, the British actress and later writer of the antislavery *Journal of a Residence on a Georgian Plantation in 1838–1839*. He had first come to Wyoming in 1885, shortly after his Harvard classmate Theodore Roosevelt moved to the area. Wister lived long enough to disapprove of Theodore's cousin, Franklin D. Roosevelt, and the reforms of the 1930s.[16]

Jack Flagg's descendants believed that he had been the model for Wister's laconic "Virginian." That may well have been possible, but Wister so completely remade his character that nothing remained of the strike leader and militant foe of the big operators. Instead, Wister's "Virginian" was a tall, dark, soft-spoken but tough-minded company

---

16 Gary Scharnhorst, *Owen Wister and the West* (Norman: University of Oklahoma, 2015).

man. The Johnson County War provided the backdrop for the romance between Wister's hero and the schoolmarm and his regular encounters with the gambler, Trampas, but the writer had no sympathy for working cowboys.

Wister's simplistic version of the West and Westerners confirmed, and ultimately comforted, the predispositions of most literate whites. It went through numerous editions and got to the stage in 1904. Dustin Farnum, who played the title role, went on to reprise that performance in Cecil B. DeMille's 1914 movie version. Other movie versions followed in 1929, 1946, 2000, and 2014, and it inspired a television series (1962–71).

The legacy of Lyman Frank Baum perhaps better explains how visions such as that of *The Virginian* came to resonate so intensely with the American psyche. Baum became famous by writing books for children, perhaps even helping to inspire Laura Ingalls Wilder to enter the field. Born in upstate New York, he survived a sickly and miserable childhood that included two years in a military academy. He made persistent ventures into writing and publishing until, at age thirty, he produced his first book, a guide to raising chickens. He also had a theatrical flare and dallied with acting in various theatrical troupes, eventually turning to playwriting. On November 9, 1882, Baum married Maud Gage, a daughter of Matilda Joslyn Gage, a famous women's suffrage and feminist activist.

Less than six years later—in July 1888—Baum and his wife moved to Aberdeen, Dakota Territory. There, he opened a store and, as it became increasingly disappointing financially, took editorial jobs for the *Aberdeen Saturday Pioneer*. He also sang in a quartet with James Kyle, one of the first Populist senators. Though reform-minded, Baum had an interest in spiritualism—he and Kyle later joined the Theosophical Society—and learned to make points in a less than straightforward way. He responded to ongoing Indian extermination with a Swiftian piece. "Having wronged them for centuries," he wrote, "we had better, in order to protect our civilization, follow it up by one more wrong and wipe these untamed and untamable creatures from the face of the earth."

In 1900, Baum produced *The Wonderful Wizard of Oz*.[17] A cyclone sweeps up a Kansas farmhouse with Dorothy and her little dog Toto inside, carrying it off to the magical land of Oz and dropping the structure on the Wicked Witch of the East, freeing her subjects, the Munchkins. The Good Witch of the North presents the magical Silver Shoes of the deceased sorceress to Dorothy, directing her to the capital, Emerald City, and the great and powerful Wizard of Oz. On her route down the yellow brick road, she encounters a Scarecrow in need of a brain, a Tin Woodman who needs a heart, and a Cowardly Lion in search of courage. The Wizard looks different to each of them, but awesome to all. He agrees to give each of them what they wanted if they can slay the Wicked Witch of the West, who rules over the Winkies. After many adventures, Dorothy angrily throws a bucket of water on the Wicked Witch, who melts away to the joy of the Winkies, who are now as free as the Munchkins.

Long after Baum's death, scholars argued that he had embedded Populist symbols and personalities into his work. Without solid documentation, these interpretations cannot be confirmed, but the contemporary literature of utopianism certainly informed his creation of Oz. Edward Bellamy's *Looking Backward* (1888), for example, enjoyed immense popularity, particularly in Theosophical circles, in which Baum, his wife, and his mother-in-law participated.[18]

Appearing almost simultaneously with Wister's *The Virginian*, the publisher presented *The Wonderful Wizard of Oz* with a printing of about 250,000 copies, partly because the Chicago Grand Opera House had already planned to make the story into a play that would become a "musical extravaganza." That musical debuted on June 16, 1902, with costumes modeled after the book's

---

17   Martin Gardner and Russel B. Nye, *The Wizard of Oz and Who He Was* (East Lansing: Michigan State University Press, 1957); Katharine M. L. Rogers, *Frank Baum, Creator of Oz: A Biography* (New York: St. Martin's Press, 2002).

18   See also John Algeo, "A Notable Theosophist: L. Frank Baum," *American Theosophist* 74 (August–September 1986): 270–3; Henry M. Littlefield, "The Wizard of Oz: Parable on Populism," *American Quarterly* 16 (Spring 1964): 47–58; David B. Parker, "The Rise and Fall of *The Wonderful Wizard of Oz* as a 'Parable on Populism,'" *Journal of the Georgia Association of Historians* 15 (1994): 49–63.

illustrations. Eight years later, the first movie version of *The Wonderful Wizard of Oz* appeared, joined by three others set in Oz in 1910. Three more followed in 1914. Persistent efforts followed to create more versions before the 1939 *Wizard of Oz* with Judy Garland, by which time the book had sold over a million copies. Other versions followed.

Most importantly, Baum played mercilessly with the distinction between reality and perception. As Dorothy and her three companions return to the Emerald City, they are again transfixed by the overwhelming image of the Wizard. At a critical junction, the playful Toto pushes over a screen, revealing an old man engineering the image of the wizard. In fact, he turns out to have been just another refugee from the plains, blown to Oz not by a cyclone but in a hot air balloon from Omaha. He provides the Scarecrow, the Tin Man, and the Lion with what amounts to various placebos, telling them that they will function as a brain, a heart, and courage. Because of their faith in the Wizard, these fixes actually work. The film and television adaptations of the book implicitly repeat this lesson.

Turner's thesis had many complex dimensions, with a subtext that reached far beyond materialism to emphasize the value of perceptions. Less tangible considerations came to have very tangible results. As we have seen, matters of race, racialized violence, violence as a means of social control, patriarchy, the quest for empire, and the profit motive all became vitally important. Of course, none of these represented particularly new considerations.

Culture hastened the nationalization—even internalization—of artificially constituted "Western values." Even as Turner wrote on the importance of the west, the various gaits of the cowboy's mount inspired a music that walked, trotted, and loped through the presentation of Western themes. Songs about westward expansion appeared early but began to make their way into songbooks around the turn of the century, notably the 1910 compilation of John Lomax, *Cowboy Songs and Other Frontier Ballads*. Phonographs and radio commercialized the music, merging it into the broader category of "country music," creating the genre of "C&W" that subsumed and repackaged the tunes and rhythms associated with the West. By mid-century, the most important remaining feature distinguishing western music seemed to be the identifying dress of "the singing cowboy," a cultural icon typified by Gene Autry, made possible by the new visual medium.

Perhaps more importantly, less than a year after Turner's paper, Thomas A. Edison's cameras recorded a short piece on Buffalo Bill and relied on his Wild West Show for additional short scenes of the West; *Bucking Broncho*, and *Annie Oakley* demonstrating her marksmanship. Two looks at the Sioux Indians accompanying Buffalo Bill followed in 1894; they performed the Ghost Dance that had inspired the last great revolt of the native people, as well as sixteen seconds of the Buffalo Dance. In 1899 Edison's company offered a forty-five-second short titled *Cripple Creek Bar-room Scene*, but then turned to documenting what they could of the Spanish–American War. In the aftermath of the war, though, the industry turned back to the West. In 1903 they released *Kit Carson*, *The Pioneers*, and, most importantly, the eight-minute *The Great Train Robbery*. From the 1910s to the 1950s a quarter of all Hollywood films were Westerns.

The Reel West

Film buffs and scholars have cranked out vast amounts of material on cinematic treatments of the West. While there is little to contribute to aesthetic evaluations or criticisms of the genre, a few observations are in order here. Moviemaking only indirectly reflects what "the people" think or believe about the West (or anything else). A successful project needs only connect enough to make itself profitable.

The fathers of the old cow towns would see their concerns well reflected almost immediately in *The Great Train Robbery* (1903). This short clearly established a vital celluloid cycle of the Western: criminal activity, chase, and retribution—the realization of a "regeneration through violence," to use Slotkin's words. Writ large, it validated a time-honored faith in sin, the community response in defense of virtue, and the painful but redeeming affirmation of universal good and evil through the victory of the former. Hundreds of these often brilliantly done morality tales built to the epic triumphalism of *How the West Was Won* (1962), national triumphalism—white nationalism, to be precise—traced the extension of Euroamerican hegemony across North America, beginning with a film's narrated dramatization of white hegemony's extension across North America begins with an explicit statement of its intent to celebrate the triumph of progress over nature and "primitive man."

While rarely so explicit, movies and television generally share the premises and assumptions of the 1903 film. Indeed, a large part of the Western genre involves police work of a particularly more violent and less cerebral order than contemporary crime stories. The 1881 shootout at the OK Corral in Tombstone occupies a key position in our collective memory of the West, and not so much because of the importance of what happened in the brief heyday of one Arizona boom town. After all, the grappling of Republican Wyatt Earp and his clan for power against Democrats from Texas played out across many communities in the Southwest.

The mechanics of the process are evident. *Frontier Marshal* (1939), *My Darling Clementine* (1946), *Gunfight at the OK Corral* (1953), *Tombstone* (1993), *Wyatt Earp* (1994), and lesser films celebrate the triumph of order and its identification with virtue. This happened primarily because we understand the story almost entirely through the eyes of Earp, who later wound up in Hollywood as a consultant in the production of Westerns, a phase of his career highlighted in the well-named *Sunset* (1988). The fame of the OK Corral also inspired a television series, *The Life and Legend of Wyatt Earp* (1955–61).

From the OK Corral emerged an iconic image, that of the laconic, reluctant lawman fighting against whatever chaos the cowboys or others passing through town might generate. None did this better than the TV series *Gunsmoke* (1955–75), which spanned two decades on law enforcement by U.S. Marshal Matt Dillon in Dodge City.

Of course, the instrumentalities of the law might not be synonymous with justice. An award-winning portrayal of Judge Roy Been in *The Westerner* (1940) depicted a possibly well-intentioned figure with too much power, which he tended to abuse. In *The Life and Times of Judge Roy Bean* (1972), the jurist seems little more than a particularly imaginative and entrepreneurial outlaw, who establishes himself as the law.

Conversely, some who hungered for justice might find themselves outlaws. *The Magnificent Seven* (1970) depicted nearly broken men who nevertheless gathered in one final self-sacrificing gamble in defense of an otherwise defenseless little town against a massively larger force of other gunmen. The 2016 remake even casts the villain as a great mining capitalist and uses rhetoric borrowed from the Occupy movement. Placing such portrayals safely in the past, though, saves the idea that "progress" and "civilization" have rescued the world from such injustices.

Movies also turn the mold inside out without breaking it. In *True Grit* (1969, 2010), the fictional Rooster Cogburn, a combination of a lawless partisan of the Lost Cause and a lawman, reflects some real people. Another John Wayne classic, *The Shootist* (1976), portrays a man without a badge whose ruthlessness serves the cause of order as surely as if he wore one. Then, too, *High Noon* (1952) returns to the Earp-like image of the single man of integrity standing in defense of order, but also raises larger questions about the communities he serves, offering us a look at a town where the much-touted sum of individual self-interest produces nothing more than self-interested abandonment of the duties of the social contract.

All of these Westerns benefitted from an overlap of interest with crime and police dramas, which have also done extremely well in the movies and television. Others overlap with entertainment centered on war and combat, which have always done well in a medium that emerged alongside the new U.S. imperial standing in the world.

Perhaps nothing touches on both themes as persistently as Jesse James and his gang, the real-life versions of Rooster Cogburn. Early depictions of this ruthless killer and his fellow cutthroats rarely ventured far from the adulation of the James boys by former Confederate officer John N. Edwards and the militant Lost Cause Democrats of Missouri in contemporary newspapers. Edwards and those who lionized the James boys recast them as poor but honest white landowners, oppressed and exploited by Yankee bankers and railroaders with their self-serving abolitionism and miscegenation. This implicit and often explicit identification with the most overtly white supremacist side of the American Civil War seems to remain an enduring feature of James, as evident in *Jesse James* (1939), *The True Story of Jesse James* (1957), *The Great Northfield, Minnesota Raid* (1972), as well as *The Long Riders* (1980), *The Assassination of Jesse James by the Coward Robert Ford* (2007), and *American Bandits: Frank and Jesse James* (2010). Indeed, *The Outlaw Josey Wales* (1976) offers a well-done variation on the misunderstood and somehow oppressed and exploited white landowner.

The career of William Bonney was popular enough to encourage more than 50 films. This started with *Billy the Kid* (1911, 1930, 1941) and *Billy the Kid Returns* (1938), and continued through Howard Hughes's *The Outlaw* (1943), *Young Guns* (1988), *Young Guns II* (1990), and *Gore Vidal's Billy the Kid* (1989) presenting him as a sympathetic, youthful victim of circumstances. Setting aside the Kid's appearances alongside Dracula and supernatural forces, *Requiem for Billy the Kid* (2006) makes a poetic presentation of his life and activities. Frederick Nolan's *Birth of a Legend: Billy the Kid and the Lincoln County War* (2011) and *Billy the Kid: Showdown in Lincoln County* (2015) provide a much more straightforward historical dramatization.

Interestingly, some of Bonney's associates lived long enough to see the beginning of this process. After participating in the Pleasant Valley War, his old friend Tom Pickett moved to Nevada and survived there until 1925. The press even noted that, in 1934, Louis Bousman turned up for the showing of *Billy the Kid* at a theater in Wichita Falls.[19]

The myth of the Rough Riders as a force for democratization resurfaced in the movies, where the wretched refuse of an American shore find their destinies as filibusterers. Old Westerners become the filibusterers *The Wild Bunch* (1969), a perspective claiming even deeper roots in American history with films like *Major Dundee* (1965), in which the warriors of North and South learn to bear the flag of their common white national identity against the more swarthy Others. Of course, this remained a central part of the industry's message, which

19   For Pickett, Forrest, *Arizona's Dark and Bloody Ground*, 183, and for Bousman, Nolan, *Tascosa*, 203.

persisted through most of what took place during what scholars have described as a "revisionist" phase in the 1970s. *Bad Company* (1972) depicts a young man evading the Civil War draft only to fall in with a dangerous crowd in the West.

Ultimately, anything touching on that period invariably faces the pervasive, tortured history of race in the United States, but rendering it essentially invisible. One of the premier directors in the field, John Ford maintained segregated outhouses on his set, casting Jewish actors as Indians and rarely portraying them as complex figures. By 1939, Ford sent one of the greatest Westerns in history across the silver screen with *Stagecoach*, a movie so iconic that it inspired overly optimistic remakes in 1966 and 1986. Careening through a dangerous world, the characters survived despite their personal foibles thanks largely to the grit of John Wayne, whose performance launched a career that carried him through movie after movie and war after war. Ford's highly praised *The Searchers* (1956) sent John Wayne to save a white woman from the Indians.

With the emergence of the civil rights movement, Hollywood entered a revisionist phase with greater sensitivity to race, though its tendency was simply to transform armed savages into "noble savages." This was, after all, the period that reduced the systemic environmental degradation of the American biosphere to a matter of personal carelessness in the disposal of paper cups and cans by presenting an Italian-American actor as a realistic and tearful Indian in a landfill.

Nevertheless, several movies hinted at a more realistic and complex history. *Cheyenne Autumn* (1964) remarkably depicts the plight of desperate Indians of that tribe on a reservation, the refusal of the government to meet its obligations to them, and the brutality of the army. *Ulzana's Raid* (1972) offers a tale of the bold Apache warriors under Geronimo, before being detourned in a test of male warriors; *Geronimo: An American Legend* (1993) tells the story more directly, albeit still from the perspective of the soldiers and scouts sent to capture the "renegades." *Little Big Man* (1970) presents the perspective of a white man raised by Indians who, among other things, witnesses the Little Big Horn. *Dances With Wolves* (1990) portrays an army officer isolated on a western assignment that inspires him to "go native," as the British used to describe it. *Buffalo Bill and the Indians, or Sitting Bull's History Lesson* (1976) showcased an imagined interaction of these two figures and their conflicting views, even as they collaborated in the Wild West Show.

African Americans fared better, but not by much. A very different sense of race appeared in *The Skin Game* (1971) and *Buck and the Preacher* (1972), which featured both an antislavery sensibility and an appreciation of the con artists' work. In the aftermath of the revisionist films of the 1970s, moviemakers finally realized the value to them of African American audiences and began showcasing black actors across a broad range of movies, though they largely linked them to military service and law enforcement. These included *Sergeant Rutledge* (1960) and *Joshua* (1976). Many, such as *Soul Soldier*, released as *The Red, White, and Black* (1970), became iconic items of "blaxploitation." At the edges, of course, these serve as something like recruitment films for the military or efforts to repair the racially tarnished U.S. image abroad. As with the movies in general, they present African Americans in positions of power and authority out of all proportion to what they have actually been accorded.

In recent years, these have branched into movies having to do with slavery. They are often remarkable for their contempt for the historical experience of African Americans. Regardless of intent, even the most explicit portrayal of brutalities can be taken as a celebration that "progress" and "civilization" have rescued the world from such injustices.

One way of dealing with historical issues of race and diversity is simply to ignore them. While that may lead to a prettification of the past that should concern thoughtful viewers, it is the essence of the commercial distillation of history into heritage. Can movies about legions of black Confederates be far off? The *Wild Wild West* (1999) resurrected a television series (1965–9), a gadget-filled bit of silliness smacking more of science fiction than a Western that told largely whites-only stories with the exception of a few Indians. After a thirty-year interlude, the gadgetry and special effects have become astronomically better and U.S. government agent Jim West himself has become an African American. Similar criticisms could be made of the diverse band of heroes depicted in a recent remake of *The Magnificent Seven* (2016), though they were much more plausibly cast as outlaws than agents of the power structure.

The Western genre also produced hybrid fields. Surely Baum would appreciate the Westernized science fiction stories, most tellingly the TV series *Firefly* (2002–3).

Going the other direction, numerous movies on the subject eventually inspired TV series. *Deadwood* (2004–6), gave us an unblinking look at the underclass, including black and Chinese people, in the region. It demonstrated that rumors of the Western's demise have been greatly exaggerated. It particularly took us into the lives of the "soiled doves" as subtle but active players in the community. In the end, it demonstrated how one could tell a more inclusive story of the West with respect for historical reality.

As to the cowboys themselves, movies and television also depicted life on a cattle drive. These included *Red River* (1948), *The Cowboys* (1972), and *The Culpepper Cattle Co.* (1972), as well as the TV series *Rawhide* (1959–65). By definition, though, any such vehicle about a sixteen-hour workday is going to have to strain to also be entertaining. The rodeo, a showcase of roundup skills, inspired its own subcategory of films, which need not be confined to the old West and usually bear great resemblance to movies about the strains of life in show business.

The category of the horse opera has done the best job, perhaps, in dealing with the very real angst of the cowboy past his age and time. Aging cowboys confront not only the impending end of their own lives but the end of their way of life in *Lonely Are the Brave* (1962), *Ride the High Country* (1962), *Will Penny* (1968), and *Monte Walsh* (1970, remade in 2003).[20]

The social tensions of the northern ranges came into sharper focus. Films such as *Shane* (1953) owed much to the experience of Johnson County and other range wars. So did *Silverado* (1985),

20 Lee Marvin's reprise in a comedy *Cat Ballou* (1965), *Support Your Local Gunfighter* (1971), and *Support Your Local Sheriff* (1969).

though both maintain the fiction that, somehow, the small ranchers triumphed over the robber barons and everyone lived happily ever after.

The memorable conflict in Wyoming found expression in the made-for-TV movie *Johnson County War* (2002), which attempted a more coherent presentation than *Heaven's Gate* (1980). Largely criticized as having singlehandedly destroyed the genre, *Heaven's Gate* muddled some of the history unnecessarily but committed the far greater crime of dramatizing the U.S. government's rescue of the hired assassins sent into the area by the Wyoming Stockgrowers Association. A darker and more realistic view of life on the northern range found its way into *Butch Cassidy and the Sundance Kid* (1969), which painted a sympathetic portrait of those trying to eke out a living on the margins of the great estates, as did *The Missouri Breaks* (1976). In the same period, Robert Altman directed *McCabe and Mrs. Miller* (1971) in Canada as what he called an anti-Western, showcasing the efforts of "the little people" to survive.

In the end, mass media is about entertainment. It measures success by audience shares, advertising potential, product placement, and profits, but it performs a much greater role in shaping a public sensibility of the past. In one of the most quotable lines from any Western, a newspaperman in *The Man Who Shot Liberty Valance* (1962) explained, "This is the west, sir. When the legend becomes fact, print the legend." He might have more honestly added, however, that the press itself establishes the legend—and later, movies and television do so even more effectively.

To an extent that Turner could never have imagined, the commercial manufacturing of American self-perception has played a vital role in shaping the course of civilization since the demise of the frontier. Our perceptions and, more importantly, misperceptions of the West have been a central part of this.

Much of this myth-making aimed at an ongoing affirmation of legitimacy that requires the projection of violent intentions onto the designated targets of institutionalized violence. From their perspective, the secessionist leaders did not instigate the

War of Northern Aggression but merely acted in self-defense against the innately violent capture of the government in Washington by antislavery voters. Later, they donned their sheets and asserted their defense of law and order against the brutality of the former slaves and their well-wishers. No less so, postwar Republican officials in Kansas presented themselves as struggling against the implicit violence of those seeking to impose an unjust collective will on the individual's right to unlimited acquisition of wealth. The imposed proscriptions against critics of the institutions precluded the need for any serious investigation of events, much less the prosecution of wrongdoers. In the wake of the terrorist attacks of 2001, the authorities declared it necessary to restrict the freedom of American citizens as a reasonable response to the invisible forces that "hate us for our freedom." Our own failure to laugh such people out of public life has deep roots in our history.

Beneath the imagery of individual opportunity, conditions in the Panhandle demonstrated that the transition from a land where Indians hunted the buffalo to large-scale, commercial livestock raising within what amounted to enclosures and a rigid class system took place in a matter of years. Getting at the meaning of the cowboy strike of 1883 requires reaching beneath the self-interested, fictionalized, and falsified accounts to draw upon the wider issues of class, power, and politics.

Long after the Green Corn Rebellion, an elderly Indian woman, who had seen it all as a child, recalled how they tried "to persuade our poor white and black brothers and sisters to rise up." "Whatever the consequences, [it] would inspire future generations. Our courage, our bravery would be remembered and copied." She continued:

That has been the Indian way for centuries, since the invasions. Fight and tell the story so that those who come after or their descendants will rise up once again. It may take a thousand years, but that is how we continue and eventually prevail.[21]

The past is not buried simply by the sedimentation of passing time, but also by the desire to entomb a living history beneath iconic and lifeless statuary. Ultimately, though, without excavating the past, no rational or coherent future can be likely.

21 Roxanne Dunbar-Ortiz, *Red Dirt: Growing Up Okie* (Norman: University of Oklahoma Press, 1997), 14.

Acknowledgements

Many years ago, as a perfectly respectable college dropout living in Texas, I stumbled onto references to the events of 1883 almost by accident. It turned out to be more than forty years before I start reconnecting these dots. In part, this happened when Rosemary Feuer asked me to contribute something on "Broncho John" Sullivan to "Labor Online," the blog of the Labor and Working-Class History Association. A paper on the strike itself was presented at the III International Conference Strikes and Social Conflicts, Barcelona, June 16 to 19, 2015, which posted a version of it; I am grateful to the Charles F. Phelps Taft Memorial Fund at the University of Cincinnati for sending me to that conference. I also presented another form of it at various locations, notably the University of North Texas, at the invitation of Professors Sandra Mendiola-Garcia and Chad Pearson of Collin College. Sebastian Budgen of Verso recognized the possibilities of the subject as the cornerstone of a book project. I am grateful to Janine Hartman for her preliminary commentary on the draft, and to my wife, Katherine Allen, for her patience and support.

The Library of Congress, Kansas State Historical Society, and the Wisconsin Historical Society provided some excellent images to supplement the story.

Index